Assessment of Student Achievement

SEVENTH EDITION

Norman E. Gronlund

Professor Emeritus
University of Illinois

Boston   New York   San Francisco
Mexico City   Montreal   Toronto   London   Madrid   Munich   Paris
Hong Kong   Singapore   Tokyo   Cape Town   Sydney

Series Editor: *Arnis E. Burvikovs*
Editorial Assistant: *Matthew Forster*
Marketing Manager: *Tara Whorf*
Editorial Production Administrator: *Joe Sweeney*
Editorial Production Service: *Walsh & Associates, Inc.*
Composition Buyer: *Linda Cox*
Manufacturing Buyer: *Chris Marson*
Cover Administrator: *Linda Knowles*

Library of Congress Cataloging-in-Publication Data

Gronlund, Norman Edward
    Assessment of student achievement / Norman E. Gronlund—7th ed.
        p.   cm.
    Includes bibliographical references and index.
    ISBN 0-205-36610-4
    1. Achievement tests—Design and construction.   2. Examinations—Design and construction.   I. Title.
    LB3060.65.G766   2003
    371.26′1—dc21   2001056626

Printed in the United States of America

10 9 8 7 6 5 4 3 2 1   06 05 04 03 02

To
Marie Ann Gronlund
and
Dave, Derek, and Erik

Contents

4 Writing Selection Items: Multiple Choice **60**

5 Writing Selection Items: True-False, Matching, and Intrepretive Exercise **83**

6 Writing Supply Items: Short Answer and Essay **100**

7 *Traditional Performance Assessments of Skills and Products* **116**

8 *Expanded Performance Assessments* **139**

9 *Portfolio Assessment* **157**

Preface

The seventh edition of *Assessment of Student Achievement* is a practical guide that focuses on how to assess all of the intended learning outcomes of instruction, from simple to complex. It describes assessment as an umbrella term that includes both testing and performance assessment, each to be used where it is most appropriate. The premise throughout the book is that valid assessment is necessary for effective instruction and that the goal of both is improved student learning.

The chapters on the preparation and use of classroom tests and performance assessments are followed by a chapter on grading and reporting. The last two chapters on how to interpret standardized test scores and validity and reliability present the more technical aspects of assessment, but the concepts and procedures can be easily grasped without any previous knowledge in the area. They were placed last so that they could be used wherever they best fit the course schedule. Brief descriptions of validity and reliability and a list of ways to build in validity and reliability during the preparation of assessment instruments is included in Chapter 2, for those who want to use the more technical chapter later in the course.

This new edition includes a number of changes:

1. A new chapter on expanded performance assessment (Chapter 8) was added that focuses on the assessment of comprehensive and complex performance outcomes.
2. A new chapter on portfolio assessment (Chapter 9) was added that describes how to prepare, use, and evaluate classroom portfolios.
3. Chapter 3 was broadened to planning for assessment, and the section on preparing an achievement test was expanded to include all aspects of the test preparation. The chapter on assembling, administering, and evaluating the test was eliminated because much of the material was now covered in Chapter 3.
4. The earlier chapter on performance assessment was revised with a more limited focus on traditional performance assessments of skills and products.
5. The chapter on assigning grades was expanded to include reporting to students and parents.

6. Numerous new boxed material was added to chapters listing steps for preparing, using, and scoring performance assessments.
7. New references were added to the "Additional Reading" lists of all chapters.

The book now presents a well-balanced treatment of testing and performance assessment and its important role in instruction. The material is presented in a simple, direct, and understandable manner without slighting basic concepts or sacrificing technical accuracy. Numerous practical examples are provided, and checklists, boxed material, and summaries of main points are used to aid in learning the content. No prior knowledge of measurement or statistics is required to understand the material in the book. In short, it is a practical guide for beginners.

I would like to thank reviewers James Tate, Southwestern Oklahoma State University, and Jane Abraham, Virginia Tech, for their time and feedback.

My appreciation is also expressed to the authors and publishers referred to in the book, to the Allyn and Bacon editorial staff, to Irene Palmer for her excellent typing, and to my wife Marie for her patience and understanding during work on this revision.

N. E. G.

1

Achievement Assessment and Instruction

Studying this chapter should enable you to[1]

1. Explain why both testing and performance assessment are important in achievement assessment.
2. Write a definition of achievement assessment.
3. Describe the relation between instruction and assessment.
4. Distinguish among the various roles of assessment in the instructional process.
5. List the ways that assessments can directly aid learning.

All of us have taken various types of paper-and-pencil tests during our many years of schooling. Some of these were teacher-made tests requiring us to select an answer (e.g., true-false, multiple choice, or matching) or to supply an answer (e.g., short answer or essay). Others were standardized tests of aptitude or achievement, primarily using multiple-choice items. The widespread use of paper-and-pencil testing in the schools was due, at least in part, to the efficiency with which they could measure a large number of learning outcomes and the ease of scoring and recording the results.

---

[1]Space does not permit using the preferred two-step method of stating intended learning outcomes described in Chapter 3. These statements, however, should provide a focus for your study and for application of the content in each chapter.

In recent years there has been a reaction to the heavy emphasis on paper-and-pencil testing. Some critics have contended that there should be more emphasis on the assessment of **authentic,** "real-life" tasks (e.g., solving problems that exist in the real world). Others have contended that paper-and-pencil testing should be replaced, at least in part, by **alternative** types of assessment. Some reactions have been extreme but they highlight the importance of focusing more attention on the actual performance of students (see Box 1.1). If you want to determine if students can write, have them write something. If you want to determine if students can operate a machine, have them operate the machine. If you want to determine if students can conduct an experiment, have them conduct an experiment. In short, if you want to determine if they can perform a task, have them perform the task. There is little doubt that more emphasis on performance assessment in the schools would improve the assessment of our intended learning outcomes. However, paper-and-pencil testing still has an important role to play, even as we focus more directly on performance-based tasks.

Most types of performance have a knowledge component that is important to the performance. Good writing includes such factors as knowledge of vocabulary, grammar, and spelling. These are not well sampled by a writing task because we tend to use only the words we know, use sentence structures that we can punctuate easily, and substitute words we can spell for those we can't spell. Thus, in writing, we can structure it to conceal our weaknesses. A separate test of vocabulary, grammar, and spelling can identify these weaknesses and be used to improve writing skill. Just don't interpret the test results as measures of "writing ability." The tests measure

---

BOX 1.1 • *Commonly Used Assessment Terms*

Performance Assessments	Assessments requiring students to demonstrate their achievement of understandings and skills by actually performing a task or set of tasks (e.g., writing a story, giving a speech, conducting an experiment, operating a machine).
Alternative Assessments	A title for performance assessments that emphasizes that these assessment methods provide an alternative to traditional paper-and-pencil testing.
Authentic Assessments	A title for performance assessments that stresses the importance of focusing on the application of understandings and skills to real problems in "real-world" contextual settings.

knowledge useful in writing but writing ability is determined by assessing the actual writing (**performance assessment**). Similarly, in operating machinery, the actual operation of the machine is the ultimate goal, but tests measuring knowledge of how to operate the machine and the safety precautions to follow may be needed before the hands-on performance assessment. Likewise, before conducting an experiment, tests can be used to determine how well students know the information needed for a well controlled experiment.

Throughout this book, the emphasis will be on achievement assessment that includes both paper-and-pencil testing and performance assessment. Tests can provide direct measures of many important learning outcomes, ranging from simple to complex, and they can provide needed information for assessing and improving actual performance tasks. Thus, although we should strive for as authentic assessment as we can obtain, within the constraints of the school setting, both tests and performance-based tasks are needed for a complete assessment of student achievement.

As used in this book, **achievement assessment** is a broad category that includes all of the various methods for determining the extent to which students are achieving the intended learning outcomes of instruction. Because we are limiting our concern to achievement assessment, the single term *assessment* is used throughout the book as a matter of convenience.

Relation Between Instruction and Assessment

In preparing for any type of instructional program our main concern is "How can we most effectively bring about student learning?" As we ponder this question, our attention is naturally directed toward the methods and materials of instruction. However, at the same time we should also consider the role of assessment in the instructional process. When properly designed and appropriately used, assessment procedures can contribute to more effective instruction and greater student learning.

The close relation between instruction and assessment can be seen in Table 1.1. Both require that we clearly specify the learning outcomes to be achieved by students, and the provisions of well-designed assessments closely parallel the characteristics of effective instruction. This relation highlights the importance of broadening instructional planning to include assessment planning. The typical procedure of limiting instructional planning to the teaching-learning process is inadequate. Effective instruction requires that we expand our concern to a teaching-learning-assessment process, with assessment as a basic part of the instructional program. As with all instructional activities, the main function of assessment is to improve learning and it can contribute to this end in a number of ways.

TABLE 1.1   *Relation between Instruction and Assessment*

Instruction	Assessment
Instruction is most effective when	*Assessment is most effective when*
1. Directed toward a clearly defined set of intended learning outcomes.	1. Designed to assess a clearly defined set of intended learning outcomes.
2. The methods and materials of instruction are congruent with the outcomes to be achieved.	2. The nature and function of the assessments are congruent with the outcomes to be assessed.
3. The instruction is designed to fit the characteristics and needs of the students.	3. The assessments are designed to fit the relevant student characteristics and are fair to everyone.
4. Instructional decisions are based on information that is meaningful, dependable, and relevant.	4. Assessments provide information that is meaningful, dependable, and relevant.
5. Students are periodically informed concerning their learning progress.	5. Provision is made for giving the students early feedback of assessment results.
6. Remediation is provided for students not achieving the intended learning.	6. Specific learning weaknesses are revealed by the assessment results.
7. Instructional effectiveness is periodically reviewed and the intended learning outcomes and instruction modified as needed.	7. Assessment results provide information useful for evaluating the appropriateness of the objectives, the methods, and the materials of instruction.

Assessment in the Instructional Process

To be fully integrated with instruction, plans for assessment should be made during the planning for instruction. From the beginning of instruction to the end there are numerous decisions that teachers need to make. Carefully planned assessment procedures can improve the effectiveness of many of these decisions by providing more objective information on which to base judgments. Let us consider some of the decisions teachers need to make at (1) the beginning of instruction, (2) during instruction, and (3) at the end of instruction.

Beginning of Instruction (Placement Assessment)

There are two major questions that teachers need to answer before proceeding with the instruction:

1. To what extent do the students possess the skills and abilities that are needed to begin instruction?
2. To what extent have the students already achieved the intended learning outcomes of the planned instruction?

Information concerning the first question is frequently obtained from *readiness* pretests. These are tests given at the beginning of a course or unit of instruction that cover those prerequisite skills necessary for success in the planned instruction. For example, a test of computational skill might be given at the beginning of an algebra course, or a test of English grammar might be given at the beginning of a German course. Students lacking in prerequisite skills could be given remedial work, or they could be placed in a special section that had lower prerequisites.

The second question is frequently answered by a *placement* pretest covering the intended learning outcomes of the planned instruction. This might very well be the same test that is given at the end of the instruction; preferably it should be another form of it. Here we are interested in determining whether students have already mastered some of the material we plan to include in our instruction. If they have, we might need to modify our teaching plans, encourage some students to skip particular units, and place other students at a more advanced level of instruction. The function of placement assessment is summarized in Figure 1.1.

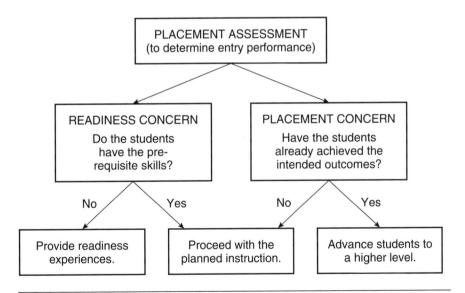

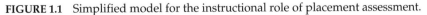

FIGURE 1.1 Simplified model for the instructional role of placement assessment.

In addition to the use of pretests, performance-based tasks may also be useful for determining entry skills. In the area of writing, for example, obtaining writing samples at the beginning of instruction can establish a base for later assessments of progress. This type of preassessment would be especially valuable if portfolios of student work were to be maintained during the instruction.

The contribution that preassessment can make to instruction depends on the nature of the instruction, how well we know students, and how the results are to be used. A pretest in arithmetic may be quite useful at the beginning of an algebra course, whereas a pretest in a course that lacks a clearly defined set of prerequisite skills (e.g., social studies) may be of little value. Similarly, the results of a test of basic skills may be of great value to a new teacher unfamiliar with the students and of less value to an experienced teacher familiar with the students' backgrounds. In addition, preassessment will contribute little to the instructional program unless plans are made to remedy deficiencies, place students in the most beneficial position in the instructional sequence, or use the results as a base for assessing future progress. To be most effective, the use of preassessment should be considered during the instructional planning stage.

During Instruction (Formative and Diagnostic Assessment)

During the instructional program our main concern is with the learning progress being made by students. Questions such as the following must be answered.

1. On which learning tasks are the students progressing satisfactorily? On which ones do they need help?
2. Which students are having such severe learning problems that they need remedial work?

Tests used to monitor student progress during instruction are called *formative* tests. Formative tests are typically designed to measure the extent to which students have mastered the learning outcomes of a rather limited segment of instruction, such as a unit or a textbook chapter. These tests are similar to the quizzes and unit tests that teachers have traditionally used, but they place greater emphasis on (1) measuring all of the intended outcomes of the unit of instruction, and (2) using the results to improve learning (rather than to assign grades). The purpose is to identify the students' learning, successes, and failures so that adjustments in instruction and learning can be made. When the majority of students fail a test item, or set of items, the material is typically retaught in a group setting. When a minority of students experience learning failures, alternate methods of study are usually prescribed for each student (for example, reading assignments in a second book, computer instruction, and visual aids). These corrective prescriptions are frequently keyed to each item, or to each set of items designed to measure a separate learning task, so that students can begin immediately after testing to correct their individual learning errors.

Formative assessment using performance-based tasks may involve periodic assessments of a product (e.g., writing sample, drawing) or of a process (e.g., giving a speech, operating a machine) with feedback to students concerning strengths and weaknesses. The aim here, as with formative testing, is to monitor learning progress and to provide corrective prescriptions to improve learning.

When a student's learning problems are so persistent that they cannot be resolved by the corrective prescriptions of formative assessment, a more intensive study of the student's learning difficulties is called for. It is here that *diagnostic* assessment is useful. Diagnostic assessment attempts to answer such questions as the following: Are the students having difficulty in addition because they don't know certain number combinations or because they don't know how to carry? Are the students' difficulties in reading German due to their inadequate knowledge of vocabulary or to their poor grasp of certain elements of grammar? Are the students unable to apply scientific principles to new situations because they don't understand the principles, because their knowledge of particular concepts is weak, or because the new situations are too unfamiliar to them? Thus, diagnostic assessment focuses on the common sources of error encountered by students, so that the learning difficulties can be pinpointed and remedied.

Diagnostic assessment can frequently be aided by the use of diagnostic tests. These tests typically include a relatively large number of test items in each specific area with slight variations from one set of items to the next so that the cause of specific learning errors can be identified. In detecting errors in the addition of whole numbers, for example, we might construct a test that includes a set of items requiring no carrying, a set that requires simple carrying, and one that requires repeated carrying to determine if carrying is the source of the difficulty. Unfortunately, diagnostic tests are difficult to construct in most areas of instruction. Therefore, we must depend more heavily on observation and judgment.

Diagnosing learning problems is a matter of degree. Formative assessment determines whether a student has mastered the learning tasks being taught and, if not, prescribes how to remedy the learning failures. Diagnostic assessment is designed to probe deeper into the causes of learning deficiencies that are left unresolved by formative assessment. Of course, this is not to imply that all learning problems can be overcome by formative and diagnostic assessment. These are simply methods to aid in the identification and diagnosis of specific learning difficulties so that appropriate remedial steps can be taken. Diagnosing and remedying severe learning problems

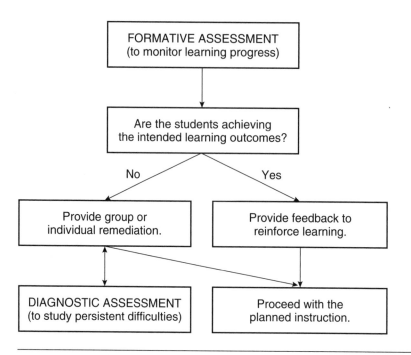

FIGURE 1.2   Simplified model for the instructional role of formative assessment.

frequently require a wide array of assessment procedures and the services of specially trained personnel. All we are attempting to do here is to show how formative and diagnostic assessment can contribute to improved student learning during instruction. The model presented in Figure 1.2 summarizes the process.

End of Instruction (Summative Assessment)

At the end of a course or unit of instruction we are concerned primarily with the extent to which the students have achieved the intended outcomes of the instruction. Questions such as the following must be answered:

1. Which students have mastered the learning tasks to such a degree that they should proceed to the next course or unit of instruction?
2. What grade should be assigned to each student?

Achievement assessment at the end of instruction for the purpose of certifying mastery or assigning grades is called *summative* assessment. This assessment is typically comprehensive in coverage and includes both tests and performance assessments. Although the results are used primarily for

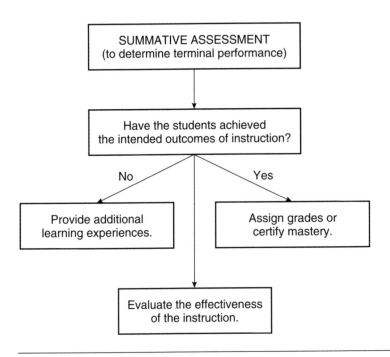

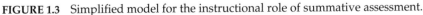

FIGURE 1.3   Simplified model for the instructional role of summative assessment.

grading, there should be some feedback to students and the results should be used for evaluating the effectiveness of the instruction. See Figure 1.3 for the summative assessment model.

Other Ways Assessments Can Aid Learning

As noted in the previous section, assessments can aid the teacher in making various instructional decisions having a direct influence on student learning. In addition, assessments can aid student learning in a number of other ways.

Student Motivation

A carefully planned assessment program can have a direct influence on student learning by (1) providing students with short-term goals, (2) clarifying the types of tasks to be learned, and (3) providing feedback concerning their learning progress. Short-term goals are more motivating than telling students "Some day you will find this knowledge or skill useful." An expected assessment stimulates learning activity and directs it toward the learning tasks to be assessed. Its contribution to learning depends to a large extent on how faithfully our assessments reflect all of the important outcomes of the instruction and how we use the results. For example, if the application of principles is stressed in our assessment as well as in our teaching, we can expect students to direct greater efforts toward learning how to apply principles. Also, if the assessment results are reported to students as soon as possible, this feedback concerning their strengths and weaknesses in the application of principles will further clarify the nature of the task and indicate what changes are needed for effective performance. Thus, properly used assessments can motivate students to work toward the instructional objectives of a course by arousing greater learning activity, by directing it toward the intended learning outcomes, and by providing prompt knowledge of results.

Retention and Transfer of Learning

Because assessments tend to direct students' learning efforts toward the intended outcomes of instruction, they can be used as tools for increasing the retention and transfer of learning. In general, learning outcomes at the understanding, application, and interpretation levels are likely to be retained longer and to have greater transfer value than outcomes at the knowledge level. By including assessments of these more complex learning outcomes, we can direct attention to their importance and provide reinforcing practice in the skills, applications, and interpretations we are attempting to develop. Thus, assessments can be used to supplement and complement our teaching efforts in these areas and thereby increase the likelihood that the learning will be of greater permanent value to the students.

Student Self-Assessment

All instruction should be directed toward helping individuals better understand themselves so that they can make more intelligent decisions. Periodic assessment and feedback of the results can help students gain insight into what they can do well, the misconceptions that need correction, and the degree of skill they have in various areas. Such information provides the students with a more objective basis for assessing their own strengths and weaknesses. Properly used assessments tend to provide evidence of learning progress in such an objective and impartial way that the results can be accepted with little resistance or distortion. This assumes, of course, that the assessments are properly prepared and are being used to improve learning rather than to threaten or label students. In the latter instance, self-assessment is apt to be distorted by the psychological defense mechanisms an individual uses to maintain a positive self-image.

Evaluating Instructional Effectiveness

Assessment results can be used to evaluate the effectiveness of various aspects of the instructional process. For example, they can help determine the extent to which the instructional objectives were realistic, whether the methods and materials of instruction were appropriate, and how well the learning experiences were sequenced. When the majority of the students do poorly on an assessment, it may be the fault of the students but the difficulty is more likely to be found in the instruction. The teacher may be striving for learning outcomes that are unattainable by the students, using inappropriate materials, or using ineffective methods for bringing about the desired changes. An analysis of the students' responses and a class discussion of the results should provide clues to the source of the instructional difficulty so that corrective steps can be taken.

Teachers' Standards for Student Assessment

It is generally agreed that student assessment plays an important role in effective teaching. A committee made up of representatives of the American Federation of Teachers, the National Council on Measurement in Education, and the National Education Association considered it so important that they came out with a report entitled *Standards for Teacher Competence in Educational Assessment of Students* (1990). In the report, they review the teacher's responsibilities for student assessment and summarize them by listing seven standards for teacher competence in student assessment. The following list, with abbreviated description of each standard, is taken from the report.

1. *Teachers should be skilled in choosing assessment methods appropriate for instructional decisions.* Skill in choosing appropriate, useful, administratively convenient, technically adequate, and fair assessment methods are prerequisite to good use of information to support instructional decisions.
2. *Teachers should be skilled in developing assessment methods appropriate for instructional decisions.* While teachers often use published or other external assessment tools, the bulk of the assessment information they use for decision making comes from approaches they create and implement.
3. *The teacher should be skilled in administering, scoring, and interpreting the results of both externally produced and teacher-produced assessment methods.* It is not enough that teachers are able to select and develop good assessment methods; they must also be able to apply them properly.

4. *Teachers should be skilled in using assessment results when making decisions about individual students, planning teaching, developing curriculum, and school improvement.* Assessment results are used to make educational decisions at several levels: in the classroom about students, in the community about a school and a school district, and in society, generally, about the purposes and outcomes of the educational enterprise. Teachers play a vital role when participating in decision making at each of these levels and must be able to use assessment results effectively.

5. *Teachers should be skilled in developing valid pupil grading procedures that use pupil assessments.* Grading students is an important part of professional practice for teachers. Grading is defined as indicating both a student's level of performance and a teacher's valuing of that performance. The principles for using assessments to obtain valid grades are known and teachers should employ them.

6. *Teachers should be skilled in communicating assessment results to students, parents, other lay audiences, and other educators.* Teachers must routinely report assessment results to students and to parents or guardians. In addition, they are frequently asked to report or to discuss assessment results with other educators and with diverse lay audiences. If the results are not communicated effectively, they may be misused or not used. To communicate effectively with others on matters of student assessment, teachers must be able to use assessment terminology appropriately and must be able to articulate the meaning, limitations, and implications of assessment results.

7. *Teachers should be skilled in recognizing unethical, illegal, and otherwise inappropriate assessment methods and uses of assessment information.* Fairness, the rights of all concerned, and professional ethical behavior must undergird all student assessment activities, from the initial planning for and gathering of information to the interpretation, use, and communication of the results.

The complete report of *Standards for Teacher Competence in Educational Assessment of Students* is presented in the Appendix of Linn and Gronlund (2000). The report is not copyrighted and reproduction and distribution of it are encouraged.

Summary of Points

1. In recent years there has been a reaction to the heavy emphasis on paper-and-pencil testing with a plea for more realistic and meaningful performance assessment.

2. A well-balanced assessment program should include both testing and performance assessment, with each used where most appropriate.

3. *Achievement assessment* is a general category that includes a broad range of methods for determining the extent to which students are achieving the intended learning outcomes of instruction.
4. Instruction is more effective when well-designed assessments are an integral part of the instructional process.
5. Assessment procedures can be used for measuring entry performance (placement assessment), monitoring learning progress (formative and diagnostic assessment), or measuring end of instruction achievement (summative assessments).
6. Achievement assessments can contribute to student motivation, the retention and transfer of learning, student self-evaluation skills, and an evaluation of instructional effectiveness.
7. Teachers' standards for student assessment focus on their competence in selecting assessment methods, developing assessment methods, administering and scoring them, interpreting and using assessment results, preparing valid grades, communicating assessment results, and recognizing inappropriate assessment methods and uses of assessment information.

References and Additional Reading

Airasian, P.W., *Classroom Assessment*, 3rd ed. (New York: McGraw-Hill, 1997).

Bloom, B. S., Madaus, G. T., and Hastings, J. T., *Evaluation to Improve Learning* (New York: McGraw-Hill, 1981).

Linn, R. L., and Gronlund, N. E., *Measurement and Assessment in Teaching*, 8th ed. (Upper Saddle River, NJ: Merrill/Prentice-Hall, 2000).

McMillan, J. H., *Classroom Assessment: Principles and Practices for Effective Instruc-tion*, 2nd ed. (Boston: Allyn and Bacon, 2001).

Popham, W. J., *Classroom Assessment: What Teachers Need to Know*, 3rd ed. (Boston: Allyn and Bacon, 2002).

Stiggins, R. J., *Student-Involved Classroom Assessment*, 3rd ed. (Upper Saddle River, NJ: Merrill/Prentice-Hall, 2001).

2

Nature of Student Assessment

Studying this chapter should enable you to

1. Describe a situation where both testing and performance assessment are needed and indicate why.
2. Describe the major types of assessment methods and give an example of each.
3. Distinguish between tests and performance assessments in terms of realism of tasks, complexity of tasks, assessment time needed, and judgment in scoring.
4. List the guidelines for effective student assessment.
5. Describe the meaning of validity and reliability and the role they play in preparing assessment procedures.
6. Distinguish between norm-referenced and criterion-referenced assessments.

As noted in the first chapter, *assessment* is used as a broad category that includes all of the various methods used to determine the extent to which students are achieving the intended learning outcomes of instruction. This includes both testing and performance assessments. To assess a student's driving ability, for example, an **objective test** is used to measure knowledge of how to drive and follow the rules of the road, and driving over a pre-scribed course (performance assessment) is used to determine skill in dri-ving the automobile. The test on rules of the road covers a much larger sample of driving rules than are likely to be encountered in the driving per-formance, but skill in driving can only be determined by sitting behind the wheel and driving. Both are important. The knowledge test tells how well the student knows what to do and the performance assessment tells how skillfully the student can do it.

Teachers have tended to favor selection-type tests (i.e., multiple choice, true-false, matching) because many questions can be asked in a relatively short time, they are easy to administer and score, and the results can be expressed in numbers that are easily recorded, compared, and reported to others. Unfortunately, teachers have also limited selection-type tests almost entirely to knowledge of facts and terms. Various studies have shown that between 80 and 90 percent of teacher-made tests focus on knowledge outcomes. There is little doubt that this overemphasis on selection-type tests and simple knowledge outcomes has led to the movement toward assessment techniques that measure more complex learning outcomes in realistic settings. The fact that paper-and-pencil tests can be designed to measure a wide array of complex learning outcomes has frequently been overlooked in the movement toward performance assessment. It is our contention that education is best served by using both paper-and-pencil testing and the assessment of actual performance, with both focusing on more complex learning tasks than typically has been the case in the past.

Major Types of Assessment Methods

Assessment methods vary widely but they can be summarized in four major categories as shown in Table 2.1. Selected-response tests require the student to choose the correct or best answer, as in multiple-choice, true-false, and matching tests. Supply-response tests require students to respond with a word, short phrase, or complete essay answer. Restricted performance assessments are concerned with the performance of a limited task that is highly structured, such as writing a brief paragraph on a given topic, selecting laboratory equipment, measuring humidity, or locating information with a computer. Extended performance assessments involve more comprehensive and less structured performance tasks, such as writing a short story, conducting a laboratory experiment, predicting weather, or using a computer to solve a problem. Besides requiring more extended performances, the assessment typically requires students to integrate and apply knowledge and skills to performance tasks in a realistic setting. If there is a product involved (e.g., a short story), students may also be expected to review and revise the product before submitting it, to add greater realism to the task.

These major types of assessment can be further clarified by reviewing some of the characteristics that are typical of each. These have been summarized in Table 2.1.

TABLE 2.1 *Summary Comparison of Assessment Methods*

Testing		Performance Assessment	
Selected Response	*Supply Response*	*Restricted Performance*	*Extended Performance*

LOW ◄——————— REALISM OF TASKS ———————► HIGH

LOW ◄——————— COMPLEXITY OF TASKS ———————► HIGH

LOW ◄——————— ASSESSMENT TIME NEEDED ———————► HIGH

LOW ◄——————— JUDGMENT IN SCORING ———————► HIGH

Realism of Tasks

By realism of assessment tasks, we mean the extent to which they simulate performance in the real world. Traditional selection-type tests are low in realism because they involve selecting a response from a given set of possible answers. The response is limited to the listed alternatives and such highly structured problems seldom occur in the real world. The extended performance assessment is high in realism because it attempts to simulate performance in the real world. Assessing how well a student can drive an automobile, operate a machine, give a speech, or apply knowledge and understanding to a real-life problem (e.g., how to protect the environment) requires comprehensive sets of responses that approximate those occurring in the real world. In between these extremes are the supply-type tests (e.g., short answer and essay) and the restricted response performance assessments that provide a moderate amount of structure but greater freedom of response and thus more realistic type problems than the selection-type tests.

In addition to the movement to increase realism in assessment by moving toward extended performance assessment, there has also been a trend toward making traditional paper-and-pencil tests more authentic (i.e., have greater realism). This has resulted in the designing of tests to measure more complex learning outcomes and in the use of problems and procedures more like those in the real world. In a math problem, for example, students may be given more facts than are needed to solve the problem to see if they can select the facts needed to solve it. In solving a science problem, students might be given the freedom to select the procedure for solving the problem and be asked to justify the procedure used. In some cases this involves a shift from selection-type items to supply-type items but in others it may be a combination of the two items types (e.g., explain why the selected answer was chosen).

Complexity of Tasks

Selected-response items tend to be low in the complexity of the problem presented and in the nature of the expected response. Although items can be designed to measure understanding and thinking skills, they typically present a single, limited problem and require choice of the correct or best answer. Extended performance problems, on the other hand, typically involve multiple learning outcome, the integration of ideas and skills from a variety of sources, the availability of various possible solutions and the need for multiple criteria for evaluating the results (e.g., preparing a plan for reducing drug traffic in the United States). Similarly, performance of a hands-on nature involves complex movement patterns that are guided by the integration of information and specific skills from various learning experiences (e.g., playing a musical instrument, operating a machine, repairing electronic equipment). As with the realism category, supply-type tests fall in between the two extremes. Essay tests, for example, can be designed to measure the ability to select, integrate, and express ideas, but the tasks are usually more limited and structured than in performance assessments.

Assessment Time Needed

A large number of selected-response items can be administered to a group of students in a relatively short time and the results can be quickly scored by hand or by machine. This efficiency has no doubt been a major factor in their widespread use. Performance assessments tend to be extremely time consuming. Some tasks may require days or even weeks to complete (e.g., conduct an experimental study) and others may require assessing students one at a time (e.g., giving a speech, operating a machine). In most cases, evaluating the process or product of the performance is also difficult and time consuming. Supply-response tests, like the essay test, require more time to score than selected-response tests but less than that of performance assessments.

The greater amount of time needed for performance assessment may result in loss of content coverage because of the limited number of assessment problems that can be included in the instructional program. This raises a question concerning the extent to which the assessment results are generalizable to other comparable tasks. We can present "real-world" problems to students, but problems are frequently unique to a particular contextual setting and the real-world changes. Thus, transfer of learning is a key consideration in performance assessment. We can justify the greater time needed only if the assessment is an integral part of instruction and transferable learning outcomes are emphasized (e.g., reasoning, critical thinking, psychomotor skills).

Judgment in Scoring

The amount of judgment involved in scoring varies widely. Each selected-response item is marked right or wrong so the scoring is completely objective (i.e., different scorers will arrive at the same score). The essay test provides more freedom of response, and this introduces greater subjectivity into the scoring. Different scorers can and do arrive at different scores as they weight elements of the answer differently (e.g., completeness, organization, clarity of writing, and the like) and introduce other personal biases into their judgments. As the tasks become more comprehensive and complex, as in performance assessment, the demands on teacher judgment become even greater. Complex performance tasks that involve the integration of various types of information and skill and may have multiple solutions make it difficult, and in many cases undesirable, to have model answers as might be used with essay testing. With performance assessment we are most likely to have to depend on identification of the **criteria** of a quality performance and then apply the criteria by means of a **rating scale** or set of **scoring rubrics.** Each of these steps is based on subjective judgment.

A review of these categories makes clear that each assessment method has its strengths and weaknesses. When we use selected-response tests, we can obtain a comprehensive coverage of a content domain, and can administer, score, and interpret it easily, but we sacrifice realism and some types of complexity. When we use extended performance assessment, we can obtain a high degree of realism and increase the complexity of the tasks we can assess, but the time needed for assessment is frequently excessive and the evaluation of the performance is highly judgmental. A useful rule would be to use the most efficient method as long as it is appropriate for assessing the intended learning outcomes, but don't neglect complex learning outcomes just because the assessment methods are time consuming and the results are difficult to score or judge.

Guidelines for Effective Student Assessment

The main purpose of a classroom assessment program is to improve student learning. This is most likely to result if assessment is closely integrated with instruction and is guided by a basic set of conditions. The following guidelines provide a general framework for using student assessment effectively.

1. *Effective assessment requires a clear conception of all intended learning outcomes.* During both instructional and assessment planning, we need to ask

ourselves—What are the intended learning outcomes of the instruction? What types of knowledge, understanding, application, and performance skills are we willing to accept as evidence that the instruction has been successful? Here, there is always the danger of focusing too narrowly on knowledge outcomes because they are easy to identify, state, and measure. Unless we include the more complex learning outcomes at this stage, they are likely to be neglected during assessment. We need to specify all intended learning outcomes in terms of student performance and make plans to assess them all.

2. *Effective assessment requires that a variety of assessment procedures be used.* The vast array of possible learning outcomes in any particular area of instruction means that various types of assessment procedures must be considered when planning for assessment. Selected-response tests may be used for some learning outcomes and essay tests for others, where ability to express ideas is important. In assessing performance skills, where we must depend largely on judgment, rating scales or checklists may be needed.

In assessing the more complex learning outcomes, a combination of methods may be most suitable. Solving a complex problem, for example, may involve gathering information from diverse sources, analyzing it, integrating it, writing out a suggested solution, and making an oral presentation to a group. Similarly, locating and correcting a malfunction in a machine may involve reading a technical manual, identifying machine sounds, selecting proper tools, testing machine parts, and making the needed repairs. In addition to correcting the malfunction, speed of performance, following the proper sequence of steps, and similar factors may be an important part of the assessment. In evaluating performance skills, multiple assessment is likely to be the rule rather than the exception.

3. *Effective assessment requires that the instructional relevance of the procedures be considered.* Instructionally relevant assessment means that the intended outcomes of instruction, the domain of learning tasks, and the assessment procedures will all be in close agreement, as shown in Figure 2.1. It also means that plans for using the assessment results in the instructional program must be considered. Will the classroom test be sufficiently diagnostic to provide for remedial action? Can the assessment of a complex performance skill be designed as an ongoing activity so that it can contribute directly to the instruction? These and similar questions are needed to obtain maximum integration of instruction and assessment. Remember, the main purpose of both instruction and assessment is to improve student learning. With a well-designed assessment program, assessment activities may become barely distinguishable from instructional activities.

4. *Effective assessment requires an adequate sample of student performance.* Assessment is always a matter of sampling. Our instruction typically covers numerous knowledge and skill outcomes, but because of the

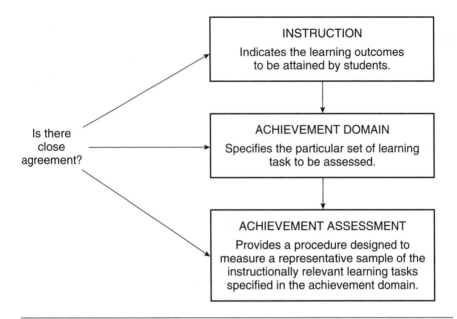

FIGURE 2.1   Sequence in preparing instructionally relevant assessment.

limited time available for assessment and other constraints, we can only measure or judge a limited sample of student performance in any particular area. In preparing a classroom test, for example, there may be 100 terms that the students should know but we only have room for 20 terms in our test. Thus, we must select a representative sample from the 100 words because we want to be able to generalize from performance on the 20 terms as to how well students know the 100 terms. If our sample is adequate, we can estimate that 18 correct answers on the 20 terms indicates that a student knows about 90 percent of the 100 terms (with allowance for a margin of error, of course).

Sampling is also a problem in performance assessment. In assessing driving skill, for example, it would be impossible to include all possible driving problems in a brief driving test so we must settle for a representative sample of them. It is interesting to note that, for licensing purposes, some states are now including driving on the expressway to obtain a more adequate sample of driving skill.

In the assessment of performance skills in the classroom there are typically two problems of sampling. In a writing project, for example, we might ask (1) does the project include a representative sample of the writing skills we are stressing in our teaching? and (2) does performance on this project represent what writing performance would be like on other similar projects? Because extended performance assessment (e.g., giving a speech, conducting an experiment, applying math to a real world problem) is so time consuming and context bound, the adequacy of sampling is always an important concern in planning the assessment.

5. *Effective assessment requires that the procedures be fair to everyone.* An assessment program that makes the intended learning outcomes clear to students, that uses assessment procedures that are instructionally relevant and adequately sample student performance, and uses assessment results to improve learning goes a long way toward creating an atmosphere of fairness. In addition, however, special efforts must be made to eliminate irrelevant sources of difficulty and bias of various types. Student performance may be inadequate because the directions were ambiguous, the reading level was inappropriate, or the performance called for knowledge or skills that were not intended as parts of the assessment task. Similarly, including racial or gender stereotypes in the assessment material may distort the results and create a feeling of unfairness. Fairness requires care in preparing and using assessment procedures, clearly communicating our intentions to students, and using the results to improve learning.

6. *Effective assessment requires the specifications of criteria for judging successful performance.* In the past, success was typically determined by comparing a student's performance to that of others (norm-referenced interpretation). If performance surpassed that of others it was considered excellent performance. If performance was lower than that of others it was considered poor performance. Although this method of judging success has its merits and is useful in certain situations, it is not satisfactory as a measure of how well students are learning the intended outcomes of instruction. For this purpose we need *criteria* that describe what students can do when they perform successfully (e.g., type 40 words per minute with no more than two errors).

Establishing performance criteria is difficult in many areas but, if the intended learning outcomes are clearly stated in performance terms, the criteria for success can be more easily established. In assessing vocabulary, for example, we can describe success in terms of how well students can define each term and use it in a sentence, how well they can distinguish between similar terms, and how well they can use the terms in a writing project. Effective laboratory performance can be described in terms of the selection and manipulation of equipment, the accuracy of measurements, the procedures followed, and the written description and interpretation of results. By specifying success in performance terms, we can describe what students are achieving and how well. The degree of success can be expressed by separate scores, scoring rubrics that describe degrees of effectiveness, rating scales, or whatever means is most useful for describing student performance.

Students should have a clear notion of what is expected of them and clearly specified criteria of successful performance can be used to clarify the learning tasks. In some cases, students may participate in defining the desired performance. In planning for oral reports, for example, a discussion of criteria and listing them on the board will cause students to focus on the criteria of a good oral report and help them improve their performance. This is one way that instruction and assessment can be blended together to the benefit of students.

7. *Effective assessment requires feedback to students that emphasizes strengths of performance and weaknesses to be corrected.* Feedback of assessment results to students is an essential factor in any assessment program. To be most effective, feedback must meet the following criteria:

A. Should be given immediately following or during the assessment.
B. Should be detailed and understandable to students.
C. Should focus on successful elements of the performance and the errors to be corrected.
D. Should provide remedial suggestions for correcting errors.
E. Should be positive and provide a guide for improving both performance and self-assessment.

In performance assessment, our immediate goal is to improve performance. But if we are to develop self-learners, who will continue to improve performance on their own, then we need to also help them develop self-assessment skills. Thus, feedback must focus on both performance skills and self-assessment skills. For example, we not only suggest how to modify performance but also how to check on the effect of the modifications on performance and ways to determine future improvement. A final question concerning feedback might be, Will this feedback to students make them more dependent on the teacher or will it contribute to more independent learning? The most desirable choice is obvious and is illustrated in Figure 2.2.

8. *Effective assessment must be supported by a comprehensive grading and reporting system.* All too frequently teachers have used various types of assessment procedures and then assigned grades on the basis of scores on an objective test. Instead, we need to have the grading and reporting system reflect the emphasis in our assessments. If half of our learning outcomes are assessed by tests and half by performance assessments, and a single grade is used, the two types of assessment should receive equal weight in the grade. With the recent emphasis on performance assessment, more elaborate grading and reporting systems are needed to describe student performance adequately. Reports based on the intended learning outcomes and portfolios of student work are becoming increasingly important for reporting learning progress to students, parents, and others. These more elaborate reports are in harmony with the more elaborate assessment procedures being used.

Because letter grades are still required for some purposes (e.g., college admission), it may be necessary to use both letter grades and a more elabo-

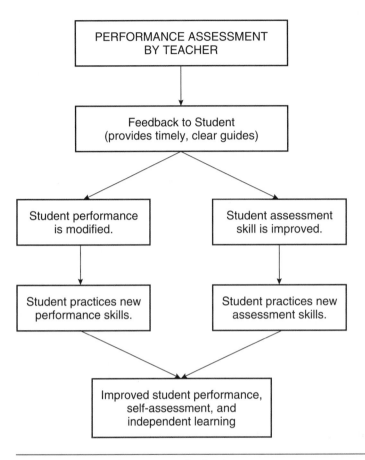

FIGURE 2.2   Role of assessment feedback.

rate report. In any event, the grading and reporting procedures should reflect and support the assessment procedures, be made clear to students at the beginning of instruction, and provide for periodic feedback to students concerning their learning progress.

Validity and Reliability in Assessment Planning

Two of the most important characteristics of a well-designed assessment procedure are **validity** and **reliability.** These characteristics are of primary concern during assessment planning and most of the suggestions in this book are directed toward preparing assessments that provide for valid and reliable interpretation of results.

Validity refers to the appropriateness and meaningfulness of the inferences we make from assessment results for some intended use. For example, if we give a vocabulary test, we would like to be able to interpret the scores as a representative sample of the terms we have been teaching. If we do a good job of (1) clearly defining the domain of vocabulary items to be measured, (2) carefully preparing the test specifications, and (3) constructiing a representative sample of relevant test items, our interpretations from the results are likely to be valid. We are now able to infer that high scores represent good knowledge of the vocabulary that has been taught. Note that it is the inference that is important. If we infer that high scores indicate good writing ability or good verbal ability, we are generalizing beyond the limited assessment domain being tested and the validity of our inference is in doubt, without further evidence. Thus, it is not the test scores that are valid or invalid but the inferences we make from them.

Performance assessments are typically viewed as providing more valid inferences concerning learning than traditional paper-and-pencil tests because they focus more directly on the types of performance tasks we are teaching. If we want to determine if students can read, we have them read something. If we want to determine if students can give a speech, we have them give a speech. If we want to determine if students can operate a computer, we have them operate a computer. In each case the task has the appearance of being valid (i.e., we have good *face* validity). However, it is not as simple as it seems. In performance assessment, the problem of defining the assessment domain, of specifying how the performance will be judged, and of obtaining a representative sample of performance tasks poses special problems. For example, there are many different types of reading, many different types of speeches, and many different types of problems to be solved on the computer. Each requires its own specifications and scoring rubrics, and because of the time-consuming nature of performance assessment, the sampling tends to be limited. This restricts the extent to which we can infer that performance on one assessment task is generalizable to performance on other assessment tasks in the same area.

With both tests and performance assessments we need to make plans and follow procedures that are most likely to yield valid inferences concerning learning. This involves selecting appropriate procedures, preparing them carefully, applying them effectively, and then interpreting the results within the limits of the particular achievement domain being assessed. In using the results we are also, of course, concerned about the consequences of the assessment. Did its use contribute to increased student learning, as intended? This is a legitimate validity-related question because our main purpose in assessing student achievement is to improve learning.

Reliability refers to the *consistency* of assessment results. For example, if a student earns a score of 60 on a test, we would like to be able to say that

60 accurately represents the student's test performance. Thus, if we tested the student at a different time or with a different sample of equivalent items, we would expect to obtain a similar score. Similarly, if a student receives a high rating on a writing project, we would like to say that it represents the student's writing skill and that if others rated the project the results would be similar. This consistency of results would indicate that they are relatively free from errors and thus we can rely on them (i.e., they have "rely-ability").

We cannot, of course, expect assessment results to be perfectly consistent over different occasions or over different samples of the same achievement domain. Such factors as ambiguities, variations in samples, fluctuations in motivation and attention, and luck can introduce errors that cause assessment results to vary. Likewise, in judging performance tasks, the personal biases of the rater can introduce error into the results. An important goal in assessment is to keep these various types of errors to a minimum so that our results are as reliable as possible.

In addition to being important in its own right, reliability is necessary to obtain valid inferences from assessment results. After all, if an individual's test score fluctuated widely on a given sample of items, we could not expect to draw valid inferences concerning the student's achievement. Similarly, if ratings varied widely on a student's writing project, valid inferences could not be made concerning writing skill. Thus, *reliability provides the consistency of results that makes valid inferences possible.* Of course, the consistency of results is just one important requirement for valid inferences. We could be consistently assessing the wrong thing, using inappropriate procedures, or generalizing beyond the achievement domain being assessed. Thus, reliability is a necessary, but not a sufficient, condition for making valid inferences.

Both the validity and reliability of assessment results can be provided for during the preparation of assessment procedures. When we clearly specify the intended learning outcomes, define the achievement domain to be assessed, and select a relevant and representative set of assessment tasks, we are providing for valid inferences concerning learning. When we include an adequate number of tasks in our assessment and we use procedures that are free from ambiguity, irrelevant sources of difficulty, unintended clues, and other factors that might distort the results, we are providing for both reliability and validity. In fact, most of the suggestions for constructing achievement tests and preparing performance assessments are directed toward improving the reliability of the assessment results and the validity of the interpretations we make from them.

A more elaborate discussion of validity and reliability and methods for determining them is presented in Chapter 12. Although high quality assessments can be made without a detailed study of validity and reliability, understanding the basic concepts involved can contribute to improved skill in preparing assessment procedures, making appropriate interpretations of the results, and using the results effectively.

Some of the most important features that enhance the validity and reliability of assessment results are presented in Table 2.2. This table makes clear that concern about validity and reliability takes place in the early stages of assessment planning and preparation, not after the assessment results have been obtained. The procedures listed in Table 2.2 will be described in more detail in the chapters on preparing tests and performance-based assessments. Here, we are simply emphasizing their importance in obtaining valid and reliable interpretations of assessment results and the need for early assessment planning to "build in" the desired features.

TABLE 2.2   *Desirable Features for Enhancing the Validity and Reliability of Assessment Results*

Desired Features	*Procedures to Follow*
1. Clearly specified set of learning outcomes.	1. State intended learning outcomes in performance terms.
2. Representative sample of a clearly defined domain of learning tasks.	2. Prepare a description of the achievement domain to be assessed and the sample of tasks to be used.
3. Tasks that are relevant to the learning outcomes to be measured.	3. Match assessment tasks to the specified performance stated in the learning outcomes.
4. Tasks that are at the proper level of difficulty.	4. Match assessment task difficulty to the learning task, the students' abilities, and the use to be made of the results.
5. Tasks that function effectively in distinguishing between achievers and nonachievers.	5. Follow general guidelines and specific rules for preparing assessment procedures and be alert for factors that distort the results.
6. Sufficient number of tasks to measure an adequate sample of achievement, provide dependable results, and allow for a meaningful interpretation of the results.	6. Where the students' age or available assessment time limit the number of tasks, make tentative interpretations, assess more frequently, and verify the results with other evidence.
7. Procedures that contribute to efficient preparation and use.	7. Write clear directions and arrange procedures for ease of administration, scoring or judging, and interpretation.

Norm-Referenced and Criterion-Referenced Assessment

An achievement assessment can be used to provide (1) a relative ranking of students or (2) a description of the learning tasks a student can and cannot perform. Results of the first type are interpreted in terms of each student's relative standing among other students (for example, "He is third highest in a class of 35 students"). This method of interpreting student performance is called **norm-referenced interpretation.** Results of the second type are expressed in terms of the specific knowledge and skills each student can demonstrate (e.g., "She can identify the parts of a microscope and demonstrate its use"). This method of interpreting assessment results is called **criterion-referenced interpretation** (see Box 2.1). Both methods of describing assessment results are useful. The first tells how an individual's performance compares with that of others. The second tells in specific performance terms what an individual can do without reference to the performance of others.

Strictly speaking, the terms *norm-referenced* and *criterion-referenced* refer only to the method of interpreting the results. Thus, both types of interpretation could be applied to the same assessment. For example, we might say, "Joan surpassed 90 percent of the students (norm-referenced interpretation) by

---

BOX 2.1 • *Terms Similar to Criterion-Referenced Interpretation*

Domain-Referenced Interpretation	Assessment results are interpreted in terms of a relevant and clearly defined set related tasks (called a *domain*). Meaning is similar to criterion-referenced interpretation but the term is less used, even though it is a more descriptive term.
Content-Referenced Interpretation	Essentially the same meaning as domain-referenced interpretation when the content domain is broadly defined to include tasks representing both content and process (i.e., reactions to the content). This term s declining in use and being replaced by criterion-referenced interpretation.
Objective-Referenced Interpretation	Assessment results are interpreted in terms of each specific objective that a set of test items represents. This is frequently called *criterion-referenced interpretation* but the more limited designation is preferable where interpretation is limited to each separate objective.

correctly completing 20 of the 25 chemical equations" (criterion-referenced interpretation). The two types of interpretation are likely to be most meaningful, however, when the assessment is designed specifically for the type of interpretation to be made. In general, norm-referenced interpretation is facilitated by a wide spread of scores so that reliable discriminations can be made among students at various levels of achievement. Criterion-referenced interpretation is facilitated by assessment tasks that provide a detailed description of student performance. In testing, this means a larger number of test items per task. In performance assessment, this means performance tasks that make clear what parts of the task a person can and cannot do.

    Although norm-referenced and criterion-referenced interpretations apply to all types of achievement assessments, the differences can be most clearly indicated when applied to testing. A summary of some common characteristics of tests specifically designed for each type of interpretation is presented in Table 2.3. It must be kept in mind, however, that these are primarily matters of emphasis. For example, norm-referenced tests are typi-

TABLE 2.3   *Summary Comparison of Two Basic Approaches to Achievement Testing*

	Norm-Referenced Testing	*Criterion-Referenced Testing*
Principal Use	Survey testing.	Mastery testing.
Major Emphasis	Measures individual differences in achievement.	Describes tasks students can perform.
Interpretation of Results	Compares performance to that of other individuals.	Compares performance to a clearly specified achievement domain.
Content Coverage	Typically covers a broad area of achievement.	Typically focuses on a limited set of learning tasks.
Nature of Test Plan	Table of specifications is commonly used.	Detailed domain specifications are favored.
Item Selection Procedures	Items are selected that provide maximum discrimination among individuals (to obtain a reliable ranking). Easy items are typically eliminated from the test.	Includes all items needed to adequately describe performance. No attempt is made to alter item difficulty or to eliminate easy items to increase the spread of scores.
Performance Standards	Level of performance is determined by *relative* position in some known group (e.g., ranks fifth in a group of 20).	Level of performance is commonly determined by *absolute* standards (e.g., demonstrates mastery by defining 90 percent of the technical terms).

cally, but not exclusively, used for surveying achievement over a broad range of learning outcomes. By the same token, criterion-referenced tests are typically, but not exclusively, used for **mastery testing.** A review of the characteristics of each testing approach in Table 2.3 will reveal the differences that exist when each test is constructed to serve its principal use. It is not uncommon, however, to view the two test types as the ends of a continuum rather than as discrete categories, and to combine the best features of each in constructing achievement tests.

For most instructional purposes, criterion-referenced assessments are to be favored. We can best help students improve learning by determining what tasks they can and cannot perform. Thus, the classroom assessment program should be based on instruments and procedures that provide for this type of interpretation. Norm-referenced interpretation is most useful when we are concerned about the relative ranking of students, as in the selection and classification of students (e.g., advance placement, grouping, giving awards, and relative grading).

Most of the discussions of procedures for constructing tests and making performance assessment will apply to all types of tests and assessments. Where there are significant differences due to the type of interpretation to be made, these will be noted.

Summary of Points

1. Student assessment needs to be expanded to include the assessment of more complex learning outcomes than has been the case in the past.
2. Assessment methods vary widely but they can be classified as selected-response tests, supply-response tests, restricted-response performance assessments, or extended-response performance assessments.
3. Selected-response tests (e.g., multiple-choice tests) are lowest in realism and complexity of the tasks assessed, but require little time to administer and can be scored quickly and objectively.
4. Supply-response tests (e.g., essay tests) are higher in realism and the complexity of tasks they can measure (e.g., ability to originate, integrate, and express ideas) than selected-response tests, but they are more time consuming to use and more difficult to score.
5. Performance assessments, both restricted response and extended response, can be designed with high degrees of realism (i.e., like real-world problems) that focus on highly complex learning tasks, but they require large amounts of time to use and the scoring is judgmental and highly subjective.
6. A sound assessment policy would be to use the most efficient method available for assessing each intended learning outcome as long as it is appropriate, but don't neglect complex learning outcomes just because

the assessment methods are more time consuming to use and more difficult to score or judge.

7. Effective assessment requires a clear conception of all intended learning outcomes, a variety of assessment procedures that are relevant to the instruction, an adequate sample of tasks, procedures that are fair to everyone, criteria for judging success, timely and detailed feedback to students, and a grading and reporting system that is in harmony with the assessment program.

8. Validity and reliability are the two most important characteristics of any assessment method and must be considered during the planning and preparation of assessment procedures.

9. Valid and reliable interpretations of assessment results require clearly defined intended learning outcomes, a representative sample of instructionally relevant tasks, a sound scoring system, and freedom from irrelevant factors that introduce error.

10. Assessment results can be interpreted by comparing a student's performance to that of others (norm-referenced) or by describing the student's performance on a clearly defined set of tasks (criterion-referenced).

11. Criterion-referenced interpretation is especially important for instructional uses of assessment results but norm-referenced interpretation may be needed for selection and classification decisions.

12. In some cases both criterion-referenced and norm-referenced interpretation may be used with the same assessment.

References and Additional Reading

Linn, R. L., and Gronlund, N. E., *Measurement and Assessment in Teaching*, 8th ed. (Upper Saddle River, NJ: Merrill/ Prentice-Hall, 2000).

McMillan, J. H., *Classroom Assessment: Principles and Practices for Effective Instruction*, 2nd ed. (Boston: Allyn and Bacon, 2001).

Oosterhoff, A. C., *Developing and Using Classroom Assessments*, 2nd ed. (Upper Saddle River, NJ: Prentice-Hall, 1999).

Smith, J. K., Smith, L. F., and DeLisi, R., *Natural Classroom Assessment*. (Thousand Oaks, CA: Corwin Press, 2001).

Stiggins, R. J., *Student-Involved Classroom Assessment*, 3rd ed. (Upper Saddle River, NJ: Merrill/Prentice-Hall, 2001).

Wiggins, G. P., *Educative Assessment: Designing Assessments to Inform and Improve Student Performance* (San Francisco, CA: Jossey-Bass, 1998).

3

Planning for Assessment

Studying this chapter should enable you to

1. List the types of learning outcomes to consider in planning for the assessment of student achievement.
2. State instructional objectives as intended learning outcomes and define them in performance terms.
3. Prepare a set of specifications for a test.
4. Describe the relative merits of selection and supply type test items.
5. Match test items to the specific learning outcomes they measure.
6. Describe the factors to consider when preparing items for a test.
7. Describe how to arrange items in a test.
8. Write clear directions for a test.
9. Review and evaluate an assembled test.
10. Administer a test properly.
11. Make a simple item analysis.

Planning for the assessment of student achievement involves a consideration of the following questions:

1. What do we expect students to learn?
2. What *types* of student performance are we willing to accept as evidence of learning?
3. What assessment instruments will best evaluate the students' performance?

The first question focuses on the goals of the curriculum as set by the school and influenced by the district and state. In recent years, states have developed **content standards** that provide guidelines for determining what students should know and be able to do. This has influenced districts and schools to modify curriculums and put greater emphasis on the more complex learning outcomes.

The second question focuses on the importance of specifying instructional objectives in performance terms and including all types of desired learning outcomes. These objectives must, of course, be in harmony with the goals of the curriculum and will reflect the state content standards to the same degree as the school curriculum. In final analysis, the assessment of student achievement is determined by what the students are expected to learn, and this is determined by the goals of the school curriculum. The instructional objectives are simply a means of stating the curriculum goals in more specific terms so that they are useful in both instruction and assessment.

The third question focuses on the match between the instructional objectives and the procedures of assessment. The objectives specify the intended learning outcomes in performance terms and the assessment method is used to determine the extent to which students' performance is satisfactory. For some performance outcomes a test will provide adequate evidence. In other cases, some type of observational technique will be needed to evaluate the ongoing nature of the performance (e.g., giving a speech) or to evaluate a resulting product (e.g., a written report). The key to effective assessment is to use the most direct and relevant method available.

Types of Intended Learning Outcomes

In planning for the assessment of student achievement, there are a number of types of learning outcomes that might be considered. Although the goals of the school and the nature of the instructional content will determine what specific types of learning outcomes are to be assessed, a review of the various types of outcomes shown in Table 3.1 will prevent any serious omissions. The list is not exhaustive, but it makes clear the range of outcomes to consider beyond that of knowledge, when preparing objectives for instruction and assessment.

Well-designed classroom tests can be used to measure many of the outcomes in the cognitive areas, but skills and products require the use of observational techniques such as checklists, rating scales, or holistic scoring rubrics.

TABLE 3.1 *Some Types of Intended Learning Outcomes*

Types	Sample Categories
Knowledge of	Facts
	Concepts
Comprehension of	Principles
	Methods
Application of	Process
	Analyzing
Reasoning	Comparing
Ability	Inferring
	Generalizing
	Evaluating
	Speaking
Observable	Oral reading
Skills	Laboratory skills
	Psychomotor skills
	Work-study skills
	Writing
	Drawing
Products	Designing
	Constructing
	Problem-solving

Role of Instructional Objectives

Well-stated instructional objectives provide a description of the intended learning outcomes in performance terms—that is, in terms of the types of performance students can demonstrate to show that they have achieved the knowledge, understanding, or skill described by the objective. By describing the performance that we are willing to accept as evidence of learning, we provide a focus for instruction, student learning, and assessment. Objectives help keep all three in close harmony. For example, for an objective emphasizing problem-solving strategies, we teach students how to apply problem-solving strategies, they practice applying the strategies, and we assess their skill in applying problem-solving strategies with new problems. Thus, the instructional targets, the learning targets, and the assessment targets are all the same. If the students are made aware of the objectives at the beginning of instruction, both teacher and students are working toward common goals and instruction and assessment are both part of the same process.

Stating Instructional Objectives

In stating instructional objectives, it is helpful to keep in mind that we are not describing the teaching procedures or the learning process. We are simply describing the student performance to be demonstrated at the end of the learning experience as evidence of learning. This permits us to use a variety of procedures, materials, and learning activities to achieve the desired outcomes.

A useful procedure is to first state the general objectives that focus on the broader learning outcomes and then define each general objective in more specific terms, as follows.

1. Understands Scientific Concepts
   1.1 Describes the concept in his or her own words.
   1.2 Describes the role of the concept in science.
   1.3 Distinguishes the concept from similar scientific concepts.
   1.4 Uses the concept in writing about science.
   1.5 Applies the concept in solving problems.

The specific learning outcomes listed under the general objective are not meant to be exhaustive, but they should provide a representative sample of the types of performance that we are willing to accept as evidence that the objective has been achieved. The general procedure for stating instructional objectives is presented in Box 3.1. The specific application of these steps is described and illustrated later for a unit on test planning.

Sources of Help in Locating Sample Objectives

In getting started with the identification and selection of instructional objectives, it helps to review various sources for ideas. Illustrative categories of intended learning outcomes and sample objectives can be found in the following sources.

1. *Taxonomy of Educational Objectives.* This is an older guide but it provides a classification of objectives in the cognitive, psychomotor, and affective domains. Each domain includes categories and subcategories that are designed to identify and classify all possible educational outcomes. For example, the cognitive domain includes the following major categories (Bloom, 1956):
   a. Knowledge (remembering previous learning material).
   b. Comprehension (grasping the meaning of material).
   c. Application (using information in concrete situation).

BOX 3.1 • *Stating Instructional Objectives*

The following steps provide guidelines for stating instructional objectives that are useful in instruction and assessment.

1. State the general objectives as follows:
   1.1 Write each as an intended learning outcome.
   1.2 State each in performance terms.
   1.3 Start each with a verb (e.g., "knows," "comprehends").
   1.4 Write each so it is general enough to identify a domain of specific learning outcomes.
2. List and state the specific learning outcomes as follows:
   2.1 Clarify each general objective with a representative sample of specific learning outcomes.
   2.2 Begin each with an action verb indicating observable student performance (e.g., "selects," "describes").
   2.3 Include a sufficient number to indicate attainment of the general objective.
   2.4 Check to be sure the specific learning outcomes are relevant to the general objectives and that the general objectives are in harmony with the school goals.

   d. Analysis (breaking down material into its parts).
   e. Synthesis (putting parts together into a whole).
   f. Evaluation (judging the value of a thing using criteria).

   These categories are listed in the order of increasing complexity and are clarified in the taxonomy by subdivisions that further describe the types of educational outcomes included. For detailed descriptions of all three domains of the taxonomy with illustrative objectives for each category see Gronlund (2000) at the end of this chapter.

2. *Instructors' guides accompanying student textbooks.* These guides typically contain objectives but they tend to focus on lower level outcomes, may be poorly stated, and are likely to lack close harmony with the goals of the curriculum. However, they are worth a review for ideas on possible learning outcomes to consider. It may be possible to modify some to put them in more usable form.
3. *Publications of educational organizations.* There are organizations in each of the main teaching areas that publish useful material on instruction that contains suggested objectives. For example, the National Science Teachers Association, the National Council of Teachers of

Mathematics, the National Council of Teachers of English, and the National Council for the Social Studies periodically issue yearbooks and other publications on instruction in their content area. The more recent publications will focus on learning outcomes that are in harmony with the newer curriculum emphasis on reasoning and problem-solving skills.

4. *State content standards.* The majority of states have developed content standards that provide guidelines for determining what students should know and be able to do in subject areas. These standards typically emphasize complex learning outcomes that focus on understanding of concepts and problem-solving skills. Thus, they may not represent a total curriculum in the content areas but serve as a framework for shaping the goals of the districts and schools. The intent is to move the school curriculum more toward a thinking curriculum and thereby improving both instruction and assessment.

Two illustrative content standards, developed by the California Department of Education, are shown in Figure 3.1. The standards are followed by examples of how students will show that they have met the standards. Although the standards are described as exemplary and compliance with them is not mandatory, schools and districts are encouraged to use them in curriculum development.

State content standards are typically reflected to some degree in the school curriculum and thus provide a valuable focus on the more complex learning outcomes. Although they are usually too general for direct use in instruction and assessment, a review of these will provide useful ideas for preparing instructional objectives. In those schools that emphasize standard-based instruction and standard-based assessment, it will be necessary to pay special attention to the content standards prepared by the state when writing instructional objectives.

Preparing and Using an Achievement Test

The preparation and use of an achievement test that measures the intended learning outcomes in a balanced manner involves the following steps:

1. Specifying the instructional objectives.
2. Preparing the test specifications.
3. Constructing relevant test items.
4. Arranging the items in the test.
5. Preparing clear directions.

Focus on Life Science

Cell Biology

1. All living organisms are composed of cells, from just one to many trillions, whose details usually are visible only through a microscope. As a basis for understanding this concept:

   a. *Students know* cells function similarly in all living organisms.

   b. *Students know* the characteristics that distinguish plant cells from animal cells, including chloroplasts and cell walls.

   c. *Students know* the nucleus is the repository for genetic information in plant and animal cells.

   d. *Students know* that mitochrondria liberate energy for the work that cells do and that chloroplasts capture sunlight energy for photosynthesis.

   e. *Students know* cells divide to increase their numbers through a process of mitosis, which results in two daughter cells with identical sets of chromosomes.

   f. *Students know* that as multicellular organisms develop, their cells differentiate.

Investigation and Experimentation

7. Scientific progress is made by asking meaningful questions and conducting careful investigations. As a basis for understanding this concept and addressing the content in the other three strands, students should develop their own questions and perform investigations. Students will:

   a. Select and use appropriate tools and technology (including calculators, computers, balances, spring scales, microscopes, and binoculars) to perform tests, collect data, and display data.

   b. Use a variety of print and electronic resources (including the World Wide Web) to collect information and evidence as part of a research project.

   c. Communicate the logical connection hypotheses, science concepts, tests conducted, data collected, and conclusions drawn from the scientific evidence.

   d. Construct scale models, maps, and appropriately labeled diagrams to communicate scientific knowledge (e.g., motion of Earth's plates and cell structure).

   e. Communicate the steps and results from an investigation in written reports and oral presentations.

FIGURE 3.1 *Sample California Science Content Standards—Grade 7.*

From *Science Content Standards for California Public Schools*, Copyright 2000, California Department of Education. Used by permission.

6. Reviewing and evaluating the assembled test.
7. Administering the test and making an item analysis.

Each of these steps will be described in turn. Performance assessment will be described in Chapters 7, 8, and 9.

Specifying the Instructional Objectives

As noted earlier, the first step in preparing instructional objectives it to list the general objectives as intended learning outcomes. The following list illustrates the procedure for a unit on planning an achievement test.

At the end of this unit in achievement test planning the student will demonstrate that he or she:

1. Knows the meaning of common terms.
2. Knows specific facts about test planning.
3. Knows the basic procedures for planning an achievement test.
4. Comprehends the relevant principles of testing.
5. Applies the principles in test planning.

These statements of general learning outcomes have been deliberately kept free of specific course content so that with only slight modification they can be used with various units of study. As we shall see later, the test specifications provide a means of relating intended outcomes to specific subject matter topics.

This list of general outcomes could, of course, be expanded by making the statements more specific, and in some cases it may be desirable to do so. The number of general learning outcomes to use is somewhat arbitrary, but somewhere between 5 and 15 items provide a list that is both useful and manageable. Typically, a shorter list is satisfactory for a unit of study, while a more comprehensive list is needed for summative testing at the end of a course.

Defining the General Outcomes in Specific Terms

When a satisfactory list of general learning outcomes has been identified and clearly stated, the next step is to list the specific types of student performance that are to be accepted as evidence that the outcomes have been achieved. For example, what specific types of performance will show that a student "knows the meaning of common terms" or "comprehends the relevant principles of testing"? For these two areas the specific learning outcomes may be listed as follows:

1. Knows the meaning of common terms.
   1.1 Identifies the correct definitions of terms.
   1.2 Identifies the meaning of terms when used in context.
   1.3 Distinguishes between terms on basis of meaning.
   1.4 Selects the most appropriate terms when describing testing procedures.
4. Comprehends the relevant principles of testing.
   4.1 Describes each principle in his or her own words.
   4.2 Matches a specific example to each principle.
   4.3 Explains the relevance of each principle to the major steps in test planning.
   4.4 Predicts the most probable effect of violating each of the principles.
   4.5 Formulates a test plan that is in harmony with the principles.

Note that the terms used to describe the specific learning outcomes indicate student performance that can be demonstrated to an outside observer. That is, they are *observable* responses that can be called forth by test items. The key terms are listed below to emphasize what is meant by defining learning outcomes in *specific performance terms.*

Identifies	Matches
Distinguishes between	Explains
Selects	Predicts
Describes	Formulates

Action verbs such as these indicate precisely what the student is able to do to demonstrate achievement. Such vague and indefinite terms as "learns," "sees," "realizes," and "is familiar with" should be avoided, since they do not clearly indicate the terminal performance to be measured.

Sample action verbs for stating specific learning outcomes at each level of the cognitive domain of the taxonomy are presented in Table 3.2. Although certain action verbs may be used at several different levels (e.g., "identifies"), the table provides a useful guide for defining intended outcomes in performance terms. For more comprehensive lists of action verbs, see Gronlund (2000) listed at the end of this chapter.

In defining the general learning outcomes in specific performance terms, it is typically impossible to list all of the relevant types of performance. The proportion that need be listed depends to a large extent on the nature of the test. In planning a test that is to be used to describe which learning tasks a student has mastered (criterion-referenced test), we should like as comprehensive a list as possible. For a test that is used to rank students in order of achievement (norm-referenced test), however, it is usually satisfactory to include a sufficient number of specific types of performance

TABLE 3.2   *Illustrative Action Verbs for Defining Objectives in the Cognitive Domain of the Taxonomy*

Taxonomy Categories	Sample Verbs for Stating Specific Learning Outcomes
Knowledge	Identifies, names, defines, describes, lists, matches, selects, outlines
Comprehension	Classifies, explains, summarizes, converts, predicts, distinguishes between
Application	Demonstrates, computes, solves, modifies, arranges, operates, relates
Analysis	Differentiates, diagrams, estimates, separates, infers, orders, subdivides
Synthesis	Combines, creates, formulates, designs, composes, constructs, rearranges, revises
Evaluation	Judges, criticizes, compares, justifies, concludes, discriminates, supports

to clarify what the typical student is like who has achieved the intended outcomes.

Preparing the Test Specifications

The writing of test items should be guided by a carefully prepared set of test specifications. The function of the specifications is to describe the achievement domain being measured and to provide guidelines for obtaining a representative sample of test tasks. Although the nature and detail of test specifications can be expected to vary considerably, here we shall describe one of the more commonly recommended procedures. In the construction of an **achievement test**, one of the most widely used devices has been a two-way chart called a *table of specifications.*

Building a Table of Specifications

Preparing a table of specifications involves (1) selecting the learning outcomes to be tested, (2) outlining the subject matter, and (3) making a two-way chart. The two-way chart describes the sample of items to be included in the test.

Selecting the Learning Outcomes to Be Tested.   The learning outcomes for a particular course will depend on the specific nature of the course, the objectives attained in previous courses, the philosophy of the school, the special needs of the students, and a host of other local factors that have a bearing on the instructional program. Despite the variation from course to course, most lists of instructional objectives will include learning outcomes in the following areas: (1) knowledge, (2) intellectual abilities and skills, (3) general skills (laboratory, performance, communication, work-study), and (4) attitudes, interests, and appreciations. It is in the first two areas covered by the cognitive domain of the taxonomy that achievement testing is most useful. Learning outcomes in the other areas are typically evaluated by rating scales, checklists, anecdotal records, inventories, and similar nontest evaluation procedures. Thus, the first step is to separate from the list of learning outcomes those that are testable by paper-and-pencil tests. The selected list of learning outcomes should, of course, be defined in specific terms, as described in the previous section. Clarifying the specific types of performance to be called forth by the test will aid in constructing test terms that are most relevant to the intended learning outcomes.

Outlining the Subject Matter.   The stated learning outcomes specify how students are expected to react to the subject matter of a course. Although it is possible to include both the student performance and the specific subject matter the student is to react toward in the same statement, it is usually desirable to list them separately. The reason for this is that the student can react in the same way to many different areas of subject matter, and he can react in many different ways to the same area of subject matter. For example, when we state that a student can "define a term in her own words," "recall a specific fact," or "identify an example of a principle," these types of performance can be applied to almost any area of subject matter. Since particular types of student performance can overlap a variety of subject matter areas, and vice versa, it is more convenient to list each aspect of performance and subject matter separately and then to relate them in the table of specifications.

The content of a course may be outlined in detail for teaching purposes, but for test planning only the major categories need be listed. The following outline of subject matter topics based on a unit on achievement testing illustrates sufficient detail for the test plan.

A. Role of testing in the instructional process
    1. Instructional decisions and test types
    2. Influence of tests on learning and instruction
B. Principles of achievement testing
    1. Relation to instructional objectives
    2. Representative sampling
    3. Relevance of items to outcomes
    4. Relevance of test to use of results
    5. Reliability of results
    6. Improvement of learning

C. Norm-referenced versus criterion-referenced testing
D. Planning the test
   1. Determining the purpose of the test
   2. Identifying the intended learning outcomes
   3. Preparing the test specifications
   4. Constructing relevant test items

Making the Two-Way Chart.   When the learning outcomes have been selected and clearly defined and the course content outlined, the two-way chart
should be prepared. This is called a **table of specifications**. It relates outcomes to content and indicates the relative weight to be given to each of the
various areas. As noted earlier, the purpose of the table is to provide assurance that the test will measure a representative sample of the learning outcomes and the subject matter topics to be measured.

An example of a table of specifications for a summative test on a unit
on achievement testing is given in Table 3.3. Note that only the general
learning outcomes and the major subject matter categories have been
included. A more detailed table may be desirable for test purposes, but this
is sufficient for illustration.

TABLE 3.3   *Table of Specifications for a Summative Test on a Unit
for Achievement Testing*

Outcomes \ Content	Knows			Comprehends Principles	Applies Principles	Total Number of Items
	Terms	*Facts*	*Procedures*			
Role of Tests in Instruction	4	4		2		10
Principles of Testing	4	3	2	6	5	20
Norm-Referenced versus Criterion-Referenced	4	3	3			10
Planning the Test	3	5	5	2	5	20
Total Number of Items	15	15	10	10	10	60

The numbers in each cell of the table indicate the number of test items to be devoted to that area. For example, 15 items in the test will measure knowledge of terms; 4 of them pertain to the "role of tests" in instruction," 4 to "principles of testing," 4 to "norm-referenced versus criterion-referenced," and 3 to "planning the test." The number of items assigned to each cell is determined by the weight given to each learning outcome and each subject matter area.

A number of factors will enter into assigning relative weights to each learning outcome and each content area. How important is each area in the total learning experience? How much time was devoted to each area during instruction? Which outcomes have the greater retention and transfer value? What relative importance do curriculum specialists assign to each area? These and similar criteria must be considered. In the final analysis, however, the weights assigned in the table should faithfully reflect the emphasis given during instruction. In Table 3.3, for example, it is assumed that twice as much emphasis was given to "planning the test" (20 items) as was given to "norm-referenced versus criterion-referenced" (10 items). Similarly, it is assumed that knowledge outcomes were given approximately two-thirds of the emphasis during instruction (40 items) and that comprehension and application outcomes were each given approximately one-sixth of the total emphasis (10 items each).

In summary, preparing a table of specifications includes the following steps:

1. Identify the learning outcomes and content areas to be measured by the test.
2. Weight the learning outcomes and content areas in terms of their relative importance.
3. Build the table in accordance with these relative weights by distributing the test items proportionately among the relevant cells of the table.

The resulting two-way table indicates the type of test needed to measure the learning outcomes and course content in a balanced manner. Thus, the table of specifications serves the test maker like a blueprint. It specifies the number and the nature of the items in the test, and it thereby provides a guide for item writing.

Considerations in Constructing Relevant Test Items

The construction of a set of relevant test items is greatly simplified if the intended learning outcomes have been clearly defined and the test specifications carefully prepared. The quality of the test will then depend on how closely the test maker can match the specifications. Here we shall confine our discussion to some of the general specifications in preparing test items. More detailed procedures and rules for item writing will be described in the chapters that follow.

Selecting the Types of Test Items to Use

The items used in achievement tests can be classified as either *selection-type* items or *supply-type* items. The selection-type item presents students with a set of possible responses from which they are to select the most appropriate answer. The supply-type item requires students to create and supply their own answers. These two major categories can be used to classify the most widely used item types as follows.

Selection-Type Items
1. Multiple choice
2. True-false
3. Matching
4. Interpretive exercise

Supply-Type Items
1. Short answer
2. Essay (restricted response)
3. Essay (extended response)

These categories are sometimes referred to as *recognition* and *recall* items. This is a case of mislabeling that confuses the method of responding with the mental reaction needed to make the response. When measuring knowledge of facts, test responses might be limited to either the recognition or recall of the answer. However, when measuring complex learning outcomes with selection-type items, the answer is not achieved through mere recognition of a previously learned answer. It typically involves some use of higher mental processes to arrive at a solution (e.g., verbal or mathematical reasoning) before the correct answer can be selected. Similarly, a short-answer item may require reasoning or problem solving rather than simply recalling and supplying factual information. Essay answers, of course, typically require analysis, synthesis, and evaluation skills in addition to recall. Using the *selection* and *supply* labels makes clear how the responses are made but it does not imply limits on the types of learning outcomes that can be measured with each.

In deciding which item types to use in a test, a guiding principle should be: *Use the item types that provide the most direct measures of student performance specified by the intended learning outcome.* Thus, if you want to determine if students can spell, have them spell from dictation. If you want to determine if students can solve mathematics problems, have them solve problems and supply the answers. If you want to determine if students can write, have them write something. Use selection-type items for supply-type outcomes only if there is a compelling reason for doing so (e.g., electronic scoring) and then take into account, during interpretation of the results, that a less direct measure has been used. In some cases, of course, both types of items are useful in the same area. For example, a writing project may provide the best evidence of writing skill but a selection-type test would provide the most systematic coverage of the elements of grammar needed for effective writing.

There are a number of achievement areas where either selection-type items or supply-type items would measure equally well. In these cases, our choice between them must be based on other item characteristics. The preparation of good selection-type items is difficult and students can get a proportion of answers correct by guessing. However, these disadvantages are offset by the fact that (1) they can be scored quickly and objectively (i.e., scorers agree on the answers), (2) they eliminate bluffing, (3) they eliminate the influence of writing skill, (4) they provide an extensive sample of student performance (because of the large number of items used), and (5) they provide for the identification of specific learning errors. In comparison, supply-type items are easier to construct (although harder than commonly believed) but more difficult to score. The scoring of short-answer items is contaminated by answers of varying degrees of correctness and by adjustments needed for misspellings. The scoring of essay tests is tedious, time consuming, and influenced by bluffing, writing skill, and the shifting of standards during scoring. Another major shortcoming of supply-type items is the limited sample of learning tasks that can be measured. The short-answer item is restricted primarily to measuring knowledge outcomes. Although the essay test is especially suited to measuring complex learning outcomes, its sampling is limited by the relatively few questions that can be included in a test.

A summary comparison of the relative merits of selection-type and supply-type items is presented in Table 3.4. Although this should serve as a guide in selecting the types of items to use in a given test, as noted earlier, the most important question to ask is: *Does this item type provide the most direct measure of the intended learning outcome?* If the various item types are equal in this regard, the selection-type items would be favored because of the broad sampling, the objective scoring, and the pinpointing of specific learning errors.

Matching Items to Specific Learning Outcomes

Effective achievement testing requires that a set of test items be constructed that calls forth the performance described in the intended learning out-

TABLE 3.4 *Summary of the Relative Merits of Selection-Type Items and Supply-Type Items*

Characteristic	Selection-Type Items	Supply-Type Items	
		Short Answer	*Essay*
Measures factual information	Yes	Yes	Yes(*)
Measures understanding	Yes	No(**)	Yes
Measures synthesis	No(**)	No(**)	Yes
Easy to construct	No	Yes	Yes
Samples broadly	Yes	Yes	No
Eliminates bluffing	Yes	No	No
Eliminates writing skill	Yes	No	No
Eliminates blind guessing	No	Yes	Yes
Easy to score	Yes	No	No
Scoring is objective	Yes	No	No
Pinpoints learning errors	Yes	Yes	No
Encourages originality	No	No	Yes

(*)The essay test can measure knowledge of facts, but because of scoring and sampling problems it probably should not be used for this purpose.

(**)These items can be designed to measure limited aspects of these characteristics.

comes. While we can never be certain of a perfect correspondence between outcome and item, the following examples illustrate how items should be written to measure the specific type of performance stated in the specific learning outcome.

EXAMPLES

Specific Learning Outcome: Defines terms in student's own words.
   Directions: Define each of the following terms in a sentence or two.
   1. Taxonomy
   2. Cognitive
   3. Measurement
   4. Evaluation

Specific Learning Outcome: Identifies procedural steps in planning for a test.
   1. Which one of the following steps should be completed first in planning for an achievement test?[1]
      A. Select the types of test items to use.
      B. Decide on the length of the test.

[1]The correct answer is indicated throughout this book by an asterisk.

   *C. Define the intended learning outcomes.
   D. Prepare the test specifications.

Specific Learning Outcome: Identifies the hierarchical order of the categories in the cognitive domain of the taxonomy.
  1. Which one of the following categories in the taxonomy indicates the highest level of learning?
   A. Analysis
   B. Application
   C. Comprehension
   *D. Synthesis

Specific Learning Outcome: Distinguishes between sound and unsound principles of achievement testing.
  Directions: Read each of the following statements. If the statement indicates a sound principle of achievement testing, circle the S; if it indicates an unsound principle, circle the U.

*S **U** **1.** The specific learning outcomes to be tested should be stated in terms of student performance.
S ***U** **2.** Achievement testing should be limited to outcomes that can be measured objectively.
*S **U** **3.** Each achievement test item should measure a clearly defined type of student performance.

Specific Learning Outcome: Identifies examples of properly stated learning outcomes.
  1. Which one of the following learning outcomes is properly stated in performance terms?
   A. Student realizes the importance of tests in teaching.
   B. Student has acquired the basic principles of achievement testing.
   C. Student demonstrates a desire for more experience in test construction.
   *D. Student predicts the most probable effect of violating a test construction principle.

It should be noted in these examples that each specific learning outcome provides a precise definition of the student performance to be measured, and the test item simply provides a task that makes measurement of the specified performance possible.

Improving the Functioning Content of Items

If test items are to call forth the performance described in the intended learning outcomes, great care must be taken in phrasing the items. We need to eliminate all barriers that might prevent a knowledgeable person from responding and all clues that might lead the uninformed to the correct answer. Only those who have achieved the outcome being measured should get the item right. All others (no matter how intelligent) should miss it.

Some of the common *barriers* to be avoided during test preparation are:

Vocabulary that is unnecessarily difficult.
Sentence structure that is unnecessarily complex.
Statements containing ambiguity.
Unclear pictorial materials.
Directions that are vague.
Material reflecting race, ethnic, or sex bias.

Awareness of such barriers during the planning and preparation of the test is the first step in their elimination. Essentially, we can avoid these barriers by (1) writing each test item so that it presents a clearly formulated task, (2) stating the items in simple, clear language, (3) keeping the items free from biased and nonfunctional material, and (4) using a test format and directions that contribute to effective test taking. Much of the material presented later in this book is directed toward constructing tests that prevent extraneous factors from distorting the test results.

Some of the common *clues* to be avoided during test preparation are:

Verbal associations that give away the answer.

Grammatical inconsistencies that eliminate wrong answers.

Specific determiners that make certain answers probable (e.g., sometimes) and others improbable (e.g., always).

Stereotyped or textbook phrasing of correct answers.

Length or location of correct answers.

Material in an item that aids in answering another item.

Just as in controlling extraneous factors that provide barriers to the correct answer, clues such as these can be eliminated by being aware of them and by following sound principles of test construction. Many of the rules for item writing and test preparation in the chapters that follow provide guidelines for this purpose.

Determining the Number of Test Items to Use

The number of items to use should be indicated in the test specifications, as noted earlier, and is modified by a number of practical constraints, such as the following:

1. Age of the students tested
2. Time available for testing
3. Type of test items used
4. Type of interpretation to be made

In the testing of elementary school students, the testing time typically should be no more than 20 or 30 minutes so that proper motivation is maintained. At the high school and college levels, students can be given tests lasting several hours (for example, a final examination), but most tests are limited to a testing time of 40 to 50 minutes because of the length of the typical class period.

In matching the number of items to available testing time, we are faced with the problem of estimating how many items students can complete per minute. Unfortunately, there are no simple answers. The size of the final product depends on the type of test item, the complexity of the learning outcome measured, and the age of the students. As a guideline, high school and college students should be able to answer one multiple-choice item, three short-answer items, or three true-false items per minute when the items are measuring knowledge outcomes. For measuring more complex learning outcomes such as comprehension and application, and for testing younger age groups, more time per item is needed. In estimating the number of items to be used, keep in mind the slower students in the group, for it is desirable to give all students an opportunity to complete the test. Experience in testing a given group of students is frequently the only dependable guide for determining proper test length.

In addition to our concern with total test length, consideration must be given to the number of test items needed for each type of interpretation to be made. This issue is especially crucial in criterion-referenced interpretation, where we want to describe student performance in terms of each intended learning outcome. For this purpose we should use at least 10 items per outcome. Where practical constraints make it necessary to use fewer than 10 items for an intended outcome, only tentative judgments should be made and these should be verified by other means. In some cases it is possible to combine items into larger item clusters for a more meaningful interpretation. See Box 3.2 for a summary checklist for evaluating the test plan.

General Guidelines for Item Writing

There are a number of general suggestions that apply to the writing of all item types. These provide a general framework for writing items that function as intended and that contribute to more valid and reliable results.

1. *Select the type of test item that measures the intended learning outcome most directly.* Use a supply-type item if supplying the answer is an important element of the task (e.g., writing). Use a selection-type item if appropriate (e.g., identification) or if both types are equally appropriate.

2. *Write the test item so that the performance it elicits matches the performance in the learning task.* The intended learning outcome specifies the

BOX 3.2 • *Checklist for Evaluating the Test Plan*

1. Is the purpose of the test clear?
2. Have the intended learning outcomes been identified and defined?
3. Are the intended learning outcomes stated in performance (measurable) terms?
4. Have test specifications been prepared that indicate the nature and distribution of items to be included in the test?
5. Does the specified set of items provide a representative sample of the tasks contained in the achievement domain?
6. Are the types of items appropriate for the learning outcomes to be measured?
7. Is the difficulty of the items appropriate for the students to be tested and the nature of the measurement (e.g., mastery or survey)?
8. Is the number of items appropriate for the students to be tested, the time available for testing, and the interpretations to be made?
9. Does the test plan include built-in features that contribute to valid and reliable scores?
10. Have plans been made for arranging the items in the test, writing directions, scoring, and using the results?

learning task in performance terms and the test task should call forth the same performance.

3. *Write the test item so that the test task is clear and definite.* Keep the reading level low, use simple and direct language, and follow the rules for correct punctuation and grammar.

4. *Write the test item so that it is free from nonfunctional material.* Material not directly relevant to the problem being presented increases the reading load and may detract from the intent of the item. Use extraneous material only where its detection is part of the task (e.g., in math problems).

5. *Write the test item so that irrelevant factors do not prevent an informed student from responding correctly.* Avoid trick questions that might cause a knowledgeable student to focus on the wrong aspect of the task. Use clear, unambiguous statements that maximize the performance to be measured and minimize all other influences. For example, word problems measuring mathematical reasoning should keep reading level and computational demands simple if an uncontaminated measure of reasoning ability is desired.

6. *Write the test item so that irrelevant clues do not enable the uninformed student to respond correctly.* Removing unwanted clues from test items requires alertness during item writing and reviewing the items after setting them aside for a while. The most common clues for each item type will be considered in the following chapters. It is also important to prevent the information given in one item from providing an answer to another item in the test.

7. *Write the test item so that the difficulty level matches the intent of the learning outcome, the age group to be tested, and the use to be made of the results.* When difficulty is being evaluated, check to be certain that it is relevant to the intended learning outcome and that the item is free from sources of irrelevant difficulty (e.g., obscure materials, overly fine discriminations).

8. *Write the test item so that there is no disagreement concerning the answer.* Typically the answer should be one that experts would agree is the correct or best answer. Most problems arise here when students are to provide the best answer (best procedure, best explanation). This involves a matter of judgment and to be defensible the answer must be clearly best and identified as such by experts in the area. Where experts disagree, it may be desirable to ask what a particular authority would consider to be the best method, the best reason, and the like. When attributed to a source, the answer can be judged as correct or incorrect.

9. *Write the test items far enough in advance that they can be later reviewed and modified as needed.* A good time to write test items is shortly after the material has been taught, while the questions and context are still clearly in mind. In any event, reviewing and editing items after they have been set aside for a while can detect flaws that were inadvertently introduced during the original item writing.

10. *Write more test items than called for by the test plan.* This will enable you to discard weak or inappropriate items during item review and make it easier to match the final set of items to the test specifications.

Arranging the Items in the Test

After the final selection of the items to be included in a test, a decision must be made concerning the best arrangement of items. This arrangement will vary with the type of test being prepared, but the following guidelines should be helpful.

1. *For instructional purposes it is usually desirable to group together items that measure the same outcome.* Each group of items can then be identified by an appropriate heading (e.g., knowledge, comprehension, application). The inclusion of the headings helps to identify the areas where students are having difficulty and to plan for remedial action.

2. *Where possible, all items of the same type should be grouped together.*
   This arrangement makes it possible to provide only one set of directions
   for each item type. It also simplifies the scoring and the analysis of the
   results.
3. *The items should be arranged in terms of increasing difficulty.* This
   arrangement has motivational effect on students and will prevent them
   from getting "bogged down" by difficult items early in the test.

Because most classroom tests include only a few item types, it is usually possible to honor all three of these guidelines. When this is not feasible,
the item arrangement that best fits the nature of the test and use to be made
of the results should be used.

Preparing Directions

The directions for an achievement test should be simple and concise and yet
contain information concerning each of the following: (1) purpose of the test,
(2) time allowed to complete the test, (3) how to record the answers, and
(4) whether to guess when in doubt about an answer. The following sample
directions for a multiple-choice test cover these four points.

EXAMPLE

Directions: This is a test of what you have learned during the first five weeks of
the course. The results of this test will be used to clarify any points of difficulty
and thus help you complete the course successfully.

There are 60 multiple-choice items, and you have one hour to complete
the test.

For each item, select the answer that *best* completes the statement, or answers the question, and circle the letter of that answer.

Since your score will be the number of items answered correctly, *be sure
to answer every item.*

When two or more item types are included in the same test, it is usually
desirable to provide general directions for the test as a whole and specific
directions for each part. When this is done, the general directions should
contain the information about purpose, time allowed, and what to do about
guessing, and the specific directions should describe how to record the
answers for that particular part. Also, some items, such as keytype exercises,
require special directions for each item.

The use of separate answer sheets requires some elaboration of the
instructions for recording the answers. If students are not familiar with the
use of separate answer sheets, it might also be desirable to present a sample
item with the correct answer properly marked. There is a variety of separate

BOX 3.3 • *Correcting for Guessing*

Use the correction for guessing formula only when students have insufficient time to consider all of the items in the test (e.g., speed test). Then, warn the students that there will be a correction for guessing. Use the following formula to correct the scores.

Score = Right – Wrong/*n*-1

In this formula, *n* equals the number of alternatives in each time, and thus:

True-false items $S = R - W$
Multiple-choice items $S = R - W/2$ (3 alternatives)
                         $S = R - W/3$ (4 alternatives)
                         $S = R - W/4$ (5 alternatives)

answer sheets, and the specific instructions will have to be adapted to the particular type used. Unless machine scoring is to be used, however, a teacher-made answer sheet that simply lists the letters of the alternatives for each item is usually satisfactory.

The Problem of Guessing

In our set of sample directions, the students were told, "Since your score will be the number of items answered correctly, be sure to answer every item." This is an attempt to equalize the variation among students in their tendency to guess when in doubt about the answer. The directions make it unnecessary to correct for guessing. Although a correction for guessing may be appropriate for standardized tests, they are not needed for classroom tests where the students have an opportunity to respond to all items. It is only where students are unable to complete the test (e.g., speed test) that the correction for guessing might be appropriate for classroom tests. Here, the purpose is to prevent students from rapidly and randomly marking the remaining items just before time is up in an attempt to improve their score (see Box 3.3 for correction formula).

Reviewing and Evaluating the Assembled Test

After assembling the items into a test, it is desirable to review the test as a whole to be sure it meets the criteria of a good test. The types of questions to consider are listed in Box 3.4.

BOX 3.4 • *Checklist for Evaluating the Assembled Test*

1. *Balance*	Do the items measure a representative sample of the learning tasks in the achievement domain?
2. *Relevance*	Do the test items present relevant tasks?
3. *Conciseness*	Are the test tasks stated in simple, clear language?
4. *Soundness*	Are the items of proper difficulty, free of defects, and do they have answers that are defensible?
5. *Independence*	Are the items free from overlapping, so that one item does not aid in answering another?
6. *Arrangement*	Are items measuring the same outcome grouped together?
	Are items of the same type grouped together?
	Are items in order of increasing difficulty?
7. *Numbering*	Are the items numbered in order throughout the test?
8. *Directions*	Are there directions for the whole test and each part?
	Are the directions concise and at the proper reading level?
	Do the directions include time limits and how to record answers?
	Do the directions tell what to do about guessing?
9. *Spacing*	Does the spacing on the page contribute to ease of reading and responding?
10. *Typing*	Is the final copy free of typographical errors?

Administering and Scoring the Test

The administration of a carefully prepared informal achievement test is largely a matter of providing proper working conditions, keeping interruptions to a minimum, and arranging enough space between students to prevent cheating. The written directions should be clear enough to make the test self-administering, but in some situations it may be desirable to give the directions orally as well. With young students a blackboard illustration may also be useful. Above all, make certain that all the students know exactly what to do, and then provide them with the most favorable conditions in which to do it.

Scoring is facilitated if all answers are recorded on the left side of each test page, as we suggested earlier. Under this arrangement, scoring is simply a matter of marking the correct answers on a copy of the test and placing it next to the column of answers on each student's paper. If a separate answer sheet is used, it is usually better to punch out the letters of the correct answers on a copy of the answer sheet and use this as a scoring stencil. The stencil is laid over each answer sheet and the correctly marked answers appear through the holes. Where no mark appears, a red line can be drawn across the hole. This indicates to the student the correct answer for each item missed. If machine scoring is to be used, simply scan the students' papers to make certain that only one answer was marked for each item.

Unless corrected for guessing, a student's score on an objective test is typically the number of answers marked correctly. Thus, each test item is counted as one point. Although teachers frequently desire to count some items more heavily than others because of their importance or difficulty, such weighting of scores complicates the scoring task and seldom results in an improved measure of achievement. A better way to increase the relative weight of an area is to construct more items in that area.

Analyzing the Effectiveness of Test Items

After a test has been administered, the items should be analyzed for their effectiveness. One method of evaluating the test is to review the test item-by-item when it is handed back to students for a discussion of the results. Significant comments made during the discussion can be recorded on a blank copy of the test. The flexibility of this procedure makes it possible to pursue comments about particular items, to ask students why they selected the response they did (both correct and incorrect selections), and to spend as much time on each item as seems warranted. This procedure may bring forth some unjustified criticisms of the test, but it will also help identify defective items in need of revision. The extra time used in discussing the test results will not be wasted because students will be obtaining a review of the course material covered by the test.

Simple Item Analysis Procedure

The discussion of test results and review of the items can be much more effective if a simple tally of student responses is made on the master copy of the test. By recording the results of the 10 highest scoring students (H) and 10 lowest scoring students (L), like that in Figure 3.2, make the results easily interpretable. The answer is circled and the numbers to the left of each alternative indicate how many students in each group selected that alternative.

The result in Figure 3.2 provides all the information we need to estimate the following types of item analysis information.

1. The difficulty of the item (percentage of students answering the item correctly).
2. The discriminating power of the item (how well the item discriminates between high and low scorers).
3. The effectiveness of each alternative (all should be chosen and each one more frequently by the low scoring group).

UNIT TEST

Name _____ Date _____

Directions:

This test measures the knowledge, understandings, and applications you have acquired during the first four weeks.

There are 65 objective items, and you will have the full class period to complete the test.

Select the best answer for each item and circle the letter of that answer.

Your score will be the number of items answered correctly, so *be sure to answer every item.*

KNOWLEDGE OF TERMS

H	L	
1	3	1. An assessment instrument is properly classified as *objective* when
1	2	A. the instrument uses objective-type questions.
0	1	B. the responses called forth by the instrument are free of opinion.
8	4	C. those preparing the instrument used standard procedures of construction.
		(D) there is agreement among scorers concerning the correctness of the answers.

FIGURE 3.2   Test copy with item analysis data to left of items (H = 10 highest scorers, L = 10 lowest scorers).

By simply looking at the answer sheet in Figure 3.2, we can see that 8 students in the high-scoring group and 4 students in the low-scoring group selected the correct answer. Also, more students in the low-scoring group selected each wrong alternative than in the high-scoring group, indicating that the distracters seem to be distracting those students who haven't learned the meaning of the term.

Because we are using 10 students in the high-scoring group and 10 students in the low-scoring group, we can mentally calculate the usual indexes of difficulty and discriminating power by using the following simple steps.

1. Determine the percentage of high scorers and low scorers passing the item by adding a zero.

   H = 8 out of 10 = 80
   L = 4 out of 10 = 40

2. Obtain *item difficulty* by adding the percentage correct in the high and low groups and dividing by 2. Add a percent sign to the answer.

$$\frac{80 + 40}{2} = 60\%$$

3. Obtain *discriminating power* by subtracting the percentage correct in the low group from the percentage correct in the high group. Add a decimal point to the answer.

$$80 - 40 = .40$$

The description of the procedure makes it sound more complicated than it is, but making a few mental calculations like this will reveal its simplicity. Item difficulty typically uses the percent sign and, of course, can range from 0% to 100%. Our **difficulty index** is based on the high- and low-scoring groups only, but this provides a satisfactory approximation of item difficulty. The **discrimination index** typically uses the decimal point and thus ranges from 0 to 1.00.

This simple method of analyzing the test results can be used as an aid in discussing the items when reviewing the test. Items that most students answer correctly can be skipped over or treated lightly, items missed by most students can be discussed in more detail, and defective items can be pointed out to students rather than defended as fair. Also, the frequency with which each incorrect answer is chosen may reveal common errors and misconceptions that can be corrected on the spot or serve as a basis for remedial work. In discussing the reasons students have selected the right or wrong answer for an item can sometimes be revealing. We assume that if they selected the correct answer they had learned the material. Not necessarily so, when using selection-type items (see Box 3.5 for common reasons for selecting alternatives). Having students discuss the reasons for their choices

BOX 3.5 • *Common Reasons for Selecting Multiple-Choice Alternatives*

Bases for Correct Choice
1. Possesses required information or skill.
2. Uses partial information that favors answer.
3. Uses clues given in the item.
4. Uses information from other items in the test.
5. Makes a blind, lucky guess.

Bases for Incorrect Choice
1. Lacks the information or skill required by the item.
2. Uses partial information that favors a distracter.
3. Uses misinformation that favors a distracter.
4. Makes a blind, unlucky guess.
5. Marks wrong answer through carelessness.

provides insights into student thinking that may contribute to both improved teaching and improved test construction skills.

Although the method of **item analysis** presented here is a crude one, it is probably satisfactory for most classroom tests. We are using it primarily as a basis for reviewing the items with students and for any insights the results might give us for improving test items in the future. A more detailed description of item analysis and cautions in interpreting item-analysis data can be found in Linn and Gronlund (2000).

Because of the small number of students involved in classroom testing, item-analysis information must be interpreted with great caution. If a test item is reused with a new group, the results may be quite different, due to changes in the instruction, the study habits of students, or some other factor. The tentative nature of the item-analysis data is not of great concern, however, when used to review tests with students for the purpose of improving learning.

Summary of Points

1. Assessment planning should be guided by what the students are expected to learn as specified by the school goals and the more specific instructional objectives.

2. Assessment planning requires a consideration of all possible types of learning outcomes in a given content area, not just those that can be measured by a test.

3. Assessment of performance skills and products typically requires some type of observation procedure, such as a checklist, rating scale, or holistic scoring rubric (see Chapter 7).

4. Preparing and using an achievement test includes specifying the instructional objectives in performance terms, preparing a table of specifications, constructing relevant test items, arranging the items in the test, preparing clear directions, reviewing and evaluating the assembled test, administering the test, and making an item analysis.

5. Test specifications typically consist of a twofold table of specifications that indicates the sample of performance tasks to be measured.

6. The types of test items used in a test should be determined by how directly they measure the intended learning outcomes and how effective they are as measuring instruments.

7. Each test item should provide a task that matches the student performance described in a specific learning outcome.

8. The functioning content of test items can be improved by eliminating irrelevant barriers and unintended clues during item writing.

9. The difficulty of a test item should match the difficulty of the learning task to be measured. Beware of irrelevant sources of difficulty (e.g., obscure material).

10. An achievement test should be short enough to permit all students to attempt all items during the testing time available.

11. A test should contain a sufficient number of test items for each type of interpretation to be made. Interpretations based on fewer than 10 items should be considered highly tentative.

12. Following a general set of guidelines during item writing will result in higher quality items that contribute to the validity and reliability of the test results.

13. Item arrangement within the test will vary with the type of test used. Where possible, items should be grouped by major learning outcome (e.g., knowledge, comprehension, application); similar items should be grouped together and should be arranged in order of increasing difficulty.

14. Test directions should clearly indicate the purpose of the test, the time allowed, how to record the answers, and to answer every item.

15. A correction for guessing should be used for speed tests only.

16. Review and evaluate the assembled test before using.

17. Administer the test under controlled conditions.

18. Item analysis provides a means of evaluating the items and is useful in reviewing the test with students.

References and Additional Reading

Bloom, B. S., et al. (ed.). *Taxonomy of Educational Objectives: Cognitive Domain* (New York: David McKay Co., 1956).

Carey, L. M., *Measuring and Evaluating School Learning*, 3rd ed. (Boston: Allyn and Bacon, 2001).

Gronlund, N. E., *How to Write and Use Instructional Objectives*, 6th ed. (Upper Saddle River, NJ: Merrill/Prentice Hall, 2000).

Linn, R. L., and Gronlund, N. E. *Measurement and Assessment in Teaching*, 8th ed. (Upper Saddle River, NJ: Merrill/Prentice-Hall, 2000).

Oosterhoff, A. C., *Classroom Application of Educational Measurement*, 3rd ed. (Upper Saddle River, NJ: Merrill/ Prentice-Hall, 2001).

Stiggins, R. J., *Student-Involved Classroom Assessment*, 3rd ed. (Upper Saddle River, NJ: Merrill/Prentice-Hall, 2001).

4

Writing Selection Items

Multiple Choice

Studying this chapter should enable you to

1. Describe the characteristics of multiple-choice items.
2. Describe the strengths and limitations of multiple-choice items.
3. Distinguish between well-stated and poorly stated multiple-choice items.
4. Identify and correct faults in poorly stated multiple-choice items.
5. Match multiple-choice items to intended learning outcomes.
6. Construct multiple-choice items that are well stated, relevant to important learning outcomes, and free of defects.

Multiple-choice items are the most widely used and highly regarded of the selection-type items. They can be designed to measure a variety of learning outcomes, from simple to complex, and can provide the highest quality items. Because they play such an important role in achievement testing, they will be treated in this chapter in considerable detail. Other selection-type items (true-false, matching, and interpretive exercise) will be described in the following chapter.

Nature of Multiple-Choice Items

The multiple-choice item consists of a *stem*, which presents a problem situation, and several *alternatives* (*options* or *choices*), which provide possible solutions to the problem. The stem may be a question or an incomplete statement. The alternatives include the correct answer and several plausible wrong answers called *distracters*. The function of the latter is to distract those students who are uncertain of the answer.

The following items illustrate the question form and the incomplete-statement form of a multiple-choice item.

EXAMPLE

Which one of the following item types is an example of a supply-type test item?
   A. Multiple-choice item.
   B. True-false item.
   C. Matching item.
   *D. Short-answer item.

An example of a supply-type test item is the:
   A. multiple-choice item.
   B. true-false item.
   C. matching item.
   *D. short-answer item.

Although stated differently, both stems pose the same problem. Note, however, that the incomplete statement is more concise. This is typically the case. The question form is easier to write and forces the test maker to pose a clear problem but tends to result in a longer stem. An effective procedure for the beginner is to start with a question and shift to the incomplete statement whenever greater conciseness can be obtained.

The alternatives in the preceding examples contain only one correct answer, and the distracters are clearly incorrect. Another type of multiple-choice item is the *best-answer* form in which the alternatives are all partially correct but one is clearly better than the others. This type is used for more complex achievement, as when the student must select the best reason for an action, the best method for doing something, or the best application of a principle. Thus, whether the correct-answer or best-answer form is used depends on the learning outcomes to be measured.

EXAMPLE

Which item is *best* for measuring computational skill?
   A. Multiple-choice item.
   B. True-false item.
   C. Matching item.
   *D. Short-answer item.

The examples given illustrate the use of four alternatives. Multiple-choice items typically include either three, four, or five choices. The larger number will, of course, reduce the student's chances of obtaining the correct answer by guessing. Theoretically, with five alternatives there is only one chance in five of guessing the answer, whereas with four alternatives there is one chance in four. It is frequently difficult to obtain five plausible choices, however, and items are not improved by adding obviously wrong answers merely to have five alternatives. There is no reason why the items in a given test should all have the same number of alternatives. Some might contain three, some four, and some five, depending on the availability of plausible distracters. This would pose a problem only if the test were to be corrected for guessing—a practice that is not recommended for informal achievement tests.

Uses of Multiple-Choice Items

The multiple-choice item can be used to measure knowledge outcomes and various types of complex learning outcomes. The single-item format is probably most widely used for measuring knowledge, comprehension, and application outcomes. The interpretive exercise consisting of a series of multiple-choice items based on introductory material (e.g., paragraph, picture, or graph) is especially useful for measuring analysis, interpretation, and other complex learning outcomes. The interpretive exercise will be described in the following chapter. Here, we confine the discussion to the use of single, independent, multiple-choice items.

Knowledge Items

Knowledge items typically measure the degree to which previously learned material has been remembered. The items focus on the simple recall of information and can be concerned with the measurement of terms, facts, or other specific aspects of knowledge.

EXAMPLES

Outcome: Identifies the meaning of a term.
  Reliability means the same as:
    *A. consistency.
    B. relevancy.
    C. representativeness.
    D. usefulness.

Outcome: Identifies the order of events.
  What is the first step in constructing an achievement test?
    A. Decide on test length.
    *B. Identify the intended learning outcomes.
    C. Prepare a table of specifications.
    D. Select the item types to use.

The wide variety of knowledge outcomes that can be measured with multiple-choice items is best shown by illustrating some of the types of questions that can be asked in various knowledge categories. Sample questions stated as incomplete multiple-choice stems are presented in the Box 4.1.

BOX 4.1 • *Illustrative Knowledge Questions**

1.11 *Knowledge of Terminology*
What word means the same as _____?
Which statement best defines the term _____?
In this sentence, what is the meaning of the word _____?

1.12 *Knowledge of Specific Facts*
Where would you find _____?
Who first discovered _____?
What is the name of _____?

1.21 *Knowledge of Conventions*
What is the correct form for _____?
Which statement indicates correct usage of _____?
Which of the following rules applies to _____?

1.22 *Knowledge of Trends and Sequences*
Which of the following best describes the trend of _____?
What is the most important cause of _____?
Which of the following indicates the proper order of _____?

1.23 *Knowledge of Classifications and Categories*
What are the main types of _____?
What are the major classifications of _____?
What are the characteristics of _____?

1.24 *Knowledge of Criteria*
Which of the following is a criterion for judging _____?
What is the most important criterion for selecting _____?
What criteria are used to classify _____?

1.25 *Knowledge of Methodology*
What method is used for _____?
What is the best way to _____?
What would be the first step in making _____?

1.31 *Knowledge of Principles and Generalizations*
Which statement best expresses the principle of _____?
Which statement best summarizes the belief that _____?
Which of the following principles best explains _____?

1.32 *Knowledge of Theories and Structures*
Which statement is most consistent with the theory of _____?
Which of the following best describes the structure of _____?
What evidence best supports the theory of _____?

*Based on Bloom (1956), *Taxonomy of Educational Objectives* (see reference list in Chapter 3).

The series of questions shown in Box 4.1, of course, provides only a sample of the many possible questions that could be asked. Also, the questions are stated in rather general terms. The stems for multiple-choice items need to be more closely related to the specific learning outcome being measured.

Comprehension Items

Comprehension items typically measure at the lowest level of understanding. They determine whether the students have grasped the meaning of the material without requiring them to apply it. Comprehension can be measured by requiring students to respond in various ways, but it is important that the items contain some *novelty.* The following test items illustrate the measurement of common types of learning outcomes at the comprehension level.

EXAMPLES

Outcome: Identifies an example of a term.
  Which one of the following statements contains a *specific determiner?*
    A. America is a continent.
    B. America was discovered in 1492.
    *****C.** America has some big industries.
    D. America's population is increasing.

Outcome: Interprets the meaning of an idea.
  The statement that "test reliability is a necessary but not a sufficient condition of test validity" means that:
    A. a reliable test will have a certain degree of validity.
    *****B.** a valid test will have a certain degree of reliability.
    C. a reliable test may be completely invalid and a valid test completely unreliable.

Outcome: Identifies an example of a concept or principle.
  Which of the following is an example of a criterion-referenced interpretation?
    A. Jorge earned the highest score in science.
    B. Erik completed his experiment faster than his classmates.
    C. Edna's test score was higher than 50 percent of the class.
    *****D.** Tricia set up her laboratory equipment in five minutes.

Outcome: Predicts the most probable effect of an action.
  What is most likely to happen to the reliability of the scores for a multiple-choice test when the number of alternatives for each item is changed from three to four?
    A. It will decrease.
    *****B.** It will increase.

C. It will stay the same.
D. There is no basis for making a prediction.

In this last example, the student must recognize that increasing the number of alternatives in the items produces the same effect as lengthening the test.

These examples would, of course, represent measurement at the comprehension level only where the situations were new to the students. If the solutions to these particular problems were encountered during instruction, the items would need to be classified as knowledge outcomes.

Some of the many learning outcomes at the comprehension level that can be measured by multiple-choice items are illustrated by the incomplete questions in Box 4.2.

BOX 4.2 • *Illustrative Comprehension and Application Questions*

Comprehension Questions

Which of the following is an example of _____?
What is the main thought expressed by _____?
What are the main differences between _____?
What are the common characteristics of _____?
Which of the following is another form of _____?
Which of the following best explains _____?
Which of the following best summarizes _____?
Which of the following best illustrates _____?
What do you predict would happen if _____?
What trend do you predict in _____?

Application Questions

Which of the following methods is best for _____?
What steps should be followed in applying _____?
Which situation would require the use of _____?
Which principle would be best for solving _____?
What procedure is best for improving _____?
What procedure is best for constructing _____?
What procedure is best for correcting _____?
Which of the following is the best plan for _____?
Which of the following provides the proper sequence for _____?
What is the most probable effect of _____?

Application Items

Application items also measure understanding, but typically at a higher level than that of comprehension. Here, the students must demonstrate that they not only grasp the meaning of information but can also apply it to concrete situations that are new to them. Thus, application items determine the extent to which students can transfer their learning and use it effectively in solving new problems. Such items may call for the application of various aspects of knowledge, such as facts, concepts, principles, rules, methods, and theories. Both comprehension and application items are adaptable to practically all areas of subject matter, and they provide the basic means of measuring understanding.

The following examples illustrate the use of multiple-choice items for measuring learning outcomes at the application level.

EXAMPLES

Outcome: Distinguishes between properly and improperly stated outcomes.
   Which one of the following learning outcomes is properly stated in terms of student performance?
   A. Develops an appreciation of the importance of testing.
   ***B.** Explains the purpose of test specifications.
   C. Learns how to write good test items.
   D. Realizes the importance of validity.

Outcome: Improves defective test items.
   Directions: Read the following test item and then indicate the best change to make to improve the item.
   Which one of the following types of learning outcomes is most difficult to evaluate objectively?
      1. A concept.
      2. An application.
      3. An appreciation.
      4. None of the above.

The best change to make in the previous item would be to:
   A. change the stem to incomplete-statement form.
   B. use letters instead of numbers for each alternative.
   C. remove the indefinite articles "a" and "an" from the alternatives.
   ***D.** replace "none of the above" with "an interpretation."

When writing application items, care must be taken to select problems that the students have not encountered previously and therefore cannot solve on the basis of general knowledge alone. Each item should be so designed that it calls for application of the particular fact, concept, principle, or procedure indicated in the intended learning outcome. See Box 4.2 for

BOX 4.3 • *Multiple-Choice Items*

Strengths
1. Learning outcomes from simple to complex can be measured.
2. Highly structured and clear tasks are provided.
3. A broad sample of achievement can be measured.
4. Incorrect alternatives provide diagnostic information.
5. Scores are less influenced by guessing than true-false items.
6. Scoring is easy, objective, and reliable.

Limitations
1. Constructing good items is time consuming.
2. It is frequently difficult to find plausible distractors.
3. This item is ineffective for measuring some types of problem solving and the ability to organize and express ideas.
4. Score can be influenced by reading ability.

some of the many questions that might be asked at the application level and Box 4.3 for strengths and limitations of multiple-choice items.

Rules for Writing Multiple-Choice Items

An effective multiple-choice item presents students with a task that is both important and clearly understood, and one that can be answered correctly by anyone who has achieved the intended learning outcome. Nothing in the content or structure of the item should prevent an informed student from responding correctly. Similarly, nothing in the content or structure of the item should enable an uninformed student to select the correct answer. The following rules for item writing are intended as guides for the preparation of multiple-choice items that function as intended.

   1. *Design each item to measure an important learning outcome.* The problem situation around which an item is to be built should be important and should be related to the intended learning outcome to be measured. The items in the previous section illustrate how to match items to intended outcomes. When writing the item, focus on the functioning content of the item and resist the temptation to include irrelevant material or more obscure and less significant content to increase item difficulty. Remember that the purpose of each item is to call forth the type of performance that will help determine the extent to which the intended learning outcomes have been achieved.

Items designed to measure complex achievement must contain some novelty. For example, where a knowledge item might require the identification of a textbook definition of a term, a comprehension item may require the identification of a modified form of it, and an application item may require the identification of an example of its proper use. Both the comprehension and application items would function as intended, however, only if the material was new to the students. Thus, items measuring complex achievement should require students to demonstrate that they have grasped the meaning of the material and can use it in situations that are new to them.

2. *Present a single clearly formulated problem in the stem of the item.* The task set forth in the stem of the item should be so clear that a student can understand it without reading the alternatives. In fact, a good check on the clarity and completeness of a multiple-choice stem is to cover the alternatives and determine whether it could be answered without the choices. Try this on the two sample items that follow.

EXAMPLE

Poor: A table of specifications:
        A. indicates how a test will be used to improve learning.
        *B.** provides a more balanced sampling of content.
        C. arranges the instructional objectives in order of their importance.
        D. specifies the method of scoring to be used on a test.

Better: What is the main advantage of using a table of specifications when preparing an achievement test?
        A. It reduces the amount of time required.
        *B.** It improves the sampling of content.
        C. It makes the construction of test items easier.
        D. It increases the objectivity of the test.

The first of these examples is no more than a collection of true-false statements with a common stem. The problem presented in the stem of the improved version is clear enough to serve as a supply-type short-answer item. The alternatives simply provide a series of possible answers from which to choose.

Note also in the second version that a *single* problem is presented in the stem. Including more than one problem usually adds to the complexity of the wording and reduces the diagnostic value of the item. When students *fail* such an item, there is no way to determine which of the problems prevented them from responding correctly.

3. *State the stem of the item in simple, clear language.* The problem in the stem of a multiple-choice item should be stated as precisely as possible and should be free of unnecessarily complex wording and sentence structure.

Anyone who possesses the knowledge measured by a test item should be able to select the correct answer. Poorly stated item stems frequently introduce sufficient ambiguity to prevent a knowledgeable student from responding correctly. Also, complex sentence structure may make the item a measure more of reading comprehension than of the intended outcome. The first of the two examples that follow is an extreme instance of this problem.

EXAMPLE

Poor: The paucity of plausible, but incorrect, statements that can be related to a central idea poses a problem when constructing which one of the following types of test items?
    A. Short answer.
    B. True-false.
    *****C.** Multiple choice.
    D. Essay.

Better: The lack of plausible, but incorrect, alternatives will cause the greatest difficulty when constructing:
    A. short-answer items.
    B. true-false items.
    *****C.** multiple-choice items.
    D. essay items.

Another common fault in stating multiple-choice items is to load the stem with irrelevant and, thus, nonfunctioning material. This is probably caused by the instructor's desire to continue to teach the students—even while testing them. The following example illustrates the use of an item stem as "another chance to inform students."

EXAMPLE

Poor: Testing can contribute to the instructional program of the school in many important ways. However, the main function of testing in teaching is:

Better: The main function of testing in teaching is:

The first version increases reading time and makes no contribution to the measurement of the specific outcome. Time spent in reading such irrelevant material could be spent more profitably in thinking about the problem presented. But if the purpose of an item is to measure a student's ability to distinguish between relevant and irrelevant material, this rule must, of course, be disregarded.

4. *Put as much of the wording as possible in the stem of the item.* Avoid repeating the same material in each of the alternatives. By moving all of the common content to the stem, it is usually possible to clarify the problem further and to reduce the time the student needs to read the alternatives. Note the improvement in the following item when this rule is followed.

EXAMPLE

Poor: In *objective* testing, the term *objective:*
    A. refers to the method of identifying the learning outcomes.
    B. refers to the method of selecting the test content.
    C. refers to the method of presenting the problem.
    *D. refers to the method of scoring the answers.

Better: In *objective* testing, the term *objective* refers to the method of:
    A. identifying the learning outcomes.
    B. selecting the test content.
    C. presenting the problem.
    *D. scoring the answers.

In many cases the problem is not simply to move the common words to the stem but to reword the entire item. The following examples illustrate how an item can be improved by revising the stem and shortening the alternatives.

EXAMPLE

Poor: Instructional objectives are most apt to be useful for test-construction purposes when they are stated in such a way that they show:
    A. the course content to be covered during the instructional period.
    *B. the kinds of performance students should demonstrate upon reaching the goal.
    C. the things the teacher will do to obtain maximum student learning.
    D. the types of learning activities to be participated in during the course.

Better: Instructional objectives are most useful for test-construction purposes when they are stated in terms of:
    A. course content.
    *B. student performance.
    C. teacher behavior.
    D. learning activities.

It is, of course, impossible to streamline all items in this manner, but economy of wording and clarity of expression are important goals to strive for in test construction. Items function better when slim and trim.

5. *State the stem of the item in positive form, wherever possible.* A positively phrased test item tends to measure more important learning outcomes than a negatively stated item. This is because knowing such things as the *best* method or the *most relevant* argument typically has greater educational significance than knowing the *poorest* method or the *least relevant* argument. The use of negatively stated items stems results all too frequently from the ease with which such items can be constructed rather than from the importance of the learning outcomes measured. The test maker who becomes frustrated by the inability to think of a sufficient number of plausible distracters for an item, as in the first following example, suddenly realizes how simple it would be to construct the second version.

EXAMPLE

Item one: Which one of the following is a category in the taxonomy of the cognitive domain?
   *A. Comprehension
   B. *(distracter needed)*
   C. *(distracter needed)*
   D. *(distracter needed)*

Item two: Which one of the following is *not* a category in the taxonomy of the cognitive domain?
   A. Comprehension
   B. Application
   C. Analysis
   *D. *(answer needed)*

Note in the second version that the categories of the taxonomy serve as distracters and that all that is needed to complete the item is a correct answer. This could be any term that appears plausible but is *not* one of the categories listed in the taxonomy. Although such items are easily constructed, they are apt to have a low level of difficulty and are likely to measure relatively unimportant learning outcomes. Being able to identify answers that do *not* apply provides no assurance that the student possesses the desired knowledge.

This solution to the lack of sufficient distracters is most likely to occur when the test maker is committed to the use of multiple-choice items only. A more desirable procedure for measuring the "ability to recognize the categories in the taxonomy of the cognitive domain" is to switch to a modified true-false form, as in the following example.

EXAMPLE

Directions: Indicate which of the following are categories in the taxonomy of the cognitive domain, by circling Y for *yes* and N for *no*.

   *Y   N   Comprehension
   Y   N*   Critical Thinking
   Y   N*   Reasoning
   *Y   N   Synthesis

In responding to this item, the student must make a separate judgment for each statement—the statement either is or is not one of the categories. Thus, the item calls for the type of performance stated in the learning outcome, yet it avoids the problems of an insufficient number of distracters and of negative phrasing.

6. *Emphasize negative wording whenever it is used in the stem of an item.* In some instances the use of negative wording is basic to the measurement of an important learning outcome. Knowing that you should *not* cross the street against a red light or should *not* mix certain chemicals, for example, is so important that these precepts might be directly taught and directly tested. Any potentially dangerous situation may require a negative emphasis. There are also, of course, less dire circumstances where negative phrasing is useful. Almost any set of rules or procedures places some emphasis on practices to be avoided.

When negative wording is used in the stem of an item, it should be emphasized by being underlined or capitalized and by being placed near the end of the statement.

EXAMPLE

Poor: Which one of the following is not a desirable practice when preparing multiple-choice items?
   A. Stating the stem in positive form.
   B. Using a stem that could function as a short-answer item.
   C. Underlining certain words in the stem for emphasis.
   ***D.** Shortening the stem by lengthening the alternatives.

Better: All of the following are desirable practices when preparing multiple-choice items EXCEPT:
   A. stating the stem in positive form.
   B. using a stem that could function as a short-answer item.
   C. underlining certain words in the stem for emphasis.
   ***D.** shortening the stem by lengthening the alternatives.

The improved version of this item assures that the item's negative aspect will not be overlooked, and it furnishes the student with the proper mind-set just before reading the alternatives.

7. *Make certain that the intended answer is correct or clearly best.* When the correct-answer form of a multiple-choice item is used, there should be only one correct answer and it should be unquestionably correct. With the best-answer form, the intended answer should be one that competent authorities would agree is clearly the best. In the latter case it may also be necessary to include "of the following" in the stem of the item to allow for equally satisfactory answers that have not been included in the item.

EXAMPLE

Poor: What is the best method of selecting course content for test items?

Better: Which one of the following is the best method of selecting course content for test items?

The proper phrasing of the stem of an item can also help avoid equivocal answers when the correct-answer form is used. In fact, an inadequately stated problem frequently makes the intended answer only partially correct or makes more than one alternative suitable.

EXAMPLE

Poor: What is the purpose of classroom testing?

Better: One purpose of classroom testing is:
                        (or)
               The main purpose of classroom testing is:

It is, of course, also necessary to check each of the distracters in the item to make certain that none of them could be defended as the correct answer. This will not only improve the quality of the item but will also prevent a disruptive argument during the discussion of the test results.

8. ***Make all alternatives grammatically consistent with the stem of the item and parallel in form.*** The correct answer is usually carefully phrased so that it is grammatically consistent with the stem. Where the test maker is apt to slip is in stating the distracters. Unless care is taken to check them against the wording in the stem and in the correct answer, they may be inconsistent in tense, article, or grammatical form. This, of course, could provide a clue to the correct answer, or at least make some of the distracters ineffective.

A general step that can be taken to prevent grammatical inconsistency is to avoid using the articles "a" or "an" at the end of the stem of the item.

EXAMPLE

Poor: The recall of factual information can be measured best with a:
               A. matching item.
               B. multiple-choice item.
               *****C.** short-answer item.
               D. essay question.

Better: The recall of factual information can be measured best with:
               A. matching items.
               B. multiple-choice items.
               *****C.** short-answer items.
               D. essay questions.

The indefinite article "a" in the first version makes the last distracter obviously wrong. By simply changing the alternatives from singular to plural, it is possible to omit the article. In other cases, it may be necessary to add an article ("a," "an," or as appropriate) to each alternative or to rephrase the entire item.

Stating all of the alternatives in parallel form also tends to prevent unnecessary clues from being given to the students. When the grammatical structure of one alternative differs from that of the others, some students may more readily detect that alternative as a correct or an incorrect response.

EXAMPLE

Poor: Why should negative terms be avoided in the stem of a multiple-choice item?
      *A. They may be overlooked.
      B. The stem tends to be longer.
      C. The construction of alternatives is more difficult.
      D. The scoring is more difficult.

Better: Why should negative terms be avoided in the stem of a multiple-choice item?
      *A. They may be overlooked.
      B. They tend to increase the length of the stem.
      C. They make the construction of alternatives more difficult.
      D. They may increase the difficulty of the scoring.

In the first version some students who lack the knowledge called for are apt to select the correct answer because of the way it is stated. The parallel grammatical structure in the second version removes this clue.

9. *Avoid verbal clues that might enable students to select the correct answer or to eliminate an incorrect alternative.* One of the most common sources of extraneous clues in multiple-choice items is the wording of the item. Some such clues are rather obvious and are easily avoided. Others require the constant attention of the test maker to prevent them from slipping in unnoticed. Let's review some of the verbal clues commonly found in multiple-choice items.

(a) *Similarity of wording in both the stem and the correct answer* is one of the most obvious clues. Key words in the stem may unintentionally be repeated verbatim in the correct answer, a synonym may be used, or the words may simply sound or look alike.

EXAMPLE

Poor: Which one of the following would you consult first to locate research articles on achievement testing?

A. *Journal of Educational Psychology*
B. *Journal of Educational Measurement*
C. *Journal of Consulting Psychology*
*D. *Review of Educational Research*

The word "research" in both the stem and the correct answer is apt to provide a clue to the correct answer to the uninformed but testwise student. Such obvious clues might better be used in both the stem and an *incorrect* answer, in order to lead the uninformed *away* from the correct answer.

(b) *Stating the correct answer in textbook language or stereotyped phraseology* may cause students to select it because it looks better than the other alternatives, or because they vaguely recall having seen it before.

EXAMPLE

Poor: Learning outcomes are most useful in preparing tests when they are:
      *A. clearly stated in performance terms.
      B. developed cooperatively by teachers and students.
      C. prepared after the instruction has ended.
      D. stated in general terms.

The pat phrasing of the correct answer is likely to give it away. Even the most poorly prepared student is apt to recognize the often repeated phrase "clearly stated in performance terms," without having the foggiest notion of what it means.

(c) *Stating the correct answer in greater detail* may provide a clue. Also, when the answer is qualified by modifiers that are typically associated with true statements (for example, "sometimes," "may," "usually"), it is more likely to be chosen.

EXAMPLE

Poor: Lack of attention to learning outcomes during test preparation:
      A. will lower the technical quality of the items.
      B. will make the construction of test items more difficult.
      C. will result in the greater use of essay questions.
      *D. may result in a test that is less relevant to the instructional program.

The term "may" is rather obvious in this example, but this type of error is common and appears frequently in a subtler form.

(d) *Including absolute terms in the distracters* enables students to eliminate them as possible answers because such terms ("always," "never," "all," "none," "only,") are commonly associated with false statements. This makes the correct answer obvious, or at least increases the chances that the students who do not know the answer will guess it.

EXAMPLE

Poor: Achievement tests help students improve their learning by:
        A. encouraging them all to study hard.
        *****B.** informing them of their progress.
        C. giving them all a feeling of success.
        D. preventing any of them from neglecting their assignments.

Such absolutes tend to be used by the inexperienced test maker to assure that the incorrect alternatives are clearly wrong. Unfortunately, they are easily recognized by the student as unlikely answers, making them ineffective as distracters.

(e) *Including two responses that are all inclusive* makes it possible to eliminate the other alternatives, since one of the two must obviously be the correct answer.

EXAMPLE

Poor: Which one of the following types of test items measures learning outcomes at the recall level?
        *****A.** Supply-type items.
        B. Selection-type items.
        C. Matching items.
        D. Multiple-choice items.

Since the first two alternatives include the only two major types of test items, even poorly prepared students are likely to limit their choices to these two. This, of course, gives them a fifty-fifty chance of guessing the correct answer.

(f) *Including two responses that have the same meaning* makes it possible to eliminate them as potential answers. If two alternatives have the same meaning and only one answer is to be selected, it is fairly obvious that both alternatives must be incorrect.

EXAMPLE

Poor: Which one of the following is the most important characteristic achievement-test results?
        A. Consistency
        B. Reliability
        *****C.** Relevance
        D. Objectivity

In this item both "consistency" and "reliability" can be eliminated because they mean essentially the same thing.

Extraneous clues to the correct answer must be excluded from test items if the items are to function as intended. It is frequently good practice, however, to use such clues to lead the uninformed away from the correct answer. If not overdone, this can contribute to the plausibility of the incorrect alternatives.

10. ***Make the distracters plausible and attractive to the uninformed.*** The distracters in a multiple-choice item should be so appealing to the students who lack the knowledge called for by the item that they select one of the distracters in preference to the correct answer. This is the ideal, of course, but one toward which the test maker must work continually. The art of constructing good multiple-choice items depends heavily on the development of effective distracters.

You can do a number of things to increase the plausibility and attractiveness of distracters:

a. Use the common misconceptions or errors of students as distracters.
b. State the alternatives in the language of the student.
c. Use "good-sounding" words ("accurate," "important,") in the distracters as well as in the correct answer.
d. Make the distracters similar to the correct answer in both length and complexity of wording.
e. Use extraneous clues in the distracters, such as stereotyped phrasing, scientific-sounding answers, and verbal associations with the stem of the item. But don't overuse these clues to the point where they become ineffective.
f. Make the alternatives homogeneous, but in doing so beware of fine discriminations that are educationally insignificant.

The greater plausibility resulting from the use of more homogenous alternatives can be seen in the improved version of the following item.

EXAMPLE

Poor: Obtaining a dependable ranking of students is of major concern when using:
        *A. norm-referenced summative tests.
        B. behavior descriptions.
        C. checklists.
        D. questionnaires.

Better: Obtaining a dependable ranking of students is of major concern when using:
        *A. norm-referenced summative tests.
        B. teacher-made diagnostic tests.
        C. mastery achievement tests.
        D. criterion-referenced formative tests.

The improved version not only increases the plausibility of the distracters but it also calls for a type of discrimination that is more educationally significant.

11. *Vary the relative length of the correct answer to eliminate length as a clue.* There is a tendency for the correct answer to be longer than the alternatives because of the need to qualify statements to make them unequivocally correct. This, of course, provides a clue to the testwise student. Learning this fact, the inexperienced test maker frequently makes a special effort to avoid ever having the correct answer longer than the other alternatives. This, of course, also provides a clue, and the alert student soon learns to dismiss the longest alternative as a possible answer.

The relative length of the correct answer can be removed as a clue by varying it in such a manner that no apparent pattern is provided. That is, it should sometimes be longer, sometimes shorter, and sometimes of equal length—but never consistently or predominantly of one relative length. In some cases it is more desirable to make the alternatives approximately equal length by adjusting the distracters rather than the correct answer.

EXAMPLE

Poor: One advantage of multiple-choice items over essay questions is that they:
  A. measure more complex outcomes.
  B. depend more on recall.
  C. require less time to score.
  *D. provide for a more extensive sampling of course content.

Better: One advantage of multiple-choice items over essay questions is that they:
  A. provide for the measurement of more complex learning outcomes.
  B. place greater emphasis on the recall of factual information.
  C. require less time for test preparation and scoring.
  *D. provide for a more extensive sampling of course content.

Lengthening the distracters, as was done in the improved version, removes length as a clue and increases the plausibility of the distracters, which are now more similar to the correct answer in complexity of wording.

12. *Avoid using the alternative "all of the above," and use "none of the above" with extreme caution.* When test makers are having difficulty in locating a sufficient number of distracters, they frequently resort to the use of "all of the above" or "none of the above" as the final option. These special alternatives are seldom used appropriately and almost always render the item less effective than it would be without them.

The inclusion of "all of the above" as an option makes it possible to answer the item on the basis of partial information. Since students are to select only one answer, they can detect "all of the above" as the correct choice simply by noting that two of the alternatives are correct. They can also detect it as a wrong answer by recognizing that at least one of the alternatives is incorrect; of course, their chance of guessing the correct answer from the remaining choices then increases proportionately. Another difficulty with this option is that some students, recognizing that the first choice is correct, will select it without reading the remaining alternatives.

Obviously, the use of "none of the above" is not possible with the best-answer type of multiple-choice item, since the alternatives vary in appropriateness and the criterion of absolute correctness is not applicable. When used as the right answer in a correct-answer type of item, this option may be measuring nothing more than the ability to detect incorrect answers. Recognizing that certain answers are wrong is no guarantee that the student knows what is correct. For example, a student may be able to answer the following item correctly without being able to name the categories in the taxonomy.

EXAMPLE

Poor: Which of the following is a category in the taxonomy of the cognitive domain?
   A. Critical Thinking
   B. Scientific Thinking
   C. Reasoning Ability
   *__D.__ None of the above

All students need to know to answer this item correctly is that the taxonomy categories are new and different from those that they have commonly associated with intellectual skills. Items such as this provide rather poor evidence for judging a student's achievement.

The alternative "none of the above" is probably used more widely with computational problems that are presented in multiple-choice form. The publishers of standardized achievement tests have resorted to multiple-choice items for such problems in order to make machine scoring possible, and they have resorted to the alternative "none of the above" in order to reduce the likelihood of the student estimating the answer without performing the entire computation. Although this use of "none of the above" may be defensible, there is seldom a need to use multiple-choice items for computational problems in classroom tests. The supply-type item that requires the student to solve the problems and record the answers provides the most direct and useful measure of computational skill. This is another case in which it is desirable to switch from multiple-choice items to another item type in order to obtain more effective measurement.

13. *Vary the position of the correct answer in a random manner.* The correct answer should appear in each alternative position about the same number of times, but its placement should not follow a pattern that may be apparent to the person taking the test. Students who detect that the correct answer never appears in the same position more than twice in a row, or that A is the correct answer on every fourth item, are likely to obtain a higher score than their knowledge would warrant. Such clues can be avoided by random placement of the correct answer.

The easiest way to randomly assign the position of the correct answer in a multiple-choice item is to develop a code with the aid of a book: simply open any book at a random place, look at the right-hand page, and let the last digit of the page number determine the placement of the correct answer. Since the right-hand page always ends in an odd number, the code might be as follows: the digit 1 indicates that the correct answer will be placed in position A, 3 = B, 5 = C, 7 = D, and 9 = E.

Sufficient variation without a discernible pattern might also be obtained by simply placing the responses in alphabetical order, based on the first letter in each, and letting the correct answer fall where it will.

When the alternative responses are numbers, they should always be listed in order of size, preferably in ascending order. This will eliminate the possibility of a clue, such as the correct answer being the only one that is not in numerical order.

14. *Control the difficulty of the item either by varying the problem in the stem or by changing the alternatives.* It is usually preferable to increase item difficulty by increasing the level of knowledge called for by making the problem more complex. However, it is also possible to increase difficulty by making the alternatives more homogeneous. When this is done, care must be taken that the finer discriminations called for are educationally significant and are in harmony with the learning outcomes to be measured.

15. *Make certain each item is independent of the other items in the test.* Occasionally information given in the stem of one item will help the students answer another item. This can be remedied easily by a careful review of the items before they are assembled into a test.

A different type of problem occurs when the correct answer to an item depends on knowing the correct answer to the item preceding it. The student who is unable to answer the first item, of course, has no basis for responding to the second. Such chains of interlocking items should be avoided. Each item should be an independently scorable unit.

16. *Use an efficient item format.* The alternatives should be listed on separate lines, under one another, like the examples in this chapter. This makes the alternatives easy to read and compare. It also contributes to ease of scoring since the letters of the alternatives all appear on the left side of the paper. A copy of the test can be used as a scoring stencil: Simply circle the letters of the correct answers on the copy, then place the copy next to the student's paper so that the columns of letters correspond.

The use of letters in front of the alternatives is preferable to the use of numbers, since numerical answers in numbered items may be confusing to the students.

17. *Follow the normal rules of grammar.* If the stem is in question form, begin each alternative with a capital letter and end with a period or other appropriate punctuation mark. Omit the period with numerical answers, however, to avoid confusion with decimal points. When the stem is an incomplete statement, start each alternative with a lower-case letter and end with whatever terminal punctuation mark is appropriate.

18. *Break (or bend) any of these rules if it will improve the effectiveness of the item.* These rules for constructing multiple-choice items are stated rather dogmatically as an aid to the beginner. As experience in item writing is obtained, situations are likely to occur where ignoring or modifying a rule may be desirable. In a problem-solving item, for example, it may be useful to include extraneous information in the stem to see if students can select what is needed to solve the problem. Until sufficient experience in item writing is gained, however, following the rules in this chapter will yield test items of fairly good quality. See Box 4.4 for summary checklist.

BOX 4.4 • *Checklist for Evaluating Multiple-Choice Items*

1. Is this type of item appropriate for measuring the intended learning outcome?
2. Does the item task match the learning task to be measured?
3. Does the stem of the item present a single, clearly formulated problem?
4. Is the stem stated in simple, clear language?
5. Is the stem worded so that there is no repetition of material in the alternatives?
6. Is the stem stated in positive form wherever possible?
7. If negative wording is used in the stem, is it emphasized (by underlining or caps)?
8. Is the intended answer correct or clearly best?
9. Are all alternatives grammatically consistent with the stem and parallel in form?
10. Are the alternatives free from verbal clues to the correct answer?
11. Are the distracters plausible and attractive to the uninformed?
12. To eliminate length as a clue, is the relative length of the correct answer varied?
13. Has the alternative "all of the above" been avoided and "none of the above" used only when appropriate?
14. Is the position of the correct answer varied so that there is no detectable pattern?
15. Does the item format and grammar usage provide for efficient test taking?

Summary of Points

1. The multiple-choice item is the most highly regarded and useful selection-type item.
2. The multiple-choice item consists of a stem and a set of alternative answers (options or choices).
3. The multiple-choice item can be designed to measure various intended learning outcomes, ranging from simple to complex.
4. Knowledge items typically measure the simple remembering of material.
5. Comprehension items measure the extent to which students have grasped the meaning of material.
6. Application items measure whether students can use information in concrete situations.
7. Items designed to measure achievement beyond the knowledge level must contain some novelty.
8. The stem of a multiple-choice item should present a single, clearly formulated problem that is related to an important learning outcome.
9. The intended answer should be correct or clearly best, as agreed upon by authorities.
10. The distracters (incorrect alternatives) should be plausible enough to lead the uninformed away from the correct answer.
11. The items should be written in simple, clear language that is free of nonfunctioning content.
12. The items should be free of irrelevant sources of difficulty (e.g., ambiguity) that might prevent an informed examinee from answering correctly.
13. The items should be free of irrelevant clues (e.g., verbal associations) that might enable an uninformed examinee to answer correctly.
14. The item format should provide for efficient responding and follow the normal rules of grammar.
15. The rules of item writing provide a framework for preparing effective multiple-choice items, but experience in item writing may result in modifications to fit particular situations.

References and Additional Reading

Carey, L. M., *Measuring and Evaluating School Learning*, 3rd ed. (Boston: Allyn and Bacon, 2001).

Haladyna, T. M., *Writing Test Items to Evaluate Higher Order Thinking* (Boston: Allyn and Bacon, 1997).

Linn, R. L., and Gronlund, N. E., *Measurement and Assessment in Teaching*, 8th ed. (Upper Saddle River, NJ: Merrill/ Prentice-Hall, 2000).

Oosterhoff, A. C., *Classroom Applications of Educational Measurement*, 3rd ed. (Upper Saddle River, NJ: Merrill/ Prentice-Hall, 2001).

5

Writing Selection Items

True-False, Matching, and Interpretive Exercise

Studying this chapter should enable you to

1. Describe the characteristics of each item type.
2. Describe the strengths and limitations of each item type.
3. Distinguish between well-stated and poorly stated items of each type.
4. Identify and correct faults in poorly stated items of each type.
5. Match each item type to intended learning outcomes.
6. Construct items of each type that are well-stated, relevant to important learning outcomes, and free of defects.

The multiple-choice item provides the most generally useful format for measuring achievement at various levels of learning. Thus, when selection-type items are to be used, an effective procedure is to start each item as a multiple-choice item and switch to another item type only when the learning outcome and content make it desirable to do so. For example, (1) when there are only two possible alternatives, a shift can be made to a true-false item; (2) when there are a number of similar factors to be related, a shift can be made to a matching item; and (3) when the items are to measure analysis, interpretation, and other complex outcomes, a shift can be made to the interpretive exercise. This procedure makes it possible to use the special strengths of the multiple-choice item and to use the other selection-type items more appropriately.

True-False Items

True-false items are typically used to measure the ability to identify whether statements of fact are correct. The basic format is simply a declarative statement that the student must judge as true or false. There are modifications of this basic form in which the student must respond "yes" or "no," "agree" or "disagree," "right" or "wrong," "fact" or "opinion," and the like. Such variations are usually given the more general name of *alternative-response* items. In any event, this item type is characterized by the fact that only two responses are possible.

EXAMPLE

T   *F   True-false items are classified as a supply-type item.

In some cases the student is asked to judge each statement as true or false, and then to change the false statements so that they are true. When this is done, a portion of each statement is underlined to indicate the part that can be changed. In the example given, for instance, the words "supply-type" would be underlined. The key parts of true statements, of course, must also be underlined.

Another variation is the cluster-type true-false format. In this case, a series of items is based on a common stem.

EXAMPLE

Which of the following terms indicate observable student performance? Circle Y for yes and N for no.

*Y	N	1. Explains
*Y	N	2. Identifies
Y	*N	3. Learns
*Y	N	4. Predicts
Y	*N	5. Realizes

This item format is especially useful for replacing multiple-choice items that have more than one correct answer. Such items are impossible to score satisfactorily. This is avoided with the cluster-type item because it makes each alternative a separate scoring unit of one point. In our example, the student must record whether each term does or does not indicate observable student performance. Thus, this set of items provides an even better measure of the "ability to distinguish between performance and nonperformance terms" than would the single answer multiple-choice item. This is a good illustration of the procedure discussed earlier—that is, starting with multiple-choice items and switching to other item types when more effective measurement will result.

Despite the limitations of the true-false item, there are situations where it should be used. Whenever there are only two possible responses, the true-false item, or some adaptation of it, is likely to provide the most effective measure. Situations of this type include a simple "yes" or "no" response in classifying objects, determining whether a rule does or does not apply, distinguishing fact from opinion, and indicating whether arguments are relevant or irrelevant. As we indicated earlier, the best procedure is to use the true-false, or alternative-response, item only when this item type is more appropriate than the multiple-choice form. See Box 5.1 for a summary of strengths and limitations.

Rules for Writing True-False Items

The purpose of a true-false item, as with all item types, is to distinguish between those who have and those who have not achieved the intended learning outcome. Achievers should be able to select the correct alternative without difficulty, while nonachievers should find the incorrect alternative at least as attractive as the correct one. The rules for writing true-false items are directed toward this end.

BOX 5.1 • *True-False Items*

Strengths
1. The item is useful for outcomes where there are only two possible alternatives (e.g., fact or opinion, valid or invalid).
2. Less demand is placed on reading ability than in multiple-choice items.
3. A relatively large number of items can be answered in a typical testing period.
4. Complex outcomes can be measured when used with interpretive exercises.
5. Scoring is easy, objective, and reliable.

Limitations
1. It is difficult to write items beyond the knowledge level that are free from ambiguity.
2. Making an item false provides no evidence that the student knows what is correct.
3. No diagnostic information is provided by the incorrect answers.
4. Scores are more influenced by guessing than with any other item type.

1. *Include only one central idea in each statement.* The main point of the item should be in a prominent position in the statement. The true-false decision should not depend on some subordinate point or trivial detail. The use of several ideas in each statement should generally be avoided because these tend to be confusing and the answer is more apt to be influenced by reading ability than the intended outcome.

EXAMPLE

Poor: T   *F   The true-false item, which is favored by test experts, is also called an alternative-response item.

Better: *T   F   The true-false item is also called an alternative-response item.

The "poor" example must be marked false because test experts do not favor the true-false item. Such subordinate points are easily overlooked when reading the item. If the point is important, it should be included as the main idea in a separate item.

2. *Keep the statement short and use simple vocabulary and sentence structure.* A short, simple statement will increase the likelihood that the point of the item is clear. All students should be able to grasp what the statement is saying. Passing or failing the item should depend solely on whether a student has achieved the necessary knowledge.

EXAMPLE

Poor: *T   F   The true-false item is more subject to guessing but it should be used in place of a multiple-choice item, if well constructed, when there is a dearth of distracters that are plausible.

Better: *T   F   The true-false item should be used in place of a multiple-choice item when only two alternatives are possible.

Long, involved statements like the "poor" version tend to contaminate the achievement measure with a measure of reading comprehension. A basic rule of item writing is to focus on the intended function of the item and remove all irrelevant influences.

3. *Word the statement so precisely that it can unequivocally be judged true or false.* True statements should be true under all circumstances and yet free of qualifiers ("may," "possible," and so on), which might provide clues. This requires the use of precise words and the avoidance of such vague terms as "seldom," "frequently," and "often." The same care, of course, must also be given to false statements so that their falsity is not too readily apparent from differences in wording. At first glance, this seems like a simple rule to follow but it causes frequent problems.

EXAMPLE

Poor: T   *F   Lengthening a test will increase its reliability.

Better: *T   F   Lengthening a test by adding items like those in the test will increase its reliability.

The "poor" version of this item must be marked false because it is not true under all conditions. For example, if items are added to the test that all students fail, reliability would not be changed. However, the "poor" version would not be a good item to use in a test because it requires students to mark a very important principle of measurement false. We could say "usually will increase" but the qualifier would encourage those who are uninformed to mark it true and they would receive an unearned point. The "better" version has no such "giveaway" to the answer. In fact, an uninformed student might think that adding similar items to a test of low reliability could not possibly increase reliability—but it does. This example illustrates the great care needed in phrasing statements so that they are unequivocally true but do not contain "giveaways" to the answer.

4. *Use negative statements sparingly and avoid double negatives.* The "no" and/or "not" in negative statements are frequently overlooked and they are read as positive statements. Thus, negative statements should be used only when the learning outcome requires it (e.g., in avoiding a harmful practice), and then the negative words should be emphasized by underlining or by use of capital letters. Statements including double negatives tend to be so confusing that they should be restated in positive form.

EXAMPLE

Poor: *T   F   Correction-for-guessing is *not* a practice that should *never* be used in testing.

Better: *T   F   Correction-for-guessing is a practice that should sometimes be used in testing.

The double negatives in the "poor" version introduce sufficient ambiguity to cause the item to be a measure of reading comprehension. The "better" version clearly states the same idea in positive form.

5. *Statements of opinion should be attributed to some source unless used to distinguish facts from opinion.* A statement of opinion is not true or false by itself, and it is poor instructional practice to have students respond to it as if it were a factual statement. Obviously, the only way students could mark such an item correctly would be to agree with the opinion of the item writer. It is much more defensible to attribute the item to some source, such as an individual or organization. It then becomes a measure of how well the student knows the beliefs or values of that individual or organization.

EXAMPLE

Poor: T   F   Testing should play a major role in the teaching-learning process.

Better: *T   F   Gronlund believes that testing should play a major role in the teaching-learning process.

In some cases, it is useful to use a series of opinion statements that pertain to the same individual or organization. This permits a more comprehensive measure of how well the student understands a belief or value system.

EXAMPLE

Would the author of your textbook agree or disagree with the following statements? Circle A for agree, D for disagree.

*A   D   **1.** The first step in achievement testing is to state the intended learning outcomes in performance terms.

A   *D   **2.** True-false tests are superior to multiple-choice tests for measuring achievement.

Using about 10 items like those listed here would provide a fairly good indication of the students' grasp of the author's point of view. Items like this are useful for measuring how well students understand a textbook without requiring them to agree with the opinions expressed. It is desirable, of course, to select opinion statements that are shared by many experts in the area.

Another valuable use of opinion statements is to ask students to distinguish between statements of fact and statements of opinion. This is an important outcome in its own right and is a basic part of critical thinking.

EXAMPLE

Read each of the following statements and circle F if it is a *fact* and circle O if it is an *opinion.*

*F   O   **1.** The true-false item is a selection-type item.
F   *O   **2.** The true-false item is difficult to construct.
F   *O   **3.** The true-false item encourages student guessing.
*F   O   **4.** The true-false item can be scored objectively.

In addition to illustrating the use of opinion statements in test items, the last two examples illustrate variations from the typical true-false format. These are more logically called *alternative-response* items.

6. When cause-effect relationships are being measured, use only true propositions. The true-false item can be used to measure the "ability to identify cause-effect relationships" and this is an important aspect of understanding. When used for this purpose, both propositions should be true and only the relationship judged true or false.

EXAMPLE

Poor:	T	*F	True-false items are classified as objective items	*because*	students must supply the answer.
Better:	T	*F	True-false items are classified as objective items	*because*	there are only two possible answers.

The "poor" version is false because of the second part of the statement. With true-false items, students must *select* the answer rather than *supply* it. However, some students may mark this item false because they think the first part of the statement is incorrect. Thus, they receive one point because they *do not know* that true-false items are classified as objective items. Obviously, an item does not function as intended if misinformation can result in the correct answer. The problem with the "poor" version is that all three elements are permitted to vary (part one, part two, and the relationship between them) and it is impossible to tell what part the student is responding to when the item is marked false. In the "better" version both parts of the statement are true and the students must simply decide if the second part explains why the first part is true. In this case it does not, so it is marked false. Typically, a series of items like this is preceded by directions that make clear that only the relationship between the two parts of each statement is to be judged true or false.

7. Avoid extraneous clues to the answer. There are a number of *specific determiners* that provide verbal clues to the truth or falsity of an item. Statements that include such absolutes as "always," "never," "all," "none," and "only" tend to be false; statements with qualifiers such as "usually," "may," and "sometimes" tend to be true. Either these verbal clues must be eliminated from the statements, or their use must be balanced between true items and false items.

EXAMPLE

Poor:	T	*F	A statement of opinion should never be used in a true-false item.
Poor:	*T	F	A statement of opinion may be used in a true-false item.
Better:	*T	F	A statement of opinion, by itself, cannot be marked true or false.

BOX 5.2 • *Checklist for Evaluating True-False Items*

1. Is this type of item appropriate for measuring the intended learning outcome?
2. Does the item task match the learning task to be measured?
3. Does each statement contain one central idea?
4. Can each statement be unequivocally judged true or false?
5. Are the statements brief and stated in simple, clear language?
6. Are negative statements used sparingly and double negatives avoided?
7. Are statements of opinion attributed to some source?
8. Are the statements free of clues to the answer (e.g., verbal clues, length)?
9. Is there approximately an even number of true and false statements?
10. When arranged in the test, are the true and false items put in random order?

The length and complexity of the statement might also provide a clue. True statements tend to be longer and more complex than false ones because of their need for qualifiers. Thus, a special effort should be made to equalize true and false statements in these respects.

A tendency to use a disproportionate number of true statements, or false statements, might also be detected and used as a clue. Having approximately, but not exactly, an equal number of each seems to be the best solution. When assembling the test, it is, of course, also necessary to avoid placing the correct answers in some discernible pattern (for instance, T, F, T, F). Random placement will eliminate this possible clue.

8. *Base items on introductory material to measure more complex learning outcomes.* True-false or alternative-response items are frequently used in interpreting written materials, tables, graphs, maps, or pictures. The use of introductory material makes it possible to measure various types of complex learning outcomes. These item types will be illustrated in the section on interpretive exercises later in this chapter. See Box 5.2 for summary checklist for evaluation of true-false items.

Matching Items

The matching item is simply a variation of the multiple-choice form. A good practice is to switch to the matching format only when it becomes apparent that the same alternatives are being repeated in several multiple-choice items. See Box 5.3 for the strengths and limitations of matching items.

EXAMPLE

Which test item is *least* useful for educational diagnosis?
   A. Multiple-choice item.
  *****B.** True-false item.
   C. Short-answer item.

BOX 5.3 • *Matching Items*

Strengths

1. A compact and efficient form is provided where the same set of responses fit a series of item stems (i.e., premises).
2. Reading and response time is short.
3. This item type is easily constructed if converted from multiple-choice items having a common set of alternatives.
4. Scoring is easy, objective, and reliable.

Limitations

1. This item type is largely restricted to simple knowledge outcomes based on association.
2. It is difficult to construct items that contain a sufficient number of homogeneous responses.
3. Susceptibility to irrelevant clues is greater than in other item types.

Which test item measures the greatest variety of learning outcomes?
    ***A.** Multiple-choice item.
    B. True-false item.
    C. Short-answer item.

Which test item is difficult to score objectively?
    A. Multiple-choice item.
    B. True-false item.
    ***C.** Short-answer item.

Which test item provides the highest score by guessing?
    A. Multiple-choice item.
    ***B.** True-false item.
    C. Short-answer item.

By switching to a matching format, we can eliminate the repetition of the alternative answers and present the same items in a more compact form. The matching format consists of a series of stems, called *premises,* and a series of alternative answers, called *responses.* These are arranged in columns with directions that set the rules for matching. The following example illustrates how our multiple-choice items can be converted to matching form.

EXAMPLE

Directions: Column A contains a list of characteristics of test items. On the line to the left of each statement, write the letter of the test item in Column B that best fits the statement. Each response in Column B may be used once, more than once, or not at all.

Column A		Column B
(B)	**1.** Least useful for educational diagnosis.	**A.** Multiple-choice item.
(A)	**2.** Measures greatest variety of learning outcomes.	**B.** True-false item.
(C)	**3.** Most difficult to score objectively.	**C.** Short-answer item.
(B)	**4.** Provides the highest score by guessing.	

The conversion to matching item illustrated here is probably the most defensible use of this item type. All too frequently, matching items consist of a disparate collection of premises, each of which has only one or two plausible answers. This can be avoided by starting with multiple-choice items and switching to the matching format only when it provides a more compact and efficient means of measuring the same achievement. In our example, we could have also expanded the item by adding other similar premises and responses.

Rules for Writing Matching Items

A good matching item should function the same as a series of multiple-choice items. As each premise is considered, all of the responses should serve as plausible alternatives. The rules for item writing are directed toward this end.

1. *Include only homogeneous material in each matching item.* In our earlier example of a matching item, we included *only* types of test items and their characteristics. Similarly, an item might include *only* authors and their works, inventors and their inventions, scientists and their discoveries, or historical events and their dates. This homogeneity is necessary if all responses are to serve as plausible alternatives (see earlier example).

2. *Keep the lists of items short and place the brief responses on the right.* A short list of items (say less than 10) will save reading time, make it easier for the student to locate the answer, and increase the likelihood that the responses will be homogeneous and plausible. Placing the brief responses on the right also saves reading time.

3. *Use a larger, or smaller, number of responses than premises, and permit the responses to be used more than once.* Both an uneven match and the possibility of using each response more than once reduces the guessing factor. As we noted earlier, proper use of the matching form requires that *all responses be plausible alternatives for each premise.* This, of course, dictates that each response be eligible for use more than once.

4. *Place the responses in alphabetical or numerical order.* This will make selection of the responses easier and avoid possible clues due to placement.

BOX 5.4 • *Checklist for Evaluating Matching Items*

1. Is this type of item appropriate for measuring the intended learning outcome?
2. Does the item task match the learning task to be measured?
3. Does each matching item contain only homogeneous material?
4. Are the lists of items short with the brief responses on the right?
5. Is an uneven match provided by making the list of responses longer or shorter than the list of premises?
6. Are the responses in alphabetical or numerical order?
7. Do the directions clearly state the basis for matching and that each response can be used once, more than once, or not at all?
8. Does the complete matching item appear on the same page?

5. *Specify in the directions the basis for matching and indicate that each response may be used once, more than once, or not at all.* This will clarify the task for all students and prevent any misunderstanding. Take care, however, not to make the directions too long and involved. The previous example illustrates adequate detail for directions.

6. *Put all of the matching item on the same page.* This will prevent the distraction of flipping pages back and forth and prevent students from overlooking responses on another page. See Box 5.4 for a summary checklist for evaluating matching items.

The Interpretive Exercise

Complex learning outcomes can frequently be more effectively measured by basing a series of test items on a common selection of introductory material. This may be a paragraph, a table, a chart, a graph, a map, or a picture. The test items that follow the introductory material may be designed to call forth any type of intellectual ability or skill that can be measured objectively. This type of exercise is commonly called an *interpretive exercise* and both multiple-choice items and alternative-response items are widely used to measure interpretation of the introductory material.

The following example illustrates the use of multiple-choice items. Note that this item type makes it possible to measure a variety of learning outcomes with the same selection of introductory material. In this particular case, item 1 measures the *ability to recognize unstated assumptions,* item 2 the *ability to identify the meaning of a term,* and item 3 the *ability to identify relationships.*

EXAMPLE

Directions: Read the following comments a teacher made about testing. Then answer the questions that follow by circling the letter of the best answer.

"Students go to school to learn, not to take tests. In addition, tests cannot be used to indicate a student's absolute level of learning. All tests can do is rank students in order of achievement, and this relative ranking is influenced by guessing, bluffing, and the subjective opinions of the teacher doing the scoring. The teacher-learning process would benefit if we did away with tests and depended on student self-evaluation."

1. Which one of the following unstated assumptions is this teacher making?
    A. Students go to school to learn.
    B. Teachers use essay tests primarily.
    *C. Tests make no contribution to learning.
    D. Tests do not indicate a student's absolute level of learning.

2. Which one of the following types of tests is this teacher primarily talking about?
    A. Diagnostic test.
    B. Formative test.
    C. Pretest.
    *D. Summative test.

3. Which one of the following propositions is most essential to the final conclusion?
    *A. Effective self-evaluation does not require the use of tests.
    B. Tests place students in rank order only.
    C. Tests scores are influenced by factors other than achievement.
    D. Students do not go to school to take tests.

The next example uses a modified version of the alternative-response form. This is frequently called a *key-type* item because a common set of alternatives is used in responding to each question. Note that the key-type item is devoted entirely to the measurement of one learning outcome. In this example the item measures the *ability to recognize warranted and unwarranted inferences.*

EXAMPLE

Directions: Paragraph A contains a description of the testing practices of Mr. Smith, a high school teacher. Read the description and each of the statements that follow it. Mark each statement to indicate the type of INFERENCE that can be drawn about it from the material in the paragraph. Place the appropriate letter in front of each statement using the following KEY:

    T—if the statement may be INFERRED as TRUE.
    F—if the statement may be INFERRED as UNTRUE.
    N—if NO INFERENCE may be drawn about it from the paragraph.

Paragraph A

Approximately one week before a test is to be given, Mr. Smith carefully goes through the textbook and constructs multiple-choice items based on the material in the book. He always uses the exact wording of the textbook for the correct answer so that there will be no question concerning its correctness. He is careful to include some test items from each chapter. After the test is given, he lists the scores from high to low on the blackboard and tells each student his or her score. He does not return the test papers to the students, but he offers to answer any questions they might have about the test. He puts the items from each test into a test file, which he is building for future use.

Statements on Paragraph A

(T)   **1.** Mr. Smith's tests measure a limited range of learning outcomes.

(F)   **2.** Some of Mr. Smith's test items measure at the understanding level.

(N)   **3.** Mr. Smith's tests measure a balanced sample of subject matter.

(N)   **4.** Mr. Smith uses the type of test item that is best for his purpose.

(T)   **5.** Students can determine where they rank in the distribution of scores on Mr. Smith's tests.

(F)   **6.** Mr. Smith's testing practices are likely to motivate students to overcome their weaknesses.

Key-type items are fairly easy to develop and can be directly related to specific learning outcomes. The key categories can, of course, be reused by simply changing the introductory material and the statements. Thus, they provide a standard framework for test preparation. Other common key categories include the following: (1) the argument is relevant, irrelevant, or neither; (2) the statement is supported by the evidence, refuted by the evidence, or neither; (3) the assumption is necessary or unnecessary; and (4) the conclusion is valid, invalid, or its validity cannot be determined. Although such standard key categories should not be applied in a perfunctory manner, they can provide guidelines to simplify the construction of the interpretive exercise. See Box 5.5 for strengths and limitations.

Rules for Constructing Interpretive Exercises

The effectiveness of interpretive exercises, such as those illustrated earlier, depends on the care with which the introductory material is selected and the skill with which the dependent items are prepared. The following rules provide guidelines for preparing high quality exercises of this type.

1. *Select introductory material that is relevant to the learning outcomes to be measured.* The introductory material may take many forms: written material, table, chart, graph, map, picture, or cartoon. In some cases the interpretation of the introductory material is an important learning outcome in its own right, as in the "interpretation of a weather map" or "the interpretation of a line graph." Here the nature of the introductory material is clearly

BOX 5.5 • *Intrepretative Exercises*

Strengths
1. An efficient means of measuring the interpretation of printed information in various forms (e.g., written, charts, graphs, maps, pictures) is provided.
2. More meaningful complex learning outcomes can be measured than with the single-item format.
3. The use of introductory material provides a common basis for responding.
4. Scoring is easy, objective, and reliable.

Limitations
1. It is difficult to construct effective items.
2. Written material is highly dependent on reading skill.
3. This item type is highly subject to extraneous clues.
4. It is ineffective in measuring the ability to originate, organize, and express ideas.

prescribed by the intended outcome. In other cases, however, the introductory material simply provides the means for measuring other important outcomes. The "ability to distinguish between valid and invalid conclusions," for example, may be measured with different types of introductory material. In this instance we should select the type of material that provides the most direct measure of the learning outcome, is familiar to the examinees, and places the least demand on reading ability. For young children this means pictorial materials should typically be favored.

2. *Select introductory material that is new to the examinees.* Although the form of the material should be familiar to the examinees, the specific content used in an exercise should be new to them. Thus, if they are asked to identify relationships shown in a graph, the type of graph should be familiar but the specific data in the graph must be new. If the data were the same as that presented in the classroom or described in the textbook, the exercise would measure nothing more than the simple recall of information. To measure complex outcomes, some novelty is necessary. How much depends on the specific nature of the intended outcome.

In some cases it is possible to locate introductory material that is new to the examinees by reviewing sources that are not readily available to them. Then it is simply a matter of adapting the material for testing purposes. In other cases it is necessary to prepare completely new material (i.e., write a paragraph, construct a graph, make a map, or draw a picture). In either case further revision will probably be needed when the dependent test items are being prepared. The process is essentially a circular one, with the writing of items requiring some changes in the introductory material and changes there providing ideas for new items. In carrying out this process of adapting and revising the material, be careful not to introduce so much novelty that the exercise no longer provides a valid measure of the intended learning outcome.

3. *Keep the introductory material brief and readable.* It is inefficient for both the test maker and the test taker to use extended introductory material and only one or two test items. If the introductory material is in written form, excessively long selections will also create problems for individuals with inadequate reading skills. Ideally, it should be a brief, concise selection that contains enough ideas for several relevant test items. Material of this type can frequently be obtained from summaries, digests, and other condensed forms of written material. In some cases pictures or diagrams may provide the most concise summary of the material. As noted earlier we should always favor the type of material that places the least demand on reading ability.

4. *Construct test items that call forth the type of performance specified in the learning outcome.* To adequately measure the intended interpretation of the introductory material requires careful phrasing of the questions and special attention to two important cautions. First, *the answer to an item should not be given directly in the material* since some mental process beyond "recognition of a stated fact" is required in measures of intellectual skills. Second, *it should not be possible to answer the question without the introductory material.* If an item can be answered on the basis of general knowledge, it is not measuring the ability to interpret the material in the exercise. A good check on this type of error is to cover the introductory material and attempt to answer the questions without it.

5. *Follow the rules of effective item writing that pertain to the type of objective item used.* All of the rules for constructing the various types of objective test items discussed in the last two chapters are applicable to the construction of items used in interpretive exercises. Even greater care must be taken to avoid extraneous clues, however, since items in interpretive exercises seem especially prone to such clues and they tend to be more difficult to detect in these items. If the introductory material includes illustrations, for example, special attention should be directed to such things as the size, shape, and position of objects as possible extraneous clues. These are frequently overlooked by the test maker who is concentrating on the intricacies of the mental response required, but not by the unprepared student who is frantically searching for any solution to the problem.

The greatest help in constructing interpretive exercises is to review a wide range of sample exercises that use different types of introductory material and different forms of dependent test items. For locating illustrative exercises, see the list of references at the end of the chapter. See Box 5.6 for a summary checklist for evaluating interpretive exercises.

BOX 5.6 • *Checklist for Evaluating Intrepretative Exercises*

---

1. Is this type of exercise appropriate for measuring the intended learning outcome?
2. Is the introductory material relevant to the learning outcomes?
3. Is the introductory material familiar but new to the examinees?
4. Is the introductory material brief and at the appropriate reading level?
5. Do the test items call forth the performance specified in the learning outcomes?
6. Do the test items call for interpretation (rather than recognition or recall)?
7. Do the test items meet the criteria of effective item writing that apply to the item type used?
8. Is the interpretive exercise free of extraneous clues?

Summary of Points

1. A good practice is to start with multiple-choice items and switch to other selection-type items when more appropriate.
2. The true-false or alternative-response item is appropriate when there are only two possible alternatives.
3. The true-false item is used primarily to measure knowledge of specific facts, although there are some notable exceptions.
4. Each true-false statement should contain only one central idea, be concisely stated, be free of clues and irrelevant sources of difficulty, and have an answer on which experts would agree.
5. Modifications of the true-false item are especially useful for measuring the ability to "distinguish between fact and opinion" and "identify cause-effect relations."
6. Modifications of the true-false item can be used in interpretive exercises to measure various types of complex learning outcomes.
7. The matching item is a variation of the multiple-choice form and is appropriate when it provides a more compact and efficient means of measuring the same achievement.
8. The matching item consists of a list of *premises* and a list of the *responses* to be related to the premises.
9. A good matching item is based on homogeneous material, contains a brief list of premises and an uneven number of responses (more or less) that can be used more than once, and has the brief responses in the right-hand column.
10. The directions for a matching item should indicate the basis for matching and that each response can be used more than once.

11. The interpretive exercise consists of a series of selection-type items based on some type of introductory material (e.g., paragraph, table, chart, graph, map, or picture).
12. The interpretive exercise uses both multiple-choice and alternative-response items to measure a variety of complex learning outcomes.
13. The introductory material used in an interpretive exercise must be relevant to the outcomes to be measured, new to examinees, at the proper reading level, and as brief as possible.
14. The test items used in an interpretive exercise should call for the intended type of interpretation, and the answers to the items should be dependent on the introductory material.
15. The test items used in an interpretive exercise should be in harmony with the rules for constructing that item type.

References and Additional Reading

Carey, L. M., *Measuring and Evaluating School Learning*, 3rd ed. (Boston: Allyn and Bacon, 2001).

Linn, R. L., and Gronlund, N. E., *Measurement and Assessment in Teaching*, 8th ed. (Upper Saddle River, NJ: Merrill/Prentice-Hall, 2000).

Mehrens, W. A., and Lehmann, I. J., *Measurement and Evaluation in Education and Psychology*, 4th ed. (New York: Holt, Rinehart and Winston, 1991).

Oosterhoff, A. C., *Developing and Using Classroom Assessments*, 2nd ed. (Upper Saddle River, NJ: Prentice-Hall, 1999).

6

Writing Supply Items

Short Answer and Essay

Studying this chapter should enable you to

1. Describe the strengths and limitations of short-answer items.
2. Distinguish between well-stated and poorly stated short-answer items.
3. Identify and correct faults in poorly stated short-answer items.
4. Match short-answer items to intended learning outcomes.
5. Construct short-answer items that are well stated, relevant to important learning outcomes, and free of defects.
6. Describe the strengths and limitations of essay questions.
7. Distinguish between restricted-response and extended-response essay questions.
8. Describe the strengths and limitations of essay questions.
9. Write essay questions that present a clear task, are relevant to important learning outcomes, and provide guidelines for scoring.
10. Score essay answers more effectively.

As noted in the last two chapters, selection-type items can be designed to measure a variety of learning outcomes, ranging from simple to complex. They tend to be favored in achievement tests because they provide (1) greater control of the type of response students can make, (2) broader sampling of achievement, and (3) quicker and more objective scoring. Despite these advantages, supply-type items can also play an important role in measuring achievement.

Supply-type items require students to produce the answer. This may be a single-word or a several-page response. Although the length of response

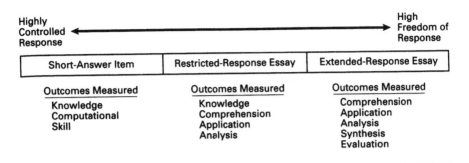

FIGURE 6.1 Supply-type items arranged along a "control of response" continuum and a list of learning outcomes typically measured by each item type.

ranges along a continuum, supply-type items are typically divided into (1) short-answer items, (2) restricted-response essay, and (3) extended-response essay (see Figure 6.1).

Short-Answer Items

The short-answer (or completion) item requires the examinee to supply the appropriate words, numbers, or symbols to answer a question or complete a statement.

EXAMPLE

What are the incorrect responses in a multiple-choice item called? *(distracters)*
The incorrect responses in a multiple-choice item are called *(distracters)*

This item type also includes computational problems and any other simple item form that requires supplying the answer rather than selecting it. Except for its use in computational problems, the short-answer item is used primarily to measure simple knowledge outcomes.

The short-answer item appears to be easy to write and use but there are two major problems in constructing short-answer items. First, it is extremely difficult to phrase the question or incomplete statement so that only one answer is correct. In the example we have noted, for instance, a student might respond with any one of a number of answers that could be defended as appropriate. The student might write "incorrect alternatives," "wrong answers," "inappropriate options," "decoys," "foils," or some other equally descriptive response. Second, there is the problem of spelling. If credit is given only when the answer is spelled correctly, the poor spellers will be prevented from showing their true level of achievement and the test scores will become an uninterpretable mixture of knowledge and spelling skill. On

BOX 6.1 • *Short-Answer Items*

Strengths
1. It is easy to write test items.
2. Guessing is less likely than in selection-type items.
3. This type is well-suited to computational problems and other learning outcomes where supplying the answer is important.
4. A broad range of knowledge outcomes can be measured.

Limitations
1. It is difficult to phrase statements so that only one answer is correct.
2. Scoring is contaminated by spelling ability when responses are verbal.
3. Scoring is tedious and time consuming.
4. This item type is not very adaptable to measuring complex learning outcomes.

the other hand, if attempts are made to ignore spelling during the scoring process, there is still the problem of deciding whether a badly spelled word represents the intended answer. This, of course, introduces an element of subjectivity that tends to make the scores less dependable as measures of achievement. See Box 6.1 for strengths and limitations.

Due to these weaknesses, the short-answer item should be reserved for those special situations where supplying the answer is a necessary part of the learning outcome to be measured; for example, where the intent is to have students *recall* the information, where computational problems are used, or where a selection-type item would make the answer obvious. In these situations, the use of the short-answer item can be defended despite its shortcomings.

Rules for Writing Short-Answer Items

1. *State the item so that only a single, brief answer is possible.* This requires great skill in phrasing and the use of precise terms. What appears to be a simple, clear question to the test maker can frequently be answered in many different ways, as we noted with the previous sample item. It helps to review the item with this rule in mind and revise as needed.

2. *Start with a direct question and switch to an incomplete statement only when greater conciseness is possible by doing so.* The use of a direct question increases the likelihood that the problem will be stated clearly and that only one answer will be appropriate. Also, incomplete statements tend to be less

ambiguous when they are based on problems that were first stated in question form.

EXAMPLE

What is another name for true-false items? *(alternative-response items)*
True-false items are also called *(alternative-response items)*.

In some cases, it is best to leave it in question form. This may make the item clearer, especially to younger students.

3. *It is best to leave only one blank and it should relate to the main point of the statement.* Leaving several blanks to be filled in is often confusing and the answer to one blank may depend on the answer in another.

EXAMPLE

Poor: In terms of type of response, the (matching) item is most like the *(multiple-choice)* item.

Better: In terms of type of responses, which item is most like the matching item? *(multiple-choice)*.

In the "poor" version, a number of different responses would have to be given credit, such as "short answer" and "essay," and "true-false" and "multiple-choice." Obviously, the item would not function as originally intended.

It is also important to avoid asking students to respond to unimportant or minor aspects of a statement. Focus on the main idea of the item and leave a blank only for the key response.

4. *Place the blanks at the end of the statement.* This permits the student to read the complete problem before coming to the blank to be filled. With this procedure, confusion and rereading of the item is avoided and scoring is simplified. Constructing incomplete statements with blanks at the end is more easily accomplished when the item is first stated as a direct question, as suggested earlier. In some cases, it may be a matter of rewording the item and changing the response to be made.

EXAMPLE

Poor: *(Reliability)* is likely to increase when a test is lengthened.

Better: When a test is lengthened, reliability is likely to *(increase)*.

With this particular item, the "better" version also provides a more clearly focused item. The "poor" version could be answered by "validity," "time for testing," "fatigue," and other unintended but clearly correct responses. This again illustrates the great care needed in phrasing short-answer items.

5. *Avoid extraneous clues to the answer.* One of the most common clues in short-answer items is the length of the blank. If a long blank is used for a long word and a short blank for a short word, this is obviously a clue. Thus, all blanks should be uniform in length. Another common clue is the use of the indefinite article "a" or "an" just before the blank. It sometimes gives away the answer, or at least rules out some possible incorrect answers.

EXAMPLE

Poor: The supply-type item used to measure the ability to organize and integrate material is called an (essay item).

Better: Supply-type items used to measure the ability to organize and integrate material are called (essay items).

The "poor" version rules out "short-answer item," the only other supply-type item, because it does not follow the article "an." One solution is to include both articles, using a(an). Another solution is to eliminate the article by switching to plural, as shown in the "better" version.

6. *For numerical answers, indicate the degree of precision expected and the units in which they are to be expressed.* Indicating the degree of precision (e.g., to the nearest whole number) will clarify the task for students and prevent them from spending more time on an item than is required. Indicating the units in which to express the answer will aid scoring by providing a more uniform set of responses (e.g., minutes rather than fractions of an hour). When the learning outcome requires knowing the type of unit in common use and the degree of precision expected, this rule must then be disregarded. See Box 6.2 for a summary checklist.

BOX 6.2 • *Checklist for Evaluating Short-Answer Items*

1. Is this type of item appropriate for measuring the intended learning outcome?
2. Does the item task match the learning task to be measured?
3. Does the item call for a single, brief answer?
4. Has the item been written as a direct question or a well-stated incomplete sentence.
5. Does the desired response relate to the main point of the item?
6. Is the blank placed at the end of the statement?
7. Have clues to the answer been avoided (e.g., "a" or "an," length of the blank)?
8. Are the units and degree of precision indicated for numerical answers?

Essay Questions

The most notable characteristic of the essay question is the freedom of response it provides. As with the short-answer item, students must produce their own answers. With the essay question, however, they are free to decide how to approach the problem, what factual information to use, how to organize the answer, and what degree of emphasis to give each aspect of the response. Thus, the essay question is especially useful for measuring the ability to organize, integrate, and express ideas. These are the types of performance for which selection-type items and short-answer items are so inadequate.

In deciding when and how to use essay questions, it may be desirable to compare their relative merits with those of selection-type items, as shown in Table 6.1. As can be seen in the table, both item types are efficient for certain purposes and inefficient for others. It is also apparent that the two types tend to complement each other in terms of the types of learning outcomes measured and the effect they are most likely to have on learning. Thus, it is not a matter of using either selection-type items or essay questions, but rather

TABLE 6.1 *Summary Comparison of Selection-Type Items and Essay*

	Selection-Type Items	Essay Questions
Learning Outcomes Measured	Good for measuring outcomes at the knowledge, comprehension, and application levels of learning; inadequate for organizing and expressing ideas.	Inefficient for measuring knowledge outcomes; best for ability to organize, integrate, and express ideas.
Sampling of Content	The use of a large number of items results in broad coverage, which makes representative sampling of content feasible.	The use of a small number of items limits coverage, which makes representative sampling of content infeasible.
Preparation of Items	Preparation of good items is difficult and time consuming.	Preparation of good items is difficult but easier than selection-type items.
Scoring	Objective, simple, and highly reliable.	Subjective, difficult, and less reliable.
Factors Distorting Scores	Reading ability and guessing.	Writing ability and bluffing.
Probable Effect on Learning	Encourages students to remember, interpret, and use the ideas of others.	Encourages students to organize, integrate, and express their own ideas.

when should each be used. Tests may frequently require both types in order to obtain adequate coverage of the intended learning outcomes.

Types of Essay Questions

The freedom of response permitted by essay questions varies considerably. Students may be required to give a brief and precise response, or they may be given great freedom in determining the form and scope of their answers. Questions of the first type are commonly called *restricted-response questions* and those of the second type are called *extended-response questions*. This is an arbitrary but convenient pair of categories for classifying essay questions.

Restricted-Response Questions.   The restricted-response question places strict limits on the answer to be given. The boundaries of the subject matter to be considered are usually narrowly defined by the problem, and the specific form of the answer is also commonly indicated (by words such as "list," "define," and "give reasons"). In some cases the response is limited further by the use of introductory material or by the use of special directions.

> **EXAMPLE**
>
> Describe the relative merits of selection-type test items and essay questions for measuring learning outcomes at the comprehension level. Confine your answer to one page.

> **EXAMPLE**
>
> Mr. Rogers, a ninth-grade science teacher, wants to measure his students' "ability to interpret scientific data" with a paper-and-pencil test.
>
> 1. Describe the steps that Mr. Rogers should follow.
> 2. Give reasons to justify each step.

Restricting the form and scope of the answers to essay questions has both advantages and disadvantages. Such questions can be prepared more easily, related more directly to specific learning outcomes, and scored more easily. On the other hand, they provide little opportunity for the students to demonstrate their abilities to organize, to integrate, and to develop essentially new patterns of response. The imposed limitations make restricted-response items especially useful for measuring learning outcomes at the comprehension, application, and analysis levels of learning. They are of relatively little value for measuring outcomes at the synthesis and evaluation levels. At these levels the extended-response question provides the more appropriate measure.

Extended-Response Questions.   The extended-response question gives students almost unlimited freedom to determine the form and scope of their responses. Although in some instances rather rigid practical limits may be imposed, such as time limits or page limits, restrictions on the material to be included in the answer and on the form of response are held to a minimum. Students must be given sufficient freedom to demonstrate skills of synthesis and evaluation, and just enough control to assure that the intended intellectual skills and abilities will be called forth by the question. Thus, the amount of structure will vary from item to item depending on the learning outcomes being measured, but the stress will always be on providing as much freedom as the situation permits.

EXAMPLE

Synthesis Outcome: For a course that you are teaching or expect to teach, prepare a complete plan for assessing student achievement. Be sure to include the procedures you would follow, the instruments you would use, and the reasons for your choices.

EXAMPLE

Evaluation Outcome: (The student is given a complete achievement test that includes errors or flaws in the directions, in the test items, and in the arrangement of the items.) Write a critical evaluation of this test using as evaluative criteria the rules and standards for test construction described in your textbook. Include a detailed analysis of the test's strengths and weaknesses and an evaluation of its overall quality and probable effectiveness.

The extended-response question provides for the creative integration of ideas, the overall evaluation of materials, and a broad approach to problem solving. These are all important learning outcomes and ones that cannot be measured by other types of test items. The biggest problem, of course, is to evaluate the answers with sufficient reliability to provide a useful measure of learning. This is a difficult and time-consuming task, but the importance of the outcomes would seem to justify the additional care and effort required (see Box 6.3).

Rules for Writing Essay Questions

The construction of clear, unambiguous easy questions that call forth the desired responses is a much more difficult task than is commonly presumed. The following rules will not make the task any easier, but their application will result in essay items of higher quality.

1. *Use essay questions to measure complex learning outcomes only.* Most knowledge outcomes profit little from being measured by easy questions.

BOX 6.3 • *Essay Questions*

Strengths
1. The highest level learning outcomes (analysis, synthesis, evaluation) can be measured.
2. Preparation time is less than that for selection-type items.
3. The integration and application of ideas is emphasized.

Limitations
1. There is an inadequate sampling of achievement due to time needed for answering each question.
2. It is difficult to relate to intended learning outcomes because of freedom to select, organize, and express ideas.
3. Scores are raised by writing skill and bluffing and lowered by poor hand-writing, misspelling, and grammatical errors.
4. Scoring is time consuming, subjective, and tends to be unreliable.

These outcomes can usually be measured more effectively by objective items that lack the sampling and scoring problems that essay questions introduce. There may be a few exceptions, as when supplying the answer is a basic part of the learning outcome, but for most knowledge outcomes essay questions simply provide a less reliable measure with no compensating benefits.

At the comprehension, application, and analysis levels of learning, both objective tests and essay tests are useful. Even here, though, the objective test would seem to have priority, the essay test being reserved for those situations that require the student to *give* reasons, *explain* relationships, *describe* data, *formulate* conclusions, or in some other way produce the appropriate answer. Where supplying the answer is vital, a properly constructed restricted-response question is likely to be most appropriate.

At the synthesis and evaluation levels of learning, both the objective test and the restricted-response test have only limited value. These tests may be used to measure some specific aspects of the total process, but the production of a complete work (such as a plan of operation) or an overall evaluation of a work (for instance, an evaluation of a novel or an experiment) requires the use of extended-response questions. It is at this level that the essay form contributes most uniquely.

2. *Relate the questions as directly as possible to the learning outcomes being measured.* Essay questions will not measure complex learning outcomes unless they are carefully constructed to do so. Each question should be specifically designed to measure one or more well-defined outcomes. Thus, the place to start, as is the case with objective items, is with a precise description of the performance to be measured. This will help determine both the content and form of the item and will aid in the phrasing of it.

The restricted-response item is related quite easily to a specific learning outcome because it is so highly structured. The limited response expected from the student also makes it possible for the test maker to phrase the question so that its intent is communicated clearly to the student. The extended-response item, however, requires greater freedom of response and typically involves a number of learning outcomes. This makes it more difficult to relate the question to the intended outcomes and to indicate the nature of the desired answer through the phrasing of the question. If the task is prescribed too rigidly in the question, the students' freedom to select, organize, and present the answer is apt to be infringed upon. One practical solution is to indicate to the students the criteria to be used in evaluating the answer. For example, a parenthetical statement such as the following might be added: "Your answer will be evaluated in terms of its comprehensiveness, the relevance of its arguments, the appropriateness of its examples, and the skill with which it is organized." This clarifies the task to the students without limiting their freedom, and makes the item easier to relate to clearly defined learning outcomes.

3. *Formulate questions that present a clear task to be performed.* Phrasing an essay question so that the desired response is obtained is no simple matter. Selecting precise terms and carefully phrasing and rephrasing the question with the desired response in mind will help clarify the task to the student. Since essay questions are to be used as a measure of complex learning outcomes, avoid starting such questions with "who," "what," "when," "where," "name," and "list." These terms tend to limit the response to knowledge outcomes. Complex achievement is most apt to be called forth by such words as "why," "describe," "explain," "compare," "relate," "contrast," "interpret," "analyze," "criticize," and "evaluate." The specific terminology to be used will be determined largely by the specific behavior described in the learning outcome to be measured (see Table 6.2).

There is no better way to check on the phrasing of an essay question than to write a model answer, or at least to formulate a mental answer, to the question. This helps the test maker detect any ambiguity in the question, aids in determining the approximate time needed by the student to develop a satisfactory answer, and provides a rough check on the mental processes required. This procedure is most feasible with the restricted-response item, the answer to which is more limited and more closely prescribed. With the extended-response form it may be necessary to ask one or more colleagues to read the question to determine if the form and scope of the desired answer are clear.

4. *Do not permit a choice of questions unless the learning outcome requires it.* In most tests of achievement, it is best to have all students answer the same questions. If they are permitted to write on only a fraction of the questions, such as three out of five, their answers cannot be evaluated on a comparative basis. Also, since the students will tend to choose those

TABLE 6.2 *Types of Complex Outcomes and Related Terms for Writing Essay Questions*

Outcome	Sample Terms
Comparing	compare, classify, describe, distinguish between, explain, outline, summarize
Interpreting	convert, draw, estimates, illustrate, interpret, restate, summarize, translate
Inferring	derive, draw, estimate, extend, extrapolate, predict, propose, relate
Applying	arrange, compute, describe, demonstrate, illustrate, rearrange, relate, summarize
Analyzing	break down, describe, diagram, differentiate, divide, list, outline, separate
Creating	compose, design, devise, draw, formulate, make up, present, propose
Synthesizing	arrange, combine, construct, design, rearrange, regroup, relate, write
Generalizing	construct, develop, explain, formulate, generate, make, propose, state
Evaluating	appraise, criticize, defend, describe, evaluate, explain, judge, write

questions they are best prepared to answer, their responses will provide a sample of their achievement that is less representative than that obtained without optional questions. As we noted earlier, one of the major limitations of the essay test is the limited and unrepresentative sampling it provides. Giving students a choice among questions simply complicates the sampling problem further and introduces greater distortion into the test results.

In some situations the use of optional questions might be defensible. For example, if the essay is to be used as a measure of writing *skill* only, some choice of topics on which to write may be desirable. This might also be the case if the essay is used to measure some aspects of creativity, or if the students have pursued individual interests through independent study. Even for these special uses, however, great caution must be exercised in the use of optional questions. The ability to organize, integrate, and express ideas is determined in part by the complexity of the content involved. Thus, an indeterminate amount of contamination can be expected when optional questions are used.

5. *Provide ample time for answering and suggest a time limit on each question.* Since essay questions are designed most frequently to measure intellectual skills and abilities, time must be allowed for thinking as well as for writing. Thus, generous time limits should be provided. For example, rather than expecting students to write on several essay questions during one class period, it might be better to have them focus on one or two. There seems to be a tendency for teachers to include so many questions in a single essay test that a high score is as much a measure of writing speed as of achievement. This is probably an attempt to overcome the problem of limited sampling, but it tends to be an undesirable solution. In measuring complex achievement, it is better to use fewer questions and to improve the sample by more frequent testing.

Informing students of the appropriate amount of time they should spend on each question will help them use their time more efficiently; ideally, it will also provide a more adequate sample of their achievement. If the length of the answer is not clearly defined by the problem, as in some extended-response questions, it might also be desirable to indicate page limits. Anything that will clarify the form and scope of the task without interfering with the measurement of the intended outcomes is likely to contribute to more effective measurement.

Rules for Scoring Essay Answers

As we noted earlier, one of the major limitations of the essay test is the subjectivity of the scoring. That is, the feelings of the scorers are likely to enter into the judgments they make concerning the quality of the answers. This may be a personal bias toward the writer of the essay, toward certain areas of content or styles of writing, or toward shortcomings in such extraneous areas as legibility, spelling, and grammar. These biases, of course, distort the results of a measure of achievement and tend to lower their reliability.

The following rules are desired to minimize the subjectivity of the scoring and to provide as uniform a standard of scoring from one student to another as possible. These rules will be most effective, of course, when the questions have been carefully prepared in accordance with the rules for construction.

1. *Evaluate answers to essay questions in terms of the learning outcomes being measured.* The essay test, like the objective test, is used to obtain evidence concerning the extent to which clearly defined learning outcomes have been achieved. Thus, the desired student performance specified in these outcomes should serve as a guide both for constructing the questions and for evaluating the answers. If a question is designed to measure "the ability to explain cause-effect relations," for example, the answer should be evaluated in terms of how adequately the student *explains the particular cause-effect relations presented in the question.* All other factors, such as interesting but extraneous factual information, style of writing, and errors in spelling and grammar, should be ignored (to the extent possible) during the evaluation. In some cases separate scores may be given for spelling or writing ability, but these should not be allowed to contaminate the scores that represent the degree of achievement of the intended learning outcomes.

2. *Score restricted-response answers by the point method, using a model answer as a guide.* Scoring with the aid of a previously prepared scoring key is possible with the restricted-response item because of the limitations placed on the answer. The procedure involves writing a model answer to each question and determining the number of points to be assigned to it and to the parts within it. The distribution of points within an answer must, of course, take into account all scorable units indicated in the learning outcomes being measured. For example, points may be assigned to the relevance of the examples used and to the organization of the answer, as well as to the content of the answer, if these are legitimate aspects of the learning outcome. As indicated earlier, it is usually desirable to make clear to the student at the time of testing the basis on which each answer will be judged (content, organization, and so on).

3. *Grade extended-response answers by the rating method, using defined criteria as a guide.* Extended-response items allow so much freedom in answering that the preparation of a model answer is frequently impossible. Thus, the test maker usually *grades* each answer by judging its quality in terms of a previously determined set of criteria, rather than *scoring* it point by point with a scoring key. The criteria for judging the quality of an answer are determined by the nature of the question, and thus, by the learning outcomes being measured. If students were asked to "describe a complete plan for preparing an achievement test," for example, the criteria would include such things as (1) the completeness of the plan (for example, whether it included a statement of objectives, a set of specifications, and the appropriate types of items), (2) the clarity and accuracy with which each step was described, (3) the adequacy of the justification for each step, and (4) the degree to which the various parts of the plan were properly integrated.

Typically, the criteria for evaluating an answer are used to establish about five levels of quality. Then as the answer to a question is read, it is assigned a letter grade or a number from 1 to 5, which designates the reader's rating. One grade may be assigned on the basis of the overall quality of the answer, or a separate judgment may be made on the basis of each criterion. The latter procedure provides the most useful information for diagnosing and improving learning and should be used wherever possible.

More uniform standards of grading can usually be obtained by reading the answers to each question twice. During the first reading the papers should be tentatively sorted into five piles, ranging from high to low in quality. The second reading can then serve the purpose of checking the uniformity of the answers in each pile and making any necessary shifts in rating. Beware of student bluffing (see Box 6.4).

BOX 6.4 • *Student Bluffing and Scoring Essays*

Students can obtain higher scores on essay questions by clever bluffing. Although this requires skill in writing and some knowledge of the topic, credit should not be given unless the question is specifically answered. Some common types of bluffing are listed below.

1. Student repeats the question in statement form (slightly paraphrased) and tells how important the topic is (e.g., "The role of assessment in teaching is extremely important. It is hard to imagine effective instruction without it, etc.").
2. Student writes on a well-known topic and fits it to the question (e.g., a student who knows testing well but knows little about performance assessment and is asked to compare testing and performance assessment might describe testing in considerable detail and frequently state that performance assessment is much superior for evaluating the type of learning measured by the test).
3. Student liberally sprinkles the answer with basic concepts whether they are understood or not (e.g., asked to write about any assessment technique the importance of "validity" and "reliability" is mentioned frequently).
4. Student includes the teacher's basic beliefs wherever possible (e.g., "The intended learning outcomes must be stated in performance terms before this type of test is constructed or selected").

Bluffing is most effective where plans have not been made for careful scoring of the answers.

4. *Evaluate all of the students' answers to one question before proceeding to the next question.* Scoring or grading essay tests question by question, rather than student by student, makes it possible to maintain a more uniform standard for judging the answers to each question. This procedure also helps offset the *halo effect* in grading. When all of the answers on one paper are read together, the grader's impression of the paper as a whole is apt to influence the grades assigned to the individual answers. Grading question by question prevents the formation of this overall impression of a student's paper. Each answer is more apt to be judged on its own merits when it is read and compared with other answers to the same question than when it is read and compared with other answers by the same student.

5. *Evaluate answers to essay questions without knowing the identity of the writer.* This is another attempt to control personal bias during scoring. Answers to essay questions should be evaluated in terms of what is written, not in terms of what is known about the writers from other contacts with them. The best way to prevent prior knowledge from biasing our judgment

BOX 6.5 • *Checklist for Evaluating Essay Questions*

1. Is this type of item appropriate for measuring the intended learning outcome?
2. Does the item task match the learning task to be measured?
3. Is the question designed to measure complex learning outcomes?
4. Does the question make clear what is being measured and how the answer will be evaluated?
5. Has terminology been used that clarifies and limits the task (e.g., "describe," not "discuss")?
6. Are all students required to answer the same questions?
7. Has an ample time limit been indicated for each question?
8. Have adequate provisions been made for scoring answers (e.g., model answers or criteria for evaluating)?

is to evaluate each answer without knowing the identity of the writer. This can be done by having the students write their names on the back of the paper or by using code numbers in place of names.

6. *Whenever possible, have two or more persons grade each answer.* The best way to check on the reliability of the scoring of essay answers is to obtain two or more independent judgments. Although this may not be a feasible practice for routine classroom testing, it might be done periodically with a fellow teacher (one who is equally competent in the area). Obtaining two or more independent ratings becomes especially vital where the results are to be used for important and irreversible decisions, such as in the selection of students for further training or for special awards. Here, the pooled ratings of several competent persons may be needed to attain a level of reliability that is commensurate with the significance of the decision being made. See Box 6.5 for a summary checklist for evaluating essay questions.

Summary of Points

1. Use supply-type items whenever producing the answer is an essential element in the learning outcome (e.g., *defines* terms, instead of *identifies* meaning of terms).
2. Supply-type items include short-answer items, restricted-response essay, and extended-response essay.
3. The short-answer item can be answered by a word, number, symbol, or brief phrase.
4. The short-answer item is limited primarily to measuring simple knowledge outcomes.

5. Each short-answer item should be so carefully written that there is only one possible answer, the entire item can be read before coming to the answer space, and there are no extraneous clues to the answer.

6. In scoring short-answer items, give credit for all correct answers and score for spelling separately.

7. Essay questions are most useful to measuring the ability to organize, integrate, and express ideas.

8. Essay questions are inefficient for measuring knowledge outcomes because they provide limited sampling, are influenced by extraneous factors (e.g., writing skills, bluffing, grammar, spelling, handwriting), and scoring is subjective and unreliable.

9. Restricted-response essay questions can be more easily written and scored, but due to limitations on the responses they are less useful for measuring the higher-level outcomes (e.g., integration of diverse material).

10. Extended-response essay questions provide the freedom to select, organize, and express ideas in the manner that seems most appropriate; therefore, they are especially useful for measuring such outcomes.

11. Essay questions should be written to measure complex learning outcomes, to present a clear task, and to contain only those restrictions needed to call forth the intended response and provide for adequate scoring.

12. Essay answers should be scored by focusing on the intended response, by using a model answer or set of criteria as a guide, by scoring question by question, and by ignoring the writer's identity. Be wary of student bluffing. If an important decision is to be based on the results, two or more competent scores should be used.

References and Additional Reading

Linn, R. L., and Gronlund, N. E. *Measurement and Assessment in Teaching*, 8th ed. (Upper Saddle River, NJ: Merrill/ Prentice-Hall, 2000).

McMillan, J. H., *Classroom Assessments: Principles and Practices for Effective Instruction*, 2nd ed. (Boston: Allyn and Bacon, 2001).

Osterhoff, A. C. *Classroom Applications of Educational Measurement*, 3rd ed. (Upper Saddle River, NJ: Merrill/Prentice-Hall, 2001).

Stiggins, R. J., *Student-Involved Classroom Assessment*, 3rd ed. (Upper Saddle River, NJ: Merrill/Prentice-Hall, 2001).

7

Traditional Performance Assessments of Skills and Products

Studying this chapter should enable you to

1. Describe how performance assessments differ from paper-and-pencil testing.
2. Identify the strengths and limitation of performance assessments.
3. Write intended performance outcomes for a performance assessment.
4. Distinguish between restricted and extended performance assessment.
5. Describe the general procedure for making a performance assessment.
6. Prepare a plan for arranging, observing, recording, and evaluating a performance task.
7. Construct a checklist that is well stated, relevant, and easy to use.
8. Construct a rating scale that is well stated, relevant, and easy to use.
9. Construct a holistic scoring rubric for some performance outcome.

Paper-and-pencil tests can measure a variety of learning tasks from simple to complex. However, performance assessment is needed when performance skills are not adequately assessed by paper-and-pencil tests alone. These performance outcomes are important in many different types of courses. For example, science courses are concerned with laboratory skills, English and foreign-language courses are concerned with communication skills, mathematics courses are concerned with various types of problem-solving skills, and social studies are concerned with skills such as map and graph construction. In addition, skill outcomes are emphasized heavily in art and music courses, industrial education, business education, agricultural

BOX 7.1 • *Performance Assessments of Skills and Products*

Strengths
1. Can evaluate complex learning outcomes and skills that cannot be evaluated with traditional paper-and-pencil tests.
2. Provides a more natural, direct, and complete evaluation of some types of reasoning, oral, and physical skills.
3. Provides greater motivation for students by clarifying goals and making learning more meaningful.
4. Encourages the application of learning to real-life situations.

Limitations
1. Requires considerable time and effort to use.
2. Judgment and scoring performance is subjective, burdensome, and typically has low reliability.
3. Evaluation must frequently be done individually, rather than in groups.

education, home economics courses, and physical education. Thus, in most instructional areas performance assessment provides a useful adjunct to paper-and-pencil tests. Although tests can tell us whether students know what to do in a particular situation, more direct assessments are needed to evaluate their actual performance skills.

This chapter will focus on the assessment of the more traditional and structured performance skills and products (see Box 7.1 for strengths and limitations). The following chapter will focus on the assessment of less structured tasks that provide for the integration of skills and ideas and the use of reasoning ability in solving problems more like those in the real world.

Components of Performance Skills

Although the focus in this chapter is on the assessment of performance skills, it is important to note that successful performance typically has several components that must be considered before and during the assessment (see Figure 7.1).

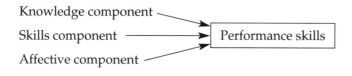

Knowledge component

Skills component → Performance skills

Affective component

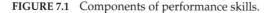

FIGURE 7.1 Components of performance skills.

In assessing writing ability, for example, we are concerned with knowledge of vocabulary, grammar, and similar basic elements needed for effective writing, as well as interests and attitudes that support good writing. In assessing laboratory skills we are concerned with the student's knowing the names and uses of the equipment and the procedures to be followed, as well as having an attitude of care in handling the equipment and making accurate measurements. The knowledge components can be measured by tests before the skill is evaluated or made a part of the evaluation. The affective component is typically made a part of the skill assessment (e.g., handles equipment in a careful manner, follows all safety precautions in operating the machine). In any event, all components of the performance must be considered when planning for the performance assessment.

Stating Objectives for Performance Assessment

In planning for instruction, the objectives for performance assessment should be developed at the same time as the objectives are being prepared for the testable learning outcomes. The same two-step procedure of stating the general objectives first and then defining them with a list of specific learning outcomes is followed. A list of objectives for a test construction unit, for example, could be stated as follows.

1. Prepares a table of specifications for an achievement test.
   1.1 Writes a clear description of the achievement domain to be tested.
   1.2 States the intended learning outcomes in performance terms.
   1.3 Lists the content areas to be covered by the test.
   1.4 Constructs a twofold table of specifications that indicates the proportion of items to be devoted to each learning outcome and each area of content.
   1.5 Checks the table of specifications with the achievement domain, to be certain the test measures a representative sample of the desired achievement.

Statements such as these clarify what is involved in preparing a table of specifications and what the final product should be like. An evaluation can be made by using the statements as they are and adding a rating scale to each item to indicate degree of success, or by developing more specific criteria in each area (e.g., Comprehensive description of achievement domain, Intended learning outcomes are clearly stated). In either case the objectives set the stage for performance assessment by focusing attention on what is to be assessed (see Box 7.2).

BOX 7.2 • *Writing Performance Objectives for Skills and Products*

1. State each general objective so that it clearly describes the skill or product to be assessed.
2. List specific performance outcomes for each objective that are most relevant to a successful performance or a satisfactory product.
3. List enough specific performance outcomes to clarify what is meant by an effective performance.
4. State the specific performance outcomes in terms of observable dimensions of the skill or product.
5. State the specific performance outcomes so that they are clear to students.

Restricted and Extended Performance Tasks

Performance tasks may be restricted to fit a specific and limited skill (e.g., measure humidity) or extended to a comprehensive performance that includes numerous specific skills (e.g., predicting weather). Although this dichotomy is somewhat arbitrary, it is useful in planning performance assessments. In some cases, it may be desirable to assess specific skills before putting them together in a more complex performance. In other cases, it may be desirable to use restricted performance tasks to diagnose problems in performing a complex task. For example, students having difficulty with laboratory procedures might benefit from a restricted assessment of measurement skills, and students having difficulty constructing a wood or metal product might need a restricted assessment of how to use a particular tool. Although our major focus is the overall performance, assessing restricted aspects of it can serve as guides for its improvement. This is another example of how teaching and assessment work together to improve learning.

Restricted performance tasks are typically highly restricted and limited in scope, as shown in the following examples.

EXAMPLES

Write a one-page report describing a field trip.
Give a one-minute speech on a given topic.
Read aloud a brief selection of poetry.
Construct a graph from a given set of data.
Demonstrate how to use a measuring instrument.

By limiting the scope of the task, it is easier to focus the observation and to judge the response. It should be recognized, however, that a series of restricted tasks do not provide sufficient evidence of a comprehensive performance. For that we need more extended tasks that integrate the specific skills into a complex pattern of movements or the production of a high quality product.

Extended performance tasks are typically less structured and broader in scope, as illustrated in the following examples.

EXAMPLES

Design and conduct an experiment.
Design and build a wood or metal product.
Write a short story.
Repair a malfunctioning motor.
Paint a picture.
Demonstrate a physical or musical performance.

Extended performance assessments typically give students greater freedom in selecting and carrying out the tasks and greater opportunity for self-assessment and self-improvement. Discussions of the ongoing performance and the final results with the teacher should focus on both the quality of the performance and the development of the students' independent learning skills.

Steps in Preparing Performance Assessments

Effective performance assessments are most likely to result when a systematic approach is used. The following procedural steps outline the main factors to consider when making performance assessments.

1. Specifying the performance outcomes.
2. Selecting the focus of the assessment (procedure, product, or both).
3. Selecting an appropriate degree of realism.
4. Selecting the performance situation.
5. Selecting the method of observing, recording, and scoring.

Each of these steps will be described in turn.

Specifying the Performance Outcomes

If the intended learning outcomes have been prespecified for the instruction, it is simply a matter of selecting those that require the use of performance assessment. If performance outcomes are not available, they should be identified and defined for the areas of performance to be assessed. Restricted performance outcomes, commonly use verbs such as *identify, con-*

struct, and *demonstrate* (and their synonyms). A brief description of these verbs and some illustrative objectives for restricted performance outcomes are shown in Table 7.1.

The specification of performance outcomes typically include a job or task analysis to identify the specific factors that are most critical in the performance. Because it is frequently impossible to focus on all of the specific procedures involved in a particular performance, it is necessary to obtain a representative sample of the most crucial ones. Keeping the list to a reasonable length increases the possibility of more accurate observations and judgments. The following examples illustrate realistic sets of performance tasks for restricted performance assessments.

TABLE 7.1   *Typical Action Verbs and Illustrative Instructional Objectives for Restricted Performance Outcomes*

Action Verbs	*Illustrative Instructional Objectives*
IDENTIFY: Selects the correct objects, part of the object, procedure, or property (typical verbs: identify, locate, select, touch, pick up, mark, describe)	Select the proper tool. Identify the parts of a typewriter. Choose correct laboratory equipment. Select the most relevant statistical procedure. Locate an automobile malfunction. Identify a musical selection. Identify the experimental equipment needed. Identify a specimen under the microscope.
CONSTRUCT: Makes a product to fit a given set of specifications (typical verbs: construct, assemble, build, design, draw, make, prepare)	Draw a diagram for an electrical circuit. Design a pattern for making a dress. Assemble equipment for an experimental study. Prepare a circle graph. Construct a weather map. Prepare an experimental design.
DEMONSTRATE: Performs a set of operations or procedures (typical verbs: demonstrate, drive, measure, operate, perform, repair, set up)	Drive an automobile. Measure the volume of a liquid. Operate a filmstrip projector. Perform a modern dance step. Repair a malfunctioning TV set. Set up laboratory equipment. Demonstrate taking a patient's temperature. Demonstrate the procedure for tuning an automobile.

Demonstrates Skill in Oral Reporting
1. Stands in a natural manner.
2. Maintains good eye contact.
3. Uses appropriate facial expressions.
4. Uses gestures effectively.
5. Speaks clearly and with good volume.
6. Speaks at an appropriate rate.
7. Presents ideas in an organized manner.
8. Uses appropriate language.
9. Maintains interest of the group.

Repairs a Malfunctioning Motor
1. Identifies the nature of the malfunction.
2. Identifies the system causing the malfunction.
3. Selects the tests to be made.
4. Conducts the tests in proper sequence.
5. Locates the malfunctioning component.
6. Replaces or repairs the component.
7. Removes and replaces parts in proper sequence.
8. Uses proper tools in a correct manner.
9. Follows safety precautions throughout procedure.

In some cases, the order in which the performance tasks are listed is unimportant, as illustrated by the first example. In other performance assessments, the sequence of steps provides a systematic approach to be followed. In these cases, as illustrated by the second example, placing the tasks in proper sequence will make it easier to observe and record the performance and to note errors in procedure.

Extended performance outcomes typically involve multiple instructional objectives and it is important to consider all of them when designing a study. A research project, for example, might include intended learning outcomes as follows:

Designs and conducts an experiment.
Writes an accurate account of the study.
States valid conclusions.
Writes a critique of the procedure and findings.
Presents and defends the study in class.

These outcomes would need to be defined in more specific terms, like the two described earlier, but stating the general objectives first and then specifying them in more detail provides a useful procedure. In defining each major outcome, it may be desirable to divide some in two (e.g., Designs an experiment, Conducts an experiment). In other cases some may be combined. For example "States valid conclusions" may be included as part of "Writes an accurate account of the study." In any event, the final list should provide a major list of the intended learning outcomes, each clearly specified by descriptions of what students can do to demonstrate achievement of the outcomes. More detailed descriptions of how to state intended learning outcomes and define them in performance terms can be found in Gronlund (2000).

Selecting the Focus of the Assessment

Performance assessment can focus on the procedure, the product, or some combination of the two. The nature of the performance frequently dictates where the emphasis should be placed, but in some cases there are also other considerations.

Assessing the Procedure

Those types of performance that don't result in a product (e.g., speaking, reading aloud, physical skills, musical performance) require that the performance be evaluated in progress.

In many cases, both procedure and product are important aspects of a performance. For example, skill in locating and correcting a malfunction in a television set involves following a systematic procedure (rather than using trial and error) in addition to producing a properly repaired set. Frequently, procedure is emphasized during the early stages of learning and products later, after the procedural steps have been mastered. In assessing typing skill, for example, proper use of the "touch system" would be evaluated at the beginning of instruction, but later evaluation would focus on the neatness and accuracy of the typed material and the speed with which it was produced. Similarly, in such areas as cooking, woodworking, and painting, correct procedure is likely to be stressed during the early stages of instruction and the quality of the product later. Procedure evaluation may also be used during later stages of instruction, of course, in order to detect errors in procedure that might account for an inferior product.

In general, focus the performance assessment on the procedure when:

1. There is no product, or product evaluation is infeasible (e.g., unavailable or too costly).
2. The procedure is orderly and directly observable.
3. Correct procedure is crucial to later success.
4. Analysis of procedural steps can aid in improving a product.

Assessing the Product

In some areas of performance, the product is the focus of attention and the procedure (or process) is of little or no significance. In evaluating a student's theme, drawing, or insect display, for example, the teacher is not likely to assess the procedures used by the student. This might be because various procedures could lead to an equally good product, or because the product was the result of a take-home project and the process was therefore not observable by the teacher. Also, some in-class activities are nonobservable because they involve primarily mental processes (such as mathematical reasoning). Some elements of the process can be obtained by having students "think aloud" and by using oral questioning, but the main focus is on the product. The quality of the product is typically guided by specific criteria that have been prepared especially for that purpose.

Where both the procedure and product are observable, the emphasis given to each will depend on the skill being assessed and the stage of skill development. However, when the procedure has been sufficiently mastered, product evaluation is favored because it typically provides a more objective basis for judgment, it can be done at a convenient time, and judgments can be rechecked if necessary.

Performance assessment should be focused on the product when:

1. Different procedures can result in an equally good product (e.g., writing a theme).
2. The procedure is not available for observation (e.g., take-home work).
3. The procedural steps have been mastered.
4. The product has qualities that can be clearly identified and judged.

Selecting an Appropriate Degree of Realism

Performance assessment in instructional settings typically falls somewhere between the usual paper-and-pencil test and performance in real-life situations. Although we can't expect to duplicate the natural situation in which the learning will later be used, we can strive for performance assessments that approximate real-world conditions. This, then, is another dimension to consider in preparing performance assessments. How much "realism" can we incorporate into our assessment? The more the better, of course, but authenticity is a matter of degree.

The presence of varying degrees of realism in a performance assessment can be illustrated by the simple example of applying arithmetic skills to the practical problem of determining correct change while shopping in a store (adapted from Fitzpatrick and Morrison, 1971). A simulation of this situation might range from the use of a story problem (low realism) to an actual purchase in a storelike situation (high realism). The various problem situations that might be contrived for this performance measure are shown in Figure 7.2. It should be noted that even though solving a story problem is relatively low in realism, it simulates the criterion situation to a greater degree than simply asking students to subtract 69 from 100. Thus, even with paper-and-pencil testing it is frequently possible to increase the degree of realism to a point where the results are useful in assessing performance outcomes.

The degree of realism selected for a particular situation depends on a number of factors. First, the nature of the instructional objectives must be considered. Acceptable performance in paper-and-pencil applications of skill, or in other measures with a low degree of realism, might be all that the instruction is intended to achieve. This is frequently the case with introductory courses that are to be followed by more advanced courses emphasizing applied performance. Second, the sequence of instruction within a particular course may indicate that it would be desirable to measure paper-and-pencil applications before "hands-on" performance is attempted. Locating the source of a malfunction on a diagram, for example, might precede working with actual equipment. Third, numerous practical constraints, such as time, cost, availability of equipment, and difficulties in administering and scoring, may limit the degree of realism that can be obtained. Fourth, the task itself may restrict the degree of realism in a test situation. In testing first aid skills, for example, it would be infeasible (and undesirable) to use actual patients

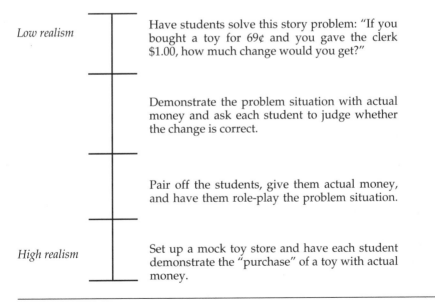

Low realism

Have students solve this story problem: "If you bought a toy for 69¢ and you gave the clerk $1.00, how much change would you get?"

Demonstrate the problem situation with actual money and ask each student to judge whether the change is correct.

Pair off the students, give them actual money, and have them role-play the problem situation.

High realism

Set up a mock toy store and have each student demonstrate the "purchase" of a toy with actual money.

FIGURE 7.2 Illustration of various degrees of realism in measuring the ability to determine correct change while making a purchase in a store.

with wounds, broken bones, and other physical conditions needed for realistic assessment. Thus, although we should strive for as high a degree of realism as the performance outcomes dictate, it is frequently necessary to make compromises in preparing performance assessments.

Selecting the Performance Situation

Performance assessments can be classified by the type of situation or setting used. The following classification system closely approximates the degree of realism present in the situation and includes the following types: (1) paper-and-pencil performance, (2) identification test, (3) structured performance test, (4) simulated performance, (5) work sample, and (6) extended research project. Although these categories overlap to some degree, they are useful for describing and illustrating the various approaches used in performance assessment.

Paper-and-Pencil Performance

Paper-and-pencil performance differs from the more traditional paper-and-pencil test by placing greater emphasis on the application of knowledge and skill in a simulated setting. These paper-and-pencil applications might result in desired terminal learning outcomes, or they might serve as an intermediate step to performance that involves a higher degree of realism (for example, the actual use of equipment).

In a number of instances, paper-and-pencil performance can provide a product of educational significance. A course in test construction, for example, might require students to perform activities such as the following:

Construct a set of test specifications for a unit of instruction.
Construct test items that fit a given set of specifications.
Construct a checklist for evaluating an achievement test.

The action verb "construct" is frequently used in paper-and-pencil performance testing. For instance, students might be asked to construct a weather map, bar graph, diagram of an electrical circuit, floor plan, design for an article of clothing, poem, short story, or plan for an experiment. In such cases, the paper-and-pencil product is a result of both knowledge and skill, and it provides a performance measure that is valued in its own right. In other cases, paper-and-pencil performance might simply provide a first step toward hands-on performance. For example, before using a particular measuring instrument, such as a micrometer, it might be desirable to have students read various settings from pictures of the scale. Although the ability to read the scale is not a sufficient condition for accurate measurement, it is necessary one. In this instance, paper-and-pencil performance would be favored because it is a more convenient method of testing a group of students. Using paper-and-pencil performance as a precursor to hands-on performance might be favored for other reasons. For example, if the performance is complicated and the equipment is expensive, demonstrating competence on paper-and-pencil situations could avoid subsequent accidents or damage to equipment. Similarly, in the health sciences, skill in diagnosing and prescribing for hypothetical patients could avoid later harm to real patients.

Identification Test

The identification test includes a wide variety of situations representing various degrees of realism. In some cases, a student may be asked simply to identify a tool or piece of equipment and to indicate its function. A more complex situation might present the student with a particular performance task (e.g., locating a short in an electrical circuit) and ask him or her to identify the tools, equipment, and procedures needed in performing the task. An even more complex type of identification test might involve listening to the operation of a malfunctioning machine (such as an automobile motor, a drill, or a lathe) and, from the sound, identifying the most probable cause of the malfunction.

Although identification tests are widely used in industrial education, they are by no means limited to that area. The biology teacher might have students identify specimens that are placed at various stations around the room, or identify the equipment and procedures needed to conduct a particular experiment. Similarly, chemistry students might be asked to identify "unknown" substances, foreign-language students to identify correct pronunciation, mathematics students to identify correct problem-solving procedures, English students to identify the "best expression" to be used in writing, and social studies students to identify various leadership roles as they are acted out in a group. Identifying correct procedures is also important, of course, in art, music, physical education, and such vocational areas as agriculture, business education, and home economics.

The identification test is sometimes used as an *indirect* measure of performance skill. The experienced plumber, for example, is expected to have a broader knowledge of the tools and equipment used in plumbing than the inexperienced plumber. Thus, a tool identification test might be used to eliminate the least skilled in a group of applicants for a position as plumber. More commonly, the identification test is used as an instructional device to prepare students for actual performance in real or simulated situations.

Structured Performance Test

A structured performance test provides for an assessment under standard, controlled conditions. It might involve such things as making prescribed measurements, adjusting a microscope, following safety procedures in starting a machine, or locating a malfunction in electronic equipment. The performance situation is structured and presented in a manner that requires all individuals to respond to the same set of tasks.

The construction of a structured performance test follows somewhat the same pattern used in constructing other types of achievement tests but there are some added complexities. The test situation can seldom be fully controlled and standardized, it typically takes more time to prepare and administer, and it is frequently more difficult to score. To increase the likelihood that the test situation will be standard for all individuals, instructions should be used that describe the test situation, the required performance, and the conditions under which the performance is to be demonstrated. Instructions for locating a malfunction in electronic equipment, for example, would typically include the following:

1. Nature and purpose of the test
2. Equipment and tools provided
3. Testing procedure:
   a. Type and condition of equipment
   b. Description of required performance
   c. Time limits and other conditions
4. Method of judging performance

When using performance tests, it may be desirable to set performance standards that indicate the minimum level of acceptable performance. These might be concerned with accuracy (e.g., measure temperature *to the nearest two-tenths of a degree*), the proper sequencing of steps (e.g., adjust a microscope *following the proper sequence of steps*), total compliance with rules (e.g., check *all safety guards* before starting a machine), or speed of performance (e.g., locate a malfunction in electronic equipment *in three minutes*). Some common **standards** for judging performance are shown in Box 7.3.

Performance standards are, of course, frequently used in combination. A particular performance may require correct form, accuracy, and speed. How much weight to give to each depends on the stage of instruction as well as the nature of the performance. In assessing laboratory measurement skills, for example, correct procedure and accuracy might be stressed early in the instruction and concern about speed of performance delayed until the later stages of instruction. The particular situation might also influence the importance of the dimension. In evaluating typing skill, for example, speed might be stressed in typing routine business letters, whereas accuracy would be emphasized in typing statistical tables for economic reports.

BOX 7.3 • *Some Common Standards for Judging Performance*

Type	*Examples*
Rate	Solve ten addition problems in two minutes.
	Type 40 words per minute.
Error	No more than two errors per typed page.
	Count to 20 in Spanish without error.
Time	Set up laboratory equipment in five minutes.
	Locate an equipment malfunction in three minutes.
Precision	Measure a line within one-eighth of an inch.
	Read a thermometer within two-tenths of a degree.
Quantity	Complete 20 laboratory experiments.
	Locate 15 relevant references.
Quality (rating)	Write a neat, well-spaced business letter.
	Demonstrate correct form in diving.
Percentage Correct	Solve 85 percent of the math problems.
	Spell correctly 90 percent of the words in the word list.
Steps Required	Diagnose a motor malfunction in five steps.
	Locate a computer error using proper sequence of steps.
Use of Material	Build a bookcase with less than 10 percent waste.
	Cut out a dress pattern with less than 10 percent waste.
Safety	Check all safety guards before operating machine.
	Drive automobile without breaking any safety rules.

Simulated Performance

Simulated performance is an attempt to match the performance in a real situation—either in whole or in part. In physical education, for example, swinging a bat at an imaginary ball, shadow boxing, and demonstrating various swimming or tennis strokes are simulated performances. In science, vocational, and business courses, skill activities are frequently designed to simulate portions of actual job performance. In mathematics, the use of computers in solving lifelike problems represents simulated performance. Similarly, in social studies, student roleplaying of a jury trial, a city council meeting, or a job interview provides the instructor with opportunities to evaluate the simulated performance of an assigned task. In some cases, specially designed equipment is used for instructional and assessment purposes. In both driver training and flight training, for example, students are frequently trained and tested on simulators. Such simulators may prevent personal injury or damage to expensive equipment during the early stages of skill development. Simulators are also used in various types of vocational training programs.

In some situations, simulated performance testing might be used as the final assessment of a performance skill. This would be the case in assessing students' laboratory performance in chemistry, for example. In many situations, however, skill in a simulated setting simply indicates readiness to attempt actual performance. The student in driver training who has demonstrated driving skill in the simulator, for example, is now ready to apply his or her skill in the actual operation of an automobile.

Work Sample

The work sample requires the student to perform actual tasks that are representative of the total performance to be measured. The sample tasks typically include the most crucial elements of the total performance and are performed under controlled conditions. In being tested for automobile driving skill, for example, the student is required to drive over a standard course that includes the most common problem situations likely to be encountered in normal driving. The performance on the standard course is then used as evidence of the ability to drive an automobile under typical operating conditions.

Performance assessments in business education and industrial education are frequently of the work-sample type. When students are required to take and transcribe shorthand notes from dictation, type a business letter, or operate a computer to analyze business data, a work-sample assessment is being employed. Similarly, in industrial education, a work-sample approach is being used when students are required to complete a metalworking or woodworking project that includes all of the steps likely to be encountered in an actual job situation (steps such as designing, ordering materials, and constructing). Still other examples are the operation of machinery, the repair of equipment, and the performance of job-oriented laboratory tasks. The work-sample approach to assessing performance is widely used in occupations involving performance skills, and many of these situations can be duplicated in the school setting.

Extended Project

One of the most comprehensive types of performance assessments involves the extended project. This approach involves a combination of academic, communication, and thinking skills in the solving of unstructured real-world problems, the construction of a unique product, or both. It typically involves multiple outcomes and criteria for each; student participation in developing criteria, selecting the problem to investigate, designing and carrying out the study, and evaluating the results; and written reports and an oral presentation and defense of the findings. Throughout, the focus is on higher-level learning outcomes used in problem solving (e.g., analysis, synthesis, evaluation), the effective use of communication skills, the development of self-assessment skills, and independent learning. This type of project will be described in the following chapter.

Selecting the Method of Observing, Recording, and Scoring

Whether judging procedures, products, or some combination of the two, some type of guided observation and method of recording and scoring the results is needed. Commonly used procedures include (1) systematic observation and anecdotal records, (2) checklists, and (3) rating scales.

Systematic Observation and Anecdotal Records

Observing students in natural settings is one of the most common methods of assessing performance outcomes. Unfortunately, the observations are typically unsystematic and frequently no record is made of the observation. For minor performance tasks that are easily corrected, like how to hold a paint brush or how to label a graph, informal observation may be all that is needed. For more comprehensive performance situations, however, the observations should be systematic and typically some record of the observation should be made. This will enhance their objectivity, meaningfulness, and usefulness at a later date.

Observations are frequently guided by checklists or rating scales, but there is some advantage in making and recording less structured observations. For example, noting how students approach a task, how persistent they are in completing it, and how carefully they work has significance for evaluating their success in performing the task. Similarly, one student may need assistance on every step of the performance, while another student completes the task early and turns to help others. These important aspects of performance are apt to be overlooked by more structured observational devices but can be described in anecdotal records.

An **anecdotal record** is a brief description of some significant event. It typically includes the observed behavior, the setting in which it occurred, and a separate interpretation of the event. Although keeping anecdotal records can be time consuming, the task can be kept manageable by limiting the records to certain types of behavior (e.g., safety) and to those individuals needing the most help (e.g., slow, careless). The records are likely to be most useful when (1) they focus on meaningful incidents, (2) they are recorded soon after the incident, (3) they contain enough information to be understandable later, and (4) the observed incident and its interpretation are kept separate. What is desired is a brief, objective, self-sufficient description of a meaningful incident and a separate interpretation (if needed) of what the incident means. As these records of events accumulate for a particular individual, a typical pattern of behavior is obtained.

Checklists

The **checklist** is basically a list of measurable dimensions of a performance or product, with a place to record a simple "yes" or "no" judgment. If a checklist were used to evaluate a set of procedures, for example, the steps to be followed might be placed in sequential order on the form; the observer would then simply check whether each action was taken or not taken. Such a checklist for evaluating the proper use of an oral thermometer is shown in Figure 7.3. A checklist for evaluating a product typically contains a list of the dimensions that characterize a good product (size, color, shape, and so on), and a place to check whether each desired characteristic is present or absent. Thus, the checklist simply directs attention to the elements to be observed and provides a convenient means of recording judgments.

Construction of a checklist for performance assessment involves the following steps.

1. List the procedural steps or product characteristics to be evaluated.
2. Add common errors to the list, if such is useful in diagnosing poor performance.
3. Arrange the list in some logical order (e.g., sequence of steps).
4. Provide instructions and a place for checking each item.
5. Add a place for comments at the bottom of the form, if needed.

Directions: Place a check in front of each step as it is performed.

_____ 1. Removes thermometer from container by grasping nonbulb end.
_____ 2. Wipes thermometer downward from nonbulb end with fresh wiper.
_____ 3. Shakes thermometer down to less than 96° while holding nonbulb end.
_____ 4. Places bulb end of thermometer under patient's tongue.
_____ 5. Tells patient to close lips but to avoid biting on thermometer.
_____ 6. Leaves thermometer in patient's mouth for three minutes.
_____ 7. Removes thermometer from patient's mouth by grasping nonbulb end.
_____ 8. Reads temperature to the nearest *two-tenths* of a degree.
_____ 9. Records temperature reading on patient's chart.
_____ 10. Cleans thermometer and replaces in container.

FIGURE 7.3   Checklist for evaluating the proper use of an oral thermometer.

Rating Scales

The **rating scale** is similar to the checklist and serves somewhat the same purpose in judging procedures and products. The main difference is that the rating scale provides an opportunity to mark the degree to which an element is present instead of using the simple "present-absent" judgment. The scale for rating is typically based on the frequency with which an action is performed (e.g., always, sometimes, never), the general quality of a performance (e.g., outstanding, above average, average, below average), or a set of descriptive phrases that indicates degrees of acceptable performance (e.g., completes task quickly, slow in completing task, cannot complete task without help). Like the checklist, the rating scale directs attention to the dimensions to be observed and provides a convenient form on which to record the judgments.

A sample rating scale for evaluating both procedures and product is shown in Figure 7.4. Although this numerical rating scale uses fixed alternatives, the same scale items could be described by descriptive phrases that vary from item to item.

Directions: Rate each of the following items by circling the appropriate number. The numbers represent the following values: 5—outstanding; 4—above average; 3—average; 2—below average; 1—unsatisfactory.

PROCEDURE RATING SCALE

How effective was the student's performance in each of the following areas?

5 4 3 2 1 (a) Preparing a detailed plan for the project.
5 4 3 2 1 (b) Determining the amount of material needed.
5 4 3 2 1 (c) Selecting the proper tools.
5 4 3 2 1 (d) Following the correct procedures for each operation.
5 4 3 2 1 (e) Using tools properly and skillfully.
5 4 3 2 1 (f) Using materials without unnecessary spoilage.
5 4 3 2 1 (g) Completing the work within a reasonable amount of time.

PRODUCT RATING SCALE

To what extent does the product meet the following criteria?

5 4 3 2 1 (a) The product appears neat and well constructed.
5 4 3 2 1 (b) The dimensions match the original plan.
5 4 3 2 1 (c) The finish meets specifications.
5 4 3 2 1 (d) The joints and parts fit properly.
5 4 3 2 1 (e) The materials were used effectively.

FIGURE 7.4   Rating scale for a woodworking project.

In this case, each rated item would be arranged as follows:

(a) Plan for the project

1	2	3	4	5
Plan is too general and vague.		Plan is in proper form but needs more detail		Plan is detailed and complete.

A space for comments might also be added under each item, or at the bottom of each set of items, to provide a place for clarifying the ratings or describing how to improve performance.

The construction of a rating scale for performance assessment typically includes the following steps.

1. List the procedural steps or product characteristics to be evaluated.
2. Select the number of points to use on the scale and define them by descriptive terms or phrases.
3. Arrange the items on the rating scale so that they are easy to use.
4. Provide clear, brief instructions that tell the rater how to mark items on the scale.
5. Provide a place for comments, if needed for diagnostic or instructional purposes.

Analytic versus Holistic Scoring

Rating scales are especially useful for **analytic scoring**. That is, when we want a judgment on each criterion by which the performance or product is to be judged. In evaluating writing skill, for example, such things as organization, vocabulary, style, ideas, and mechanics might be judged separately. The rating scale then becomes an instrument for directing observation to these criteria and provides a convenient means of recording and scoring our judgments.

Holistic scoring is based on an overall impression of the performance or product rather than a consideration of the individual elements. The global judgment is made by assigning a numerical score to each performance or product. Typically, between 4 and 8 points are used, and an even number of points is favored to avoid a "middle dumping ground." Evaluation consists of quickly examining the performance or product and assigning the number that matches the general impression of the performance or product. In the case of writing assessment, for example, the reader will read each writing sample quickly for overall impression and place it in one of the piles ranging from 4 to 1. It is assumed that good writing is more than a sum of the individual elements that go into writing and that holistic scoring will capture this total impression of the work.

Holistic scoring can be guided by scoring rubrics that clarify what each level of quality is like. **Scoring rubrics** (i.e., scoring guides) for writing and a

BOX 7.4 • *Sample Scoring Rubric for Writing*

4— Interesting throughout
   Flows smoothly, good transitions
   Well-organized for topic
   Good use of mechanics and sentence structure
3— Interesting most of the time
   Flows smoothly but some poor transitions
   Organized but some weaknesses
   Minor mechanical errors
2— Interest lowered by lapses in focus
   Flow is interrupted by many poor transitions
   Organization weak, strays from topic
   Some serious mechanical errors
1— No clear focus
   Jerky and rambling
   Poorly organized
   Many mechanical errors and weak sentence structure

psychomotor skill are shown in Boxes 7.4 and 7.5. These descriptions of each level do not provide for analysis of the product or the performance but simply list the criteria to keep in mind when making the overall judgment. Another way to clarify the meaning of each score level for a product is to use a *product scale.* This consists of a series of sample products that represent various degrees of quality. In writing assessment, for example, a writing sample representing each level of quality from 4 to 1 are reviewed and each writing product is compared to the sample models and assigned the number of the

BOX 7.5 • *General Scoring Rubric for a Psychomotor Skill*

EXCELLENT	Uses procedure rapidly and skillfully
	Explains function of each step in procedure
	Modifies procedure to fit changing conditions
GOOD	Uses procedure correctly but with some hesitation
	Gives general explanation of steps in procedure
	Modifies procedure but needs some instructor guidance
ACCEPTABLE	Uses procedure correctly but is slow and clumsy
	Explanation of procedure is limited
	Modifies procedures but only after demonstration by instructor
INADEQUATE	Fails to use procedure correctly
	Explanation of procedure shows lack of understanding
	Uses trial and error in adjusting procedure

sample it matches most closely. Product scales are especially useful where the quality of the product is difficult to define (e.g., art, creative writing).

For most instructional purposes, both holistic and analytic scoring are useful. One gives the global judgment of the performance or product and the other provides diagnostic information useful for improving performance. Where both are used, the global judgment should be made first so some specific element does not distort the general impression of the product.

Improving Performance Assessments

Performance assessments can provide useful information concerning student achievement, but they are subject to all of the errors of observation and judgment, such as personal bias, generosity error (tendency to overrate), and halo effect (judging individual characteristics in terms of a general impression). Thus, if performance assessments are to provide valid information, special care must be taken to improve the objectivity, reliability, and meaningfulness of the results. The guidelines listed in Box 7.6 enumerate ways to improve the usefulness of performance assessments.

BOX 7.6 • *Improving Performance Assessments*

1. Specify the intended performance outcomes in observable terms and describe the use to be made of the results.
2. Limit the observable dimensions of the performance to a reasonable number.
3. Provide clear, definite criteria for judging the procedure or product.
4. Select the performance setting that provides the most relevant and realistic situation.
5. If a structured performance situation is used, provide clear and complete instructions.
6. Be as objective as possible in observing, judging, and recording the performance.
7. Observe the performance under various conditions and use multiple observations whenever possible.
8. Make a record as soon as possible after an observation.
9. Use evaluation forms that are clear, relevant, and easy to use.
10. Use a scoring procedure that is appropriate for the use to be made of the results (e.g., holistic for global evaluation, analytic for diagnostic purposes).
11. Inform students of the method and criteria to be used in evaluating the performance.
12. Supplement and verify performance assessments with other evidence of achievement.

Summary of Points

1. Performance assessments provide direct evidence of valued learning outcomes that cannot be adequately assessed by traditional paper-and-pencil testing, but they are time consuming to use and require greater use of judgment in scoring.

2. Performance tasks contain knowledge and affective components as well as the skill component. All three components must be considered when planning performance assessments.

3. Writing performance objectives involves stating each general objective so that it describes a skill or product and then defining it by a list of specific performance outcomes that are relevant, clarify an effective performance, and are stated in observable terms that are easily understood by students.

4. Restricted performance tasks are highly structured and limited in scope (e.g., construct a graph). Extended performance tasks are typically less well structured and broad in scope (e.g., design and conduct an experiment).

5. The first step in performance assessment is to specify the intended performance outcome.

6. Performance assessment may focus on a procedure (e.g., giving a speech), a product (e.g., a theme), or both (e.g., using tools properly in building a bookcase).

7. In some cases, it may be desirable to emphasize procedure evaluation during the early stages of instruction (e.g., touch system in typing) and product evaluation later (typed letter).

8. There are varying degrees of realism in performance assessment, and the aim is to obtain as high a degree of realism as possible within the various constraints operating (e.g., time, cost, availability of equipment).

9. Paper-and-pencil performance assessment is useful as a terminal measure in many areas (e.g., writing, drawing, problem solving) and can serve as a first step toward hands-on performance in others (e.g., procedure for repairing an automobile engine).

10. The identification test is typically concerned with identifying the tools, equipment, and procedures needed for a performance task and serves as an *indirect* measure of performance, or as an instructional device to prepare students for actual performance.

11. A structured performance test provides for an assessment under standard, controlled conditions (e.g., locating a malfunction in electronic equipment). The tools, equipment, conditions, and standards of performance are all carefully prescribed.

12. Performance assessment based on simulated performance (e.g., driver's training simulator) and the work sample (e.g., analyze business data on

a computer) has a high degree of realism. Many performance skills in laboratory courses, business education, and industrial education can be evaluated at this level.

13. Observing students in natural settings and keeping anecdotal records can aid in evaluating aspects of performance that are likely to be overlooked by more structured methods (e.g., work habits).

14. Rating scales provide for analytic scoring, direct attention to the performance dimensions to be observed, and provide a convenient form on which to record the judgments.

15. Holistic scoring rubrics and product scales are especially useful where global judgments are being made (e.g., creative writing, works of art).

16. Improving performance assessments involves making clear what is to be observed, how it is to be observed, how the observations are to be recorded, and how the results are to be scored and used. In addition, any procedure that contributes to more objective observations and records will aid in increasing the reliability and meaningfulness of the results.

References and Additional Reading

Arter, J., and McTighe, J., *Scoring Rubrics in the Classroom* (Thousand Oaks, CA: Corwin Press, 2001).

Chase, C. I., *Contemporary Assessment for Educators* (New York: Longman, 1999).

Fitzpatrick, R., and Morrison, E. J., "Performance and Product Evaluation." Chapter 9 in R. L. Thorndike, Ed., *Educational Measurement*, 2nd ed. (Washington, DC: American Council on Education, 1971).

Gronlund, N. E., *How to Write and Use Instructional Objectives*, 6th ed. (Upper Saddle River, NJ: Merrill/Prentice-Hall, 2000).

Linn, R. L., and Gronlund, N. E. *Measurement and Assessment in Teaching*, 8th ed. (Upper Saddle, NJ: Merrill/Prentice-Hall, 2000).

Oosterhoff, A. C., *Classroom Applications of Educational Measurement*, 3rd ed. (Upper Saddle River, NJ: Merrill/Prentice-Hall, 2001).

8

Expanded Performance Assessments

Studying this chapter should enable you to

1. Describe the nature of expanded performance assessments.
2. Describe ways to expand traditional performance assessments.
3. Prepare a performance-based prompt for use in a subject you are now teaching or plan to teach.
4. Describe how a project can be used to expand performance assessments.
5. Write a plan for a project in a subject you are now teaching or plan to teach.
6. Prepare a rating scale or holistic scoring rubric for a performance-based task and project.

Education has frequently been criticized for putting too much emphasis on *knowing* and too little emphasis on *doing*. This was at least partly due to the wide use of objective tests that were designed primarily to measure the knowledge of facts. Although objective tests can be designed to measure more complex learning outcomes, they were seldom used that way by classroom teachers. With the wider use of criterion-referenced measurement (describing what students can do, rather than just ranking them in order of achievement), there is a greater need for direct assessment of how well students can perform. This has resulted in renewed interest in assessing performance skills in the classroom. All too frequently, however, traditional assessment of performance skill has focused too narrowly on the skill activity, to the neglect of the role of the performance in the general education of students. Limiting the focus to the routine learning and assessment of the skill is appropriate for some training programs and for some classroom activities (e.g., learning to operate a computer or set up laboratory equipment). However, for most educational programs a broader focus is needed—one that emphasizes complex learning outcomes, integrates skills and understandings, and gives students greater responsibility for selecting, organizing, and evaluating educational activities.

This broader conception of performance assessment and its role in the teaching-learning process is supported by the more recent conceptions of how students learn. Modern learning theory emphasizes the need for focusing on more complex learning outcomes, using more comprehensive student activities, engaging students in the activities and obtaining meaning from them, and using more realistic types of problem solving. This emphasis requires more elaborate performance assessments that integrates the various skills and ideas imbedded in the activities. Properly done these expanded assessments can make a significant contribution to the improvement of students' understanding and to their general educational development, in addition to their improvement of the particular skill activity (see Box 8.1).

BOX 8.1 • *Skill Execution versus Expanded Assessment*

Performing a Skill	*Expanded Assessment*
1. Write a short story on a given topic.	1. Plan a short story, outline the plot and characters, write the story, review and critique the story, and rewrite it.
2. Construct a bar graph from a given set of data.	2. Analyze a set of data and select the best type of graph to illustrate it. Construct the graph and give reasons for selecting this type of graph.
3. Set up laboratory equipment and follow the steps of an assigned exercise.	3. Design an experiment for comparing two products, complete the experiment, and write a summary of the findings. Make recommendations concerning the two products and give reasons.
4. Construct a bird house to fit a given set of plans.	4. Make a study of the birds that are most prevalent in your area. Design and build a bird house for one of the most common types. Explain to the class why you selected this model and where would be the best place to locate it.

Ways to Expand Traditional Performance Assessment

In harmony with modern learning theory, performance assessments have been broadened in scope. The newer version is expected to contribute more to the development of cognitive skills, communication skills, problem-solving skills, group-working skills, self-assessment skills, and independent learning—in short, to help move learning toward a higher level of learning outcomes. Following are some ways that the assessment of performance skills can be expanded.

Increase the Emphasis on Cognitive Skills

A common way to increase cognitive skills is to go beyond the *how to do it* aspect of the skill and give more attention to the *why* aspect. For example, why did you select this problem or project to work on, why were these tools or laboratory instruments selected, why use these strategies rather than others, why should this be considered a quality performance or product? These are just a few of the many types of questions that could be asked before, during, and after a performance. Such questions can increase the students' understanding of the performance and move the learning task from limited skill training to an educative activity. A technician may be able to perform a skill expertly, but an educated person should have a conceptual understanding of the process and be able to explain it to others.

Questions are most useful for developing a full understanding if they focus on reflection and thought rather than factual information. For example, asking students to analyze problems or procedures, compare strategies, draw inferences, and evaluate procedures or products is more likely to introduce complex cognitive skills into the process and enhance student reasoning ability. This is a major focus of the trend toward expanded performance assessments.

Increase the Role of Communication Skills

Oral communication can enhance an assessment by asking students to explain what they are doing and why they are doing it. A more comprehensive type of oral communication can also be added by asking students to demonstrate and explain the performance to other students. Requiring students to write an analysis and critique of their performance, to write laboratory reports, to write research reports, and to write other types of relevant reports can also provide a means of broadening performance assessments. Although communication skills are important performance targets in their own right, they also are a useful adjunct to other performance assessments.

They provide opportunities for focusing the performance and the assessment on the more complex learning outcomes and requiring students to reflect on their work.

Increase the Use of Visual Materials

The construction of maps, charts, graphs, slides, posters, and models can be useful for expanding various types of performance assessments. In some cases, the display materials may be part of a written report (e.g., use of graphs with a research report); in others, it may be the main focus with an oral report explaining and interpreting it (e.g., construction of a weather map as part of a weather prediction project). The use of visual materials can aid in analyzing the ability to integrate and express concepts in easily understandable form. In some cases they can also help assess creative abilities, which tend to be neglected in other forms of assessment.

Increase the Participation of Students

There are a number of ways that students can participate in the performance assessment process. They can participate in the development of the criteria to be used, in the preparation of the assessment instruments, and in the use of the instruments (e.g., peer evaluations and self-evaluations). They can compare their self-assessments with the teachers' assessments and peer assessments and discuss the agreements and discrepancies. They can keep a record of progress in the development of a performance and write a paper describing improvement in the performance and factors contributing to it. How much students can, or should, participate is determined by the nature of the performance, the age of the students, and the purpose of the assessment. Where the assessment is to be used to improve learning, students should be encouraged to participate in the process to the extent of their capabilities.

Increase the Realism of Tasks

Assessment **tasks** that are more like those in the real world are apt to be more meaningful to students and to provide understandings, strategies, and skills that are useful in solving other life-like problems (e.g., how to change zoning laws, or how to protect the environment). Real-world problems are likely to be ambiguous and complex, having no set strategies for solving them and no clearly right or wrong solutions. Thus, they can provide for an array of complex learning outcomes that emphasize the integration of cognitive, communication, and problem-solving skills.

Increase the Complexity of Tasks

There are many ways to increase the complexity of the performance tasks that students are expected to master. For restricted performance tasks, a common procedure is to present students with a performance-based prompt and, by means of questions or directions, indicate what the students are expected to do. The tasks are to be complex and thought provoking and may require the use of various skills and strategies. For extended performance tasks, one of the most comprehensive procedures is the use of student projects. An elaborate problem-solving project might involve such things as identifying and defining a problem, consulting many different types of resources, analysis and interpretation of the information, the writing of a report describing possible solutions, preparing visual materials, presenting and defending the project to a group, and critiquing and revising the final report. Such a project might also include an experimental study based on the findings. How elaborate the project is to be depends on the age of the students, the content area, and the instructional objectives.

Using Performance Tasks as Prompts

Direct questions concerning how to solve a problem serve as a type of performance assessment because they ask students to write an answer that requires them to organize, integrate, and express ideas. This role can be enhanced, however, by using performance tasks as prompts for a set of questions. Typically, the performance task describes a problem using a realistic contextual setting with questions based on the problem situation. This makes the questions more meaningful to students because they are based on real situations they are likely to face in the future. The following performance task and questions illustrates this procedure.

> You are employed as a new teacher of science at Jefferson High School. At the beginning of the year the department chairman asks you to describe how the department's assessment program might be improved. The current program uses multiple-choice questions based on the book and ratings of laboratory work, each to count 50 percent of the grade.
>
> What are the weaknesses in the current assessment program? Give reasons you think these are weaknesses.
>
> What procedures would you suggest the department follow in developing an effective assessment program? List the steps that should be taken and the reasons for each step. Describe what the final program should be like. Your responses will be judged using the scoring rubric given to you (see Box 8.2).

BOX 8.2 • *Scoring Rubric for Student Responses*

EXCELLENT 4	Complete analysis of program weaknesses with sound justification for each. Comprehensive and well-organized description of procedures for improving program. Supports each step with sound reasons. Complete and clear description of final program.
ADEQUATE 3	Describes major program weaknesses with good justification. Fairly complete and organized description of procedures for improving program. Supports most steps with sound reasons. Good general description of final program.
MINIMAL 2	Lists several program weaknesses with minimum justification. Describes or lists procedures for improving program, without elaboration. Supports steps with some fairly good reasons. General and limited description of final program.
INADEQUATE 1	States only general and vague program weaknesses. Incomplete description of procedures for improving program. Supports steps with reasons that are general, vague, incomplete, or irrelevant. Description of final program is missing, unclear, or inappropriate.

Using performance tasks as prompts makes the nature of the task clear and yet provides the freedom needed to demonstrate higher level learning outcomes. The scoring rubric lets students know how their responses will be judged.

Guidelines for Preparing Performance Tasks

Effective performance tasks are more time consuming to use and the scoring is subjective, so they need to be constructed with great care. The following guidelines provide the most important factors to consider when writing the performance tasks.

1. *The task should be relevant to the instructional objectives.* The objectives specify the intended learning outcomes in performance terms and thus indicate what performance should be like. Performance tasks frequently involve more than one objective, however, and all of them need to be considered when writing the task (e.g., cognitive skills and communication skills).

2. *The task should focus on complex learning outcomes.* Lower level outcomes (e.g., factual knowledge) can be more effectively measured with objective tests, so performance tasks should be designed for those outcomes that cannot be measured by objective tests. Higher level outcomes such as analysis, synthesis, and evaluation should be the focus of the performance to be assessed.

3. *The task should provide for the integration of understandings and skills.* The task should require the students to combine and use their understanding and skills in new ways. Thus, the task must have enough novelty to prevent students from using ready-made answers to routine problems.

4. *The task should be realistic and meaningful to students.* In performance assessment there is much stress on using real-world problems. This is a worthy goal, but a proviso should be added—providing it is realistic and meaningful to students. Some life-like problems are of little interest or concern to students.

5. *The task should be clearly understood by students.* This means using descriptions that make the problem clear and directions that tell students exactly what to do. Performance tasks should provide the student with some freedom in how to deal with the problem, but the degree of freedom should be clearly indicated in the directions.

6. *The task should be free of factors irrelevant to the task performance.* Students may perform poorly on a performance task because of some factor irrelevant to the learning outcomes being assessed. In a mathematics reasoning problem, for example, keep the demands on computation skills low enough that they don't contaminate the measure of reasoning ability. In final analysis, we want the task performance to provide valid evidence of the intended learning outcomes and not be distorted by irrelevant sources of difficulty.

7. *The task should be feasible in terms of the constraints of time, equipment, and available resources.* This is a rather obvious guideline to apply but performance tasks can vary widely in terms of complexity and the demands on time and other factors. In preparing a performance task, it may be necessary to pare it back to fit the classroom schedule. In other cases, it might be more desirable to assign it as an out-of-class activity so that students have more time and can use community resources.

8. *The task should be developmentally appropriate for the students being assessed.* This means taking into account the students' present knowledge and skill. It's important to strive for difficult and complex performance tasks, but a basic level of knowledge and skill is needed to successfully complete performance tasks. When writing the task, ask yourself whether students have the needed background knowledge, skill in using the equipment, and the like. If not, you will need to modify the task or increase the students' required knowledge and skill before using it.

9. *The task should call forth performance that is generalizable to other similar tasks.* Because of the time required for using performance tasks, relatively few tasks can be used in each area of instruction. Thus, it is important to write tasks so that they have the greatest transfer value. Are the understandings and skills being assessed those that are most likely to be generalizable to comparable tasks? In general, complex learning outcomes (e.g., reasoning ability) tend to have the greatest transferability in problem solving and should receive special attention when writing the task.

10. *The task should be accompanied by the method of scoring the performance.* The scoring involves identifying the criteria to be used in judging the performance and preparing a rating scale or holistic scoring rubric. This needs to be done at the time the task is being developed so that it can be given to students with the task. The scoring procedure lets the students know how the performance will be judged and provides them with an instrument for self-evaluation. Preparing the scoring method at the same time as writing the task provides an opportunity to check on their agreement. It also may require some rewriting of the task to better fit the evaluative criteria.

Developing Criteria for Assessing Performance Tasks

Criteria make clear to teacher and students alike the dimensions of a quality performance. They serve as a guide for both instruction and assessment and a basis for providing feedback to students. Thus, it is important to develop the criteria carefully. The characteristics of sound performance criteria listed in Box 8.3 provide guidelines for this purpose. It may not be possible to match all of these characteristics for some performance tasks (e.g., experts may disagree on the most important aspects of a performance in a given area), but attempts should be made to provide criteria that clearly describe the most important dimensions of the performance.

The best way to start is to review the specific learning outcomes described in the instructional objectives. If the objectives have been well stated, they frequently can be used directly as criteria (e.g., distinguishes between statements of fact and opinion). In other cases the intended learning outcomes may be only slightly modified to become sound criteria. If the objectives are not stated in usable form, it may be necessary to start with the completed task and ask "What are the main attributes that distinguish a satisfactory performance from an unsatisfactory one?" A careful analysis of the task and a review of criteria developed by others should result in a usable list. Just make sure the criteria are in harmony with the instructional objectives, regardless of how the objectives are stated.

BOX 8.3 • *Characteristics of Sound Performance Criteria*

1. They describe the components that are most crucial to satisfactory completion of the performance (e.g., beware of peripheral activities that are trivial).
2. They focus on observable aspects of the performance (e.g., "Follows safety procedures," not "Demonstrates safety consciousness").
3. They apply in various contextual settings (e.g., "skill in computation" is applicable in all contexts).
4. They represent aspects of performance that experts would agree are necessary for a successful performance (e.g., "Good organization" would be recognized by experts as basic in all types of writing).
5. They are stated in terms that are readily understood and usable by students in evaluating performance (e.g., for self-evaluation and peer evaluation).
6. They are in harmony with the instructional objectives and the use to be made of the assessment results (e.g., criteria used in judging writing skills and their improvement over time).

The type of scoring method used will also influence how the criteria are stated. For a rating scale, a detailed list of criteria is desired to pinpoint specific areas of strength and weakness. For a holistic scoring rubric, it is desirable to combine specific criteria into broader statements for an overall evaluation. For example, in assessing skills used in analyzing an argument for or against a proposal, the outcomes might be listed as follows: distinguishes between facts and inferences, relevant and irrelevant, cause and effect, consistent and inconsistent, essential and nonessential, and supportive and nonsupportive. Each of these elements might be stated as a criterion for a rating scale. For a scoring rubric, however, it would be necessary to use a broader statement, such as "Evaluates the applicability and validity of statements used to support or refute a proposal." In some cases both a rating scale and holistic scoring rubric are used, so both types of statements might be needed, one to provide a detailed analysis and the other to provide an overall judgment. When both are used, the holistic scoring rubric is responded to first to avoid specific items from distorting the general impression of the performance.

Using Student Projects for Performance Assessment

As noted earlier, a project can provide for a comprehensive form of performance assessment. It can be designed to include a combination of academic, communication, thinking, and related skills that result in a complex performance, product, or problem-solving activity. Ideally, it involves

BOX 8.4 • *Characteristics of a Good Student Project*

1. It focuses on multiple learning outcomes.
2. It includes the integration of understandings, skills, and strategies.
3. It is concerned with problems and activities that relate to out-of-school life.
4. It involves the active participation of students in all phases of the project.
5. It provides for student self-assessment and independent learning.
6. It requires performance skills that are generalizable to similar situations.
7. It is feasible within the constraints of the students' present knowledge, time limits, and available resources and equipment.
8. It is both challenging and motivating to students.
9. It is fair and doable by all students.
10. It provides for collaboration between the students and the teacher.

multiple outcomes and criteria for each and student participation in all phases of the project, including its assessment (see Box 8.4).

To illustrate the use of projects in assessment, we will focus on a problem-solving type of project. Typically, an unstructured problem, like those in the real world, is used so that there is no simple or single solution. This increases the complexity of the problem and provides for greater focus on higher-level learning outcomes (e.g., analysis, synthesis, evaluation). It also provides for the assessment of a greater range of skills useful later in life (e.g., locating resources, writing, speaking, self-assessment).

A common outline for a problem-solving project includes the following items.

1. Establishing criteria and standards.
2. Selecting and stating the problem.
3. Locating and selecting resources.
4. Writing the report.
5. Designing and completing a research study or making a product.
6. Orally presenting and defending the project.

Each of these steps is guided by the teacher and involves considerable student-teacher collaboration.

Establishing Criteria and Standards

Because of the multiple outcomes expected from a project, criteria must be established in many areas. For example, criteria for each of the major areas (i.e., problem selection, research skills, report writing, product design and construction, and oral presentation). Throughout these areas, or as separate categories, criteria must also be established for level of thinking shown and general problem-solving skills. These criteria may be developed by the teacher or they may be cooperatively prepared with the students. The latter procedure tends to provide greater understanding of the criteria by students and tends to be more motivating. The final list of criteria should be checked against the instructional objectives to be sure they are in agreement.

Standards that describe levels of success on each criterion should be set at the same time as the criteria are prepared. These may be stated for use in holistic scoring rubrics or may be included as part of a rating scale to be used in evaluating the project.

Selecting and Stating the Problem

Students should be free to select a problem that interests them, but the selection may require considerable help from the teacher. In a traditional classroom, many students are in the "tell me what to do" mode and one or two conferences may be needed to help them think about possible problems to study. In helping students select a problem, it is important to keep in mind how suitable the problem is for the student. Is it too difficult or too easy for the student? Does it provide an opportunity for new learning, or is it one the student already has studied? Will the problem be motivating to the student or one that is done grudgingly? Will the problem provide significant learning experiences that are in harmony with the intended learning outcomes? These and similar concerns will aid in helping the student select an appropriate and worthwhile problem to study.

Students also typically need help in phrasing the problem so that it is clear, objective, and realistic. Stating the problem in question form usually provides the crux of the problem most effectively. For example, changing "Study of the Environment" to "How Can We Improve the Environment?" helps provide a focus on a major problem. From here it is possible to go to more specific statements, such as "How Can We Improve the Air or Water?" Asking students to put their topics in question form forces them to pose problems. It is then just a matter of helping them refine the statements until they are clear and realistic.

If criteria for selecting and stating a problem have been developed beforehand, as should be done, they can be stated in evaluation form and serve as an aid in the process. They can also, of course, provide a basis for later assessment of the project. Criteria such as the following can be combined with other project criteria and used as a basis for a rating scale.

1. Selects and states a realistic problem.
   1.1. Is the problem in harmony with the student's present knowledge and skill?
   1.2. Does the problem provide opportunities for the student to learn new knowledge and skills?

   1.3. Does the problem provide opportunities for assessing cognitive and communication skills?

   1.4. Does the problem relate to real-world situations?

   1.5. Does the problem have more than one possible solution?

   1.6. Is the problem stated clearly?

   1.7. Is the statement of the problem free from bias and distortion?

In stating the criteria, it is important that they be understandable to the students. This can be accomplished by having the students help develop the criteria. If the problem requires teacher-prepared criteria, they can be presented to the students for clarification and rewording as needed. In any event, criteria should be clear to students and available to them at the beginning of the project. This will provide a focus for doing the project and a guide for self-assessment and peer assessment later.

Locating and Selecting Resources

After stating the problem clearly, the student is expected to go to reference books and other sources to gather information. Other sources might include interviews with knowledgeable people in the community (e.g., banker, accountant, doctor, scientist), observation of a process (e.g., council meeting, trial, bakery operation), or writing a letter to a congressional representative requesting information. The point is, students are expected to obtain information from any source that can provide help with the problem—as we do in real life.

   This phase of the project might include criteria similar to the following.

  2. Selects appropriate resource material.

   2.1. Has a variety of resources been selected?

   2.2. Is the resource material relevant to the problem?

   2.3. Do the resources provide various possible solutions to the problem?

   2.4. Does the resource material include evidence supporting the suggested solutions?

   2.5. Is there enough resource material to provide for valid conclusions?

Writing the Report

The written report provides an opportunity for students to combine ideas from various sources, analyze and interpret the findings, and summarize and draw conclusions. The criteria for judging the report should be used as a guide for writing it. The written report provides an important means of assessing higher-order thinking skills and, thus, they should be reflected in the criteria.

   The following list illustrates how criteria might be stated for the written report.

3. Writes a clear and effective report.
   3.1. Has the problem been clearly stated?
   3.2. Have the study procedures been adequately described?
   3.3. Has the material from various sources been analyzed, compared, and evaluated?
   3.4. Have the findings been integrated into a well-organized report?
   3.5. Have the findings been supported by adequate and relevant information?
   3.6. Does the summary include the main points?
   3.7. Are the conclusions in harmony with the findings and the limits of the study?
   3.8. Does the report exhibit good reasoning ability?

The specific nature of the criteria will, of course, be influenced by the content, instructional objectives, and level of the instruction. Emphasis on reasoning ability might require more specific criteria on the quality of the questions raised, the relevance of the arguments, and distinctions between supported and unsupported statements. Emphasis on communication skills might call for criteria on the clarity of the writing and on grammar and on spelling. At lower grades, the criteria would, of course, need to be modified to fit the age level of the students. Our illustrative criteria are general and simply show how the intended learning outcomes might be stated so that they are most useful for instruction, learning, and assessment. If properly stated, they can be easily converted to a rating scale by adding numbers from 1 to 4, representing different levels of performance, as shown later in the section on Preparing a Rating Scale and in Box 8.5.

In any event, the student should be aware of the completed list of criteria before writing this report, use them to evaluate the report, and then to revise the report as needed. It is helpful for the teacher to evaluate the report and compare the ratings with those of the student in a conference before the student revises the report. Peer evaluations, of course, may also be used.

Designing and Completing a Research Study or Making a Product

In some cases the written report may serve as a basis for a research study. In others, the written report may serve as a basis for constructing a product. This might be a map, poster, chart, graph, model, or some other type of exhibit illustrating the findings. Or it might be a wood or metal product, as in the vocational area. In this case, the focus of the project may be on designing and constructing the product, but the study phase is still important. For a woodworking project, for example, the study phase may involve a comparison of different types of wood, various construction procedures, or a history of the product (e.g., making a replica of an antique chair). The study phase provides for the combining of academic and vocational skills in carrying out the project and increases the opportunity for including higher level thinking skills in the project.

Criteria for assessing the research or product should be stated in the same manner as those listed earlier. The specific nature of the criteria for a research study will depend on the type of problem being studied. However, there are some general criteria that should be considered, such as the use of proper procedures, control of variables, selection and use of equipment, accuracy of measurements, adequacy of interpretation of results, and the validity of conclusions. Adapting these and similar criteria to the specific research project and phrasing them in terms the students can understand provide a sound basis for conducting the research and for its later assessment.

The criteria for a product will depend on the type of product that is being constructed and its relation to the written report. If an exhibit, such as a graph or poster, is being constructed as part of the project, for example, the criteria will include how well it illustrates the findings, its ease of interpretation, and the like. For a woodworking project, the criteria might be concerned with both the procedure (e.g., selection of tools and materials, the use of tools and machines, etc.) and the product (e.g., appearance, meeting specifications, and functioning properly). As indicated earlier, the criteria should be known to students before starting on the construction project. It is also helpful to put the criteria in rating form, as illustrated later in the chapter to clarify how they will be used in the assessment.

Orally Presenting and Defending the Project

Upon completion of the project, it may be desirable to have each student describe the procedures and findings to a group of students, parents, or members of the community. The nature of the group depends on the purpose of the assessment, the type of project, and how the school is organized.

The final presentation gives the student practice in public speaking and in defending his or her work. This, of course, also provides another opportunity to evaluate higher order thinking skills through use of questions that require the student to defend the procedures, findings, and products of the project. As with other phases of the project, evaluation of the presentation is guided by a set of criteria developed at the beginning of the project and fully shared with the students.

The expanded project described here includes multiple outcomes, such as research skills, writing skills, speaking skills, thinking skills, self-assessment skills, and, in some cases, vocational skills. The specific nature of such a project will, of course, vary with the area of instruction and the purpose of the project. It is helpful to review descriptions of how this and other types of expanded performance assessments are functioning in the schools.

The list of references at the end of the chapter provides numerous descriptions and examples of performance assessment in action.

Evaluating Student Projects

Student projects can be evaluated by rating scales or holistic scoring rubrics, depending on the use to be made of the results and the complexity of the project. For diagnosis and correction of specific weaknesses, the rating scale would be favored. The numerous tasks involved in a complex project may also suggest a rating scale for each major phase. A holistic scoring rubric might be favored where the integration of understandings and skills makes a rating scale less useful, or it violates the wholeness of the performance. In some cases it may be desirable to develop a holistic scoring rubric for each phase of the project (e.g., problem identification, using resources, writing the report). If the assessment is for grading or recording purposes, a holistic scoring rubric may be satisfactory for assessing the overall quality of the project or might be used in addition to the rating scale.

Preparing a Rating Scale

If the specific criteria have been listed for each phase of the project, as illustrated earlier, it is simply a matter of adding to each specific criterion the method of rating desired and adding appropriate directions. The use of a four-point scale is fairly common and is illustrated in Box 8.5. The entire scale would have to be completed, of course. All we are doing here is demonstrating how simple the procedure is once the criteria have been specified for the performance or product.

The rating scale provides a focus for judging the project and a convenient place to record the judgments. It is important to state the rating scale items in simple clear language so that they are understandable to students. This makes it a useful device for both student self-evaluation and peer evaluation, as well as teacher evaluation. In some cases, it may be desirable to use all three types of ratings and compare the results in a student-teacher conference. Discussing the agreements and discrepancies should contribute to student learning and to improvement in self-evaluation skills.

Preparing Holistic Scoring Rubrics

Because of the complex nature of the project described earlier, it may be desirable to prepare a holistic scoring rubric for each phase of the project (e.g., selecting and stating the problem, locating and selecting resources, writing the report, etc.). A sample scoring rubric for the first phase of a project

BOX 8.5 • *Sample Rating Scale Form for a Project*

Directions: Rate each item by circling the appropriate number. The numbers represent the following values: 4—excellent; 3—good; 2—satisfactory, 1—weak (needs modification).

Selecting and Stating the Problem

4 3 2 1   (a) Is the problem in harmony with the student's present knowledge and skill?

4 3 2 1   (b) (add others)

Locating and Selecting Resources

4 3 2 1   (a) Has a variety of resources been selected?

4 3 2 1   (b) (add others)

Writing the Report

4 3 2 1   (a) Has the problem been clearly stated?

4 3 2 1   (b) (add others)

Conducting a Research Study

4 3 2 1   (a) Have proper procedures been followed?

4 3 2 1   (b) (add others)

Building a Product

4 3 2 1   (a) Did the product match the specifications?

4 3 2 1   (b) (add others)

Oral Presentation of Project

4 3 2 1   (a) Did the oral presentation reflect understanding of the problem studied?

4 3 2 1   (b) (add others)

is shown in Box 8.6. A similar type rubric for each of the other phases of project would then provide a profile of judgments on each phase of the project, as shown below.

Problem selection	— Good
Use of resources	— Acceptable
Written report	— Excellent
Research study	— Acceptable
Constructed product	— Good
Oral report	— Inadequate

Such a profile would help identify where improvement is most needed, but a more detailed study of the inadequate area would be required. The criteria listed in the scoring rubric would help focus on the nature of the problem.

BOX 8.6 • *Scoring Rubric for Selecting and Stating a Problem for a Project*

EXCELLENT 4	Selects a complex problem that is solvable. Selects a problem that challenges his or her knowledge and skill. States the problem clearly and objectively.
GOOD 3	Selects a fairly complex problem that is solvable. Selects a problem that is appropriate but could be more challenging. States the problem clearly and objectively.
ACCEPTABLE 2	Selects a solvable problem that is not very complex. Selects a problem of moderate difficulty. States the problem fairly clearly and objectively.
INADEQUATE 1	Selects a problem that is too simple or too complex. Selects a problem that is unchallenging or beyond his or her knowledge or skill. Statement of problem lacks clarity and objectivity.

Summary of Points

1. Expanded performance assessments focus on complex learning outcomes that integrate skills and understandings and involve students' active participation in the learning process.
2. Expanded performance assessments are supported by modern learning theory.
3. Traditional performance assessment can be expanded by increasing the emphasis on cognitive skills, communication skills, visual materials, realism of tasks, complexity of tasks, and student participation in the assessment process.
4. Two common ways of expanding performance assessments are through the use of performance tasks as prompts and through the use of student projects.
5. Performance tasks provide useful prompts for performance assessment. They typically present a realistic problem situation that describes the type of performance to be assessed and the method of scoring to be used.
6. Performance tasks should be relevant to the instructional objectives; focus on complex learning outcomes; provide for the integration of understandings and skills; be realistic and meaningful, clear, free of irrelevant factors, feasible, and developmentally appropriate for students;

be based on generalizable performance; and be accompanied by the method of scoring.

7. Criteria make clear the dimensions of a quality performance and, thus, play a key role in performance assessment. Effective performance criteria describe the crucial components of the performances, focus on observable elements, apply in various contexts, are agreed upon by experts, are stated in understandable and usable terms, and are in harmony with the instructional objectives and use to be made of the results.

8. Preparing assessment criteria involves reviewing the instructional objectives and relevant specific learning outcomes, analyzing the performance called forth by the task, consulting criteria developed by others, and considering the type of scoring method to be used.

9. Student projects provide for the assessment of multiple learning outcomes (e.g., research, writing, speaking, thinking, and self-assessment skills), are adaptable to various areas of instruction, and typically use realistic problems.

10. A problem-solving project includes the establishing of criteria and standards for assessing the project, selecting and stating the problem, locating and selecting resources, writing the report, designing and completing a research study or making a product (e.g., model), and orally presenting and defending the project.

11. The criteria for evaluating the project should be converted into a rating scale or holistic scoring rubric for assessment purposes.

12. Students should actively participate in stating the criteria and preparing the assessment instruments, to the extent possible. The completed assessment instruments should be available to students before starting work on the project.

References and Additional Reading

Airasian, P. W., *Classroom Assessment*, 3rd ed. (New York: McGraw Hill, 1997).

Arter, J., and McTighe, J., *Scoring Rubrics in the Classroom* (Thousand Oaks, CA: Corwin Press, 2001).

Darling-Hammond, L., Ancess, J., and Falk, B., *Authentic Assessment in Action: Studies of Schools and Students at Work* (New York: Teachers College Press, Columbia University, 1995).

Johnson, B., *Performance Assessment Handbook: Volume 2, Performances and Exhibitions* (Princeton, NJ: Eye on Education, 1996).

McMillan, J. H., *Classroom Assessment: Principles and Practices for Effective Instruction*, 2nd ed. (Boston: Allyn and Bacon, 2001).

Stiggins, R. J., *Student-Involved Classroom Assessment*, 3rd ed. (Upper Saddle River, NJ: Merrill/Prentice-Hall, 2001).

Wiggins, G. P. *Educative Assessment: Designing Assessments to Inform and Improve Student Performance* (San Francisco, CA: Jossey-Bass, 1998).

9

Portfolio Assessment

Studying this chapter should enable you to

1. Describe the advantages of using a portfolio as a means of assessment.
2. Distinguish between a developmental portfolio and a showcase portfolio.
3. List the types of portfolio entries that should be considered in your teaching area.
4. Describe the factors to consider in planning a portfolio.
5. Describe a procedure for getting started in the use of a portfolio in the classroom.
6. Prepare a rating scale for the structural evaluation of a portfolio in your teaching area.
7. Prepare a rating scale for evaluating a student's learning progress shown in a portfolio in your teaching area.
8. Prepare a holistic scoring rubric for evaluating a student's final level of performance shown in a portfolio, in your teaching area.

Portfolios are becoming an important means of assessment in many schools. In some cases, they are used as a basic, or sole, method of performance assessment. In others, they provide another useful tool in the teacher's assessment kit. A portfolio is a collection of student work that has been selected and organized to show student learning progress (developmental portfolio) or to show samples of the student's best work (showcase portfolio). A common practice is to use the developmental portfolio throughout an instructional program and the showcase portfolio at the end. Thus, the showcase portfolio provides a collection of work that indicates the student's final level of performance. Some schools have used the showcase portfolio as a basis for high school graduation. Some states have used them on a statewide basis as a means of assessing performance in basic skills. Our focus will be on **portfolio assessment** in the classroom instructional program.

BOX 9.1 • *What a Student Portfolio Can Show*

1. Learning progress over time.
2. Student's current best work.
3. Comparison of best work to past work.
4. Development of self-assessment skills.
5. Development of reflective learning.
6. Individual's level and pace of work.
7. Clear evidence of learning to parents and others.
8. The amount of teacher-student collaboration involved.

The assessment value of portfolios is found in the variety of types of evidence that are available for judging student performance. They typically include various types of independent work (e.g., writing samples, drawings, research reports, computer worksheets, projects) as well as assessment results in the form of written comments, checklists, rating scales, test scores, and conference reports. The assessment data is also likely to include the student's self-assessments, peer assessments, and teacher's assessments. See Box 9.1 for what portfolios can show.

Students play an active role in selecting the entries and maintaining the portfolio. This provides for another important item to be included in a portfolio—that is, the student's reflections on such things as why the entry was chosen, what it illustrates, what was learned, and what might be done to improve performance. These written reflections cause students to focus on the learning process, the changes taking place, and the growth in their learning.

The active participation of students in selecting entries for the portfolio helps them focus on the criteria of successful performance, and their reflections on the criteria provides a basis for developing critical thought and deeper understanding. The criteria also make students aware of their responsibility for participating fully in the learning process, an important step toward becoming independent learners.

Advantages of Using Classroom Portfolios

Portfolios have a number of specific advantages as a means of assessing classroom learning.

1. Learning progress over times can be clearly shown (e.g., changes in writing, thinking, or research skills).
2. Focus on students' best work provides a positive influence on learning (e.g., best writing samples, best examples of reasoning and problem solving).

3. Comparing work to past work provides greater motivation than comparison to the work of others (e.g., growth in knowledge and skills).
4. Self-assessment skills are increased due to the student selection of best samples of work (e.g., focus is on criteria of good performance).
5. Reflective learning is encouraged as students are asked to comment on each portfolio entry (e.g., why do you consider this your best work?)
6. Providing for adjustment to individual differences (e.g., students work at their own levels but work toward common goals).
7. Providing for clear communication of learning progress to students, parents, and others (e.g., work samples obtained at different times can be shown and compared).
8. Increasing teacher-student collaboration in the teaching-learning-assessment process.

Despite the numerous advantages of using portfolios, they are time consuming to maintain and use. Assisting students in the selection of portfolio entries, providing feedback on the students' work, and periodically reviewing the students' learning progress requires considerable student-teacher conference time. Simply collecting samples of student work and putting it in a file does not constitute a portfolio. Much greater care is required in the development of a portfolio that will be useful in instruction and assessment.

Planning for the Use of Portfolios

There are a number of factors to keep in mind when planning for the use of portfolios in the classroom. A careful consideration of them will increase a portfolio's value as an instructional and assessment tool. The major considerations are:

1. Purpose of the portfolio.
2. Types of entries to include.
3. Guidelines for selecting and evaluating the entries.
4. Maintaining and using the portfolio.
5. Evaluating the portfolio.

Each of these will be discussed in turn.

Purpose of the Portfolio

The main purpose of the classroom portfolio, as with any method of assessment, is to improve student learning. As noted earlier, it provides unique contributions to this goal by showing actual samples of student work, providing for comparisons of work in different areas and progress over time, providing opportunities for students to evaluate their own work and reflect on it, conveying clear evidence of learning to all interested persons, and increasing students' participation in the learning process.

Although the main purpose of the assessment portfolio is to improve student learning, a secondary purpose is to help students become responsible for their own learning. This means active participation of the students in selecting the samples to be included in the portfolios, in assessing the quality of entries, in reflecting on what was learned and how to improve performance, in maintaining the portfolio and evaluating it. All of this is done under the guidance of the teacher, of course, but there should be a weaning away of control as students become increasingly capable of independent learning.

In some schools the students have limited opportunity to participate because of the requirements set by the department, school, or district. All a teacher can do in these cases, obviously, is to provide the students with as much freedom of choice as is allowed by the constraints. For example, if the nature of the task and the criteria for the assessment are predetermined, provide students with a limited choice of tasks within that framework.

Portfolios may be set up for more specific purposes than the assessment portfolio we have been discussing. For example, a portfolio may be used to showcase only the student's best work for use in grading, accountability, or placement in permanent school records. A portfolio may be limited to evidence that shows the development of student self-assessment skills and growth toward becoming an independent learner. A portfolio may be limited to the development of research skills only. We have been stressing the comprehensive use of portfolios in assessing student learning, but portfolios can serve a variety of purposes. Thus, it is important to be clear about the purpose of the portfolio. This will help answer the following basic questions.

1. What understandings and skills should result from the use of the portfolio?
2. What types of performance tasks are best for providing the needed evidence?
3. Who are the users of the portfolio and how will they use them?

Types of Entries to Include

The selection of entries for the portfolio is guided by the purpose, the intended learning outcomes, and the use to be made of the results. If the portfolio is limited to a specific area such as writing skill, the entries might be limited to one type of writing (e.g., narrative) or include different types of writing tasks (e.g., letters, essays, poetry). They might also include writing on different topics or in specific content areas (e.g., scientific writing). Both the first draft of the writing and later revisions also might be included. The specific types of entries will depend on the goals of instruction, how the information is to be used in the instructional programs, and with whom the information will be shared.

A more comprehensive portfolio will include samples of various types of student work, depending on the area of instruction. In math, for example, entries might include samples of problem solving, written explanations of how to solve problems, mathematical charts and graphs, and computer printouts of problem solving. Science entries might include examples of experimental studies, laboratory skills, evidence of conceptual understandings, student-designed projects, and field studies. The types of entries to include will, of course, vary with the purpose of the portfolio, the grade level, the instructional objectives, and any school requirements concerning the nature of the portfolio.

As noted earlier, each entry should be accompanied by the students' reflections on the entry. A brief form can be designed that provides questions and a space for answering. For example, What did I do? What did I learn? How would I improve it? Such questions cause students to think about their learning and their need to take responsibility for it.

In addition to the other entries, portfolios should also include test scores, checklists, rating scales, and other types of relevant data used for assessing learning (see Box 9.2).

Guidelines for Selecting and Evaluating the Entries

The portfolio should not be a repository for all of the student's work. If this is done, it becomes too cumbersome and unmanageable. Its content should be a sample of the student's best work, or latest work in progress, in selected areas. The areas may be determined by the teacher or by school requirements. In any event, the selection and evaluation of the portfolio entries should be determined by guidelines such as the following.

BOX 9.2 • *What Types of Entries Should Be Included*

---

1. Entries selected by students (e.g., work samples, writing samples, drawings, performance tasks, projects, assessment results).
2. Student reflections on the entries:
   2.1 Why was this entry selected?
   2.2 What was done to accomplish it?
   2.3 What was learned from it?
   2.4 What changes would improve it?

---

1. Entries should be in harmony with the goals of instruction and the use to be made of the portfolio (e.g., to improve learning, for use in parent-teaching conferences, as part of a schoolwide assessment).
2. Entries should provide a variety of types of evidence (e.g., written, oral, exhibits, projects).
3. Entries should be selected in terms of the criteria to be used in judging them.
4. Entries should be selected by students, or at least they should be involved in the process.
5. Entries should be complex enough to allow for students' self-evaluations and their reflections on the learning that resulted.
6. Entries should be started early in the instructional program to better show growth in learning.
7. Entries should be evaluated by using the criteria and standards established for the performance tasks.

The procedure for developing criteria for evaluating the portfolio entries is the same here as for any performance task, like those discussed in the last two chapters. The criteria should specify the types of performance we are willing to accept as evidence of a quality product, and the standards should identify the various levels of acceptable performance. These are then used in preparing rating scales or holistic scoring rubrics to be used in the assessments.

The criteria can aid students in selecting, preparing, and evaluating the samples to be entered in the portfolio by focusing their attention on the elements to be included in the product. In working on a problem-solving project, for example, criteria like those discussed in the last chapter make clear to the students that the project requires a realistic problem, the selection and use of various resources, a written report, the preparation of an exhibit, and an oral report to a group. The specific criteria in each area make clear how the project will be judged and thus provide direction for student learning. Within the framework provided by the criteria, the students are still free to select a problem that interests them.

Our discussion makes clear why the criteria and standards must be shared with students at the beginning of the instruction. They provide guidelines for the preparation of the portfolio entries, for the students' self-assessments and reflections, and for the final assessment of the performance.

Maintaining and Using the Portfolios

The portfolio entries are typically placed in file folders or notebooks and stored in a cabinet. As noted earlier, it is important to keep the portfolio entries down to a manageable number, so that they can be arranged in an orderly and useful manner. A hodgepodge collection of material is apt to defeat the purpose of using portfolios. Arranging the entries by sections and placing a table of contents in front of the file makes it easier to maintain the file and to locate material when evaluating learning progress or reporting to parents. Each entry should be dated and labeled before placing it in the file.

Students should actively participate in the maintenance of the portfolio. It is a collection of their work, so they should aid in setting the guidelines for what goes into the portfolio, selecting the portfolio samples, and evaluating the progress reflected in the samples of work. Unless a student is an active participant, he or she is likely to feel that it is not a personal portfolio.

The portfolio is to be reviewed periodically during a student-teacher conference. Here, student and teacher can view the content together, compare evaluations, and discuss strengths in learning progress and areas where improvement is needed. The portfolio is also used in parent-teacher conferences to demonstrate and discuss student achievement. There is no better way to make clear to parents what a student is learning than by the use of actual samples of student work.

If portfolios have not been used in the school before, one might start on a small scale. A safe approach is to start with one specific area such as writing, drawing, problem solving, laboratory work, or some other relevant learning activity. This makes it possible to obtain practice in use of the procedure with a limited and clearly defined task. The goals and criteria can be more easily specified, the nature of the entries are more readily identifiable, and the entire process is more manageable. Once experience is obtained in helping students select entries, evaluate and reflect on their work, and maintain the portfolio, other content and skills can be added.

The specific nature of the portfolio entries varies so widely from one instructional area to another and one level of instruction to another that it is wise to consult some of the numerous references on portfolio design and use before getting started. Especially useful are those illustrating the criteria, forms, and procedures used in specific content areas. The references at the end of this chapter provide a sample of helpful resource material.

Evaluating the Portfolio

As noted earlier, criteria for each performance task that is to serve as an entry should be clearly specified beforehand, as is done with any performance assessment. The criteria provide guidelines for preparing and evaluating the entry and should be shared with students early in the process. They are typically converted to rating scales or other scoring rubrics that can be used in self-assessment, peer assessment, and teacher assessment. The specification of criteria and their use in task assessment have been discussed and illustrated earlier and need not be repeated here. In addition to these specific performance assessments, however, there is a need to evaluate the portfolio structure and the students' overall performance.

Evaluating the Portfolio Structure

The criteria for evaluating the structure of the portfolio should clarify the main features of an effective portfolio. Although these will vary somewhat with the content and level of instruction, there are some general criteria that should apply to all portfolios. The list in Box 9.3 includes some of main ones to be considered.

General criteria, such as these, provide guidelines for both developing a portfolio and for detecting shortcomings in its makeup. Criteria for evaluating a portfolio in a given content area could be made more specific and content oriented. For example, in a science course, item 2 might be stated as "Does the portfolio provide evidence of understandings, laboratory skills, and research skills?" Thus, the general criteria can serve as a guide for developing a more content-relevant set of criteria.

Evaluating the Student's Overall Portfolio Performance

In addition to the evaluation of individual samples as they are entered in the portfolio, there is a need to evaluate the student's overall performance. Criteria concerning the improvement in performance during the year and the final level of performance can provide the basis for a rating scale or holistic scoring rubric.

BOX 9.3 • *General Criteria for Evaluating the Portfolio's Structure*

---

1. Has the purpose of the portfolio been clearly stated?
2. Does the portfolio provide evidence of various types of student learning?
3. Does the portfolio include evidence of complex learning in realistic settings?
4. Does the portfolio include enough entries in each area to make valid judgments?
5. Does the portfolio include students' self-evaluations and their reflections on what was learned?
6. Does the portfolio enable one to determine learning progress and current level of learning?
7. Does the portfolio provide clear evidence of learning to users of the portfolio?
8. Does the portfolio provide for student participation and responsibility?
9. Does the portfolio provide guidelines for the student participation?
10. Does the portfolio present the entries in a well-organized and useful manner?
11. Does the portfolio include assessments based on clearly stated criteria of successful performance?
12. Does the portfolio provide for greater interaction between instruction and assessment?

Evaluating Student Improvement.   For evaluating student's improvement over the school year, a rating scale is typically favored because it can focus attention on the student's strengths and weaknesses. A rating scale based on general criteria is shown in Box 9.4.

The items in our illustrative rating scale are, obviously, very general but they illustrate the types of items to consider when preparing this form of assessment instrument. The specific items to include would be determined by the instructional area, the intended learning outcomes of the instruction, and the purpose of the portfolio. A set of items for a writing portfolio, for example, would focus on the improvement of specific writing skills (e.g., word choice, sentence structure, organization, flow of ideas, etc.). A language arts portfolio would not only include specific items on writing skills but also on reading skills, reading comprehension, and speaking and listening skills. In addition to the specific items needed to fit the nature of the instruction, however, some of the general criteria still should be considered. Growth in self-assessment skills, reflective skills, and independent learning should be of interest in all areas of instruction.

The unique advantage of the portfolio in assessing student growth is that the entries over the school year provide sequential evidence of changes in student performance that can be examined and reexamined, if needed, when judging the degree of improvement. The rating scale simply provides

---

BOX 9.4 • *Portfolio Ratings of Student Improvement*

Directions: Rate each of the following items by circling the appropriate number. The numbers represent the following values: 4—outstanding progress; 3—good progress; 2—satisfactory progress; 1—unsatisfactory progress.

To what extent does the student show improvement in:

4	3	2	1	Understanding of concepts
4	3	2	1	Application of information
4	3	2	1	Reasoning ability
4	3	2	1	Writing skills
4	3	2	1	Speaking skills
4	3	2	1	Problem-solving skills
4	3	2	1	Performance skills
4	3	2	1	Computational skills
4	3	2	1	Computer skills
4	3	2	1	Self-assessment skills
4	3	2	1	Reflection skills
4	3	2	1	Work-study skills
4	3	2	1	Independent learning

a convenient place to record the judgments. As with the assessment of individual entries, the students can also use the rating scale to rate their own overall improvement and, if desired, compare it to the teacher's ratings.

Evaluating the Student's Final Level of Performance.   For an evaluation of the student's final level of performance, a holistic scoring rubric is preferred. Here we are interested in an overall impression of each student's terminal performance. If the portfolio is focused on one limited area of instruction such as narrative writing, a single scoring rubric may suffice. However, for most courses of instruction several scoring rubrics would be needed. In science, for example, a separate scoring rubric for understanding science concepts, application of concepts and methods, scientific research skills, and process skills may be needed. In math, separate scoring rubrics for conceptual understanding, problem solving, reasoning ability, and using math in communications might be needed.

The preparation of scoring rubrics for an overall evaluation of a student's final level of performance is time consuming but the following outline of steps should help.

1. *Prepare a list of criteria for each scoring rubric to be prepared.* A review of the instructional objectives and the criteria used for portfolio entries should help here. For overall assessment of a student's final level of performance in the portfolio, however, there is a problem of selecting a limited number of criteria. A list of six or fewer is desirable so that the scoring rubric does not become too cumbersome. This means focusing on the most important criteria for judging the quality of the performance. A common procedure is to state the criteria you think are most important and then consult the literature to get help on how to combine them into a list of major criteria.

2. *Select the number of categories of performance to be used.* A good procedure is to start with four categories and expand it to six or eight if finer distinctions are needed. It is frequently difficult to describe more than four discrete levels of performance. A guide for preparing holistic scoring rubrics, using four categories, is presented in Box 9.5. The commonly used category labels and the frequently used terms for stating criteria were gleaned from currently used scoring rubrics in various content areas. The lists are not meant to be exhaustive and should not be used in a perfunctory manner, but they should be helpful in getting started.

3. *Adapt scoring rubrics from published sources.* The literature on portfolios and scoring rubrics provide numerous examples of scoring rubrics in various areas of instruction that might be adapted for use in an overall evaluation of student performance. Because of the difficulty of preparing holistic scoring rubrics, selecting those rubrics that seem most

BOX 9.5 • *Guide for Preparing Holistic Scoring Rubrics*

Level Number	Category Labels	Frequently Used Terms When Stating Criteria	
4	Exemplary	Sophisticated	Thorough
	Superior	Extensive	Deep
	Distinguished	Comprehensive	Elegant
	Excellent	Unique	Perceptive
		Clear	Efficient
3	Satisfactory	Appropriate	Mostly
	Adequate	Consistent	Clear
	Competent	Relevant	Accurate
	Good	Acceptable	Broad
		Detailed	Variety
2	Minimal	Paraphrases	Inconsistent
	Borderline	Shallow	Incomplete
	Marginal	Limited	Basic
	Fair	Weak	Minor
		Minimal	Conventional
1	Unsatisfactory	Trivial	Incoherent
	Inadequate	Unclear	Lacks
	Incomplete	Vague	Disorganized
	Poor	General	Irrelevant
		Inaccurate	Superficial

appropriate and then adapting them by modifying the criteria to fit your particular instructional situation and type of portfolio can provide a good way to start. When completed, check to be sure they are appropriate for your use.

4. *Check your prepared scoring rubrics to see if they work as intended.* When you have completed the sets of scoring rubrics, try them out by evaluating students' sample portfolios. This will help you determine if the criteria focus on the most important areas of performance and provide clear distinctions between the various levels of performance. At this point you might just need some fine-tuning.

Summary of Points

1. A portfolio is a collection of student work that has been selected and organized to show learning progress (developmental portfolio) or to show the student's best work (showcase portfolio).

2. Both types of portfolios are useful in the classroom—the developmental to show student growth during the school year and the showcase to indicate final level of learning.
3. The assessment value of portfolios is found in the vast array of evidence of learning they provide, the actual use of students' samples of work, the active participation of students in selecting entries and maintaining the portfolio, and the variety of types of assessment data included.
4. The specific advantages of using a portfolio in the classroom are that it shows actual samples of student work, provides for comparisons of work in different areas and growth over time, provides students with an opportunity to evaluate and reflect on their work, provides clear evidence of learning to all interested persons, and provides for increased participation of students in the teaching-learning-assessment process.
5. Planning for the use of portfolios involves determining the purpose, the types of entries to include, the guidelines for selecting and evaluating the entries, the procedures for maintaining and using the portfolio, and the criteria for an overall evaluation of the portfolio.
6. Although the main purpose of using a portfolio is to improve student learning, a secondary purpose is to encourage students to participate more actively in the learning process and become more responsible for their own learning. This is an important step in becoming independent learners.
7. The structural evaluation of a portfolio can be accomplished by considering a series of questions concerning its makeup, organization, and content.
8. The overall evaluation of student progresses shown in the portfolio can be determined by a rating scale that focuses on the learning outcomes being assessed by the portfolio.
9. The final level of student performance can best be determined by holistic scoring rubrics for each of the major areas of instruction included in the portfolio.

References and Additional Reading

Arter, J., and McTighe, J., *Scoring Rubrics in the Classroom* (Thousand Oaks, CA: Corwin Press, 2001).

Cole, D. J., Ryan, C. W., Kick, F., and Mathies, B. K., *Portfolios across the Curriculum and Beyond*, 2nd ed. (Thousand Oaks, CA: Corwin Press, 2000).

Johnson, B., *Performance Assessment Handbook: Volume 1, Portfolios and Socratic Seminars* (Princeton, NJ: Eye on Education, 1996).

Linn, R. L., and Gronlund, N. E., *Measurement and Assessment in Teaching*, 8th ed. (Upper Saddle River, NJ: Merrill/ Prentice-Hall, 2000).

McMillan, J. H., *Classroom Assessment: Principles and Practices for Effective Instruction*, 2nd ed. (Boston: Allyn and Bacon, 2001).

10

Grading and Reporting

Studying this chapter should enable you to

1. Distinguish between absolute grading and relative grading.
2. Describe how to select a proper frame of reference, or standard, for assigning grades.
3. Explain why learning ability, improvement, and effort provide a poor basis for grading.
4. Describe and defend the grading system you would use in your area of instruction.
5. Demonstrate how to properly weight components to be included in a grade.
6. Describe a rationale for making the pass-fail decision.
7. Write a statement, to be given to students, that describes your grading procedures.
8. Report learning progress to students and parents.

Grades assigned to student work should represent the extent to which the instructional objectives (i.e., the intended learning outcomes) have been achieved and should be in harmony with the grading policies of the school. Some schools have both clearly defined objectives and grading policies; many schools have neither. With or without the guidance of clear-cut policies and procedures, the assigning of grades is a difficult and frustrating task. It is somewhat easier if valid evidence of achievement has been gathered throughout the course.

Assessment of learning during instruction might include the use of objective and essay tests, ratings, papers, and various types of performance assessment. The problem of grading is that of summarizing this diverse collection of information into a single letter grade or brief report. Because the single letter grade (e.g., A, B, C, D, F) is the most widely used grading system, we shall focus on how best to assign such grades. This involves several important considerations: (1) What frame of reference, or standard, should be used to report level of performance? (2) How should the performance data be combined for grading? (3) What guidelines should be followed to provide the most effective and fair grading system? Each of these will be discussed in turn.

Selecting the Basis for Grading

Letter grades are typically assigned by comparing a student's performance to a prespecified standard of performance (absolute grading) or to the performance of the members of a group (relative grading). In some cases, grades are based on or modified by the learning ability of the student, the amount of improvement shown over a given instructional period, or student effort. As we shall see later, these factors provide an inadequate basis for assigning grades.

Absolute Grading

A common type of absolute grading is the use of letter grades defined by a 100-point system. Whether assigning grades to an individual set of test scores or as a basis for the final grades in a course, the set of grades might be expressed as one of the following:

	Points	Points	Points
A =	90–100	95–100	91–100
B =	80–89	85–94	86–90
C =	70–79	75–84	81–85
D =	60–69	65–74	75–80
F =	below 60	below 65	below 75

In the case of an individual test, this 100-point system might represent the percentage of items correct or the total number of points earned on the test. When used as a final grade, it typically represents a combining of scores from various tests and other assessment results. In any event, it provides an absolute basis for assigning letter grades.

Which set of points provides the best basis for assigning grades? There is no way of knowing. The distribution of points is arbitrary. Whatever distribution is used, however, should be based on the teacher's experience with this and past groups of students, knowledge concerning the difficulty of the intended learning outcomes, the difficulty of the tests and other assessments used, the conditions of learning, and the like. These are all subjective judgments, however, and shifts in the proportion of students getting the letter grade of A or F are difficult to evaluate. Do a larger number of grades of A represent improved instruction and better study habits by students, or easier tests and less rigid grading of papers and projects? Do more failures indicate poor teaching, inadequate study, or assessments that have inadvertently increased in difficulty?

Despite the problem of setting meaningful standards for an absolute grading system, this method is widely used in schools. It is most appropriate in programs where the set of learning tasks has been clearly specified, the standards have been defined in terms of the learning tasks, and the tests and other assessment techniques have been designed for criterion-referenced interpretation. All too frequently, however, absolute grading is based on some hodgepodge of ill-defined achievement results. When the distribution of points does not fit the grading scale, the points are adjusted upward or downward by some obscure formula to get a closer fit. Needless to say, such grades do not provide a meaningful report of the extent to which the intended learning outcomes have been achieved.

Relative Grading

When assigning grades on a relative basis, the students are typically ranked in order of performance (based on a set of test scores or combined assessment results) and the students ranking highest receive a letter grade of A, the next highest receive a B, and so on. What proportion of students should receive each grade is predetermined and might appear as one of the following:

	Percent of Students	*Percent of Students*
A	15	10–20
B	25	20–30
C	45	40–50
D	10	10–20
F	5	0–10

The percent of students to be assigned each grade is just as arbitrary as the selection of points for each grade in the absolute grading system. The use of a range of percents (e.g., A = 10–20 percent) should probably be favored because it makes some allowance for differences in the ability level of the class. It does not make sense to assign 15 percent As to both a regular class and a gifted class. Likewise, in an advanced course a larger proportion of As and Bs should be assigned and fewer (if any) Fs because the low-achieving students have been "weeded out" in earlier courses. When these percentages have been set by the school system, one has little choice but to follow the school practice—at least until efforts to change it are successful.

Older measurement books recommended using the normal curve to assign grades. This resulted in the same percent of As and Fs (e.g., 7 percent) and Bs and Ds (e.g., 38 percent). Although some teachers may still use such a system, its use should be discouraged. Measures of achievement in classroom groups seldom yield normally distributed scores. Also, to maintain the same proportion of grades, especially failures, at different grade levels does not take into account that the student population is becoming increasingly select as the failing students are held back or drop out of school.

The relative grading system requires a reliable ranking of students; thus, it is most meaningful when the achievement measures provide a wide range of scores. This makes it possible to draw the lines between grades with greater assurance that misclassifications will be kept to a minimum. Ideally, of course, the spread of scores should be based on the difficulty and complexity of the material learned. For example, an A should not simply represent more knowledge of factual material, but a higher level of understanding, application, and thinking skills. Thus, although norm-referenced interpretation is being utilized, the real meaning of the grades comes from referring back to the nature of the achievement that each grade represents. See Box 10.1 for a summary comparison of absolute and relative grading.

BOX 10.1 • *Absolute Grading and Relative Grading*

ABSOLUTE GRADING

Strengths
1. Grades can be described directly in terms of student performance, without reference to the performance of others.
2. All students can obtain high grades if mastery outcomes are stressed and instruction is effective.

Limitations
1. Performance standards are set in an arbitrary manner and are difficult to specify and justify.
2. Performance standards tend to vary unintentionally due to variations in test difficulty, assignments, student ability, and instructional effectiveness.
3. Grades can be assigned without clear reference to what has been achieved (but, of course, they should not be).

RELATIVE GRADING

Strengths
1. Grades can be easily described and interpreted in terms of rank in a group.
2. Grades distinguish among levels of student performance that are useful in making prediction and selection decisions.

Limitations
1. The percent of students receiving each grade is arbitrarily set.
2. The meaning of a grade varies with the ability of the student group.
3. Grades can be assigned without clear reference to what has been achieved (but, of course, they should not be).

Learning Ability, Improvement, and Effort

In some cases, attempts are made to base grades on achievement in relation to learning ability, the amount of improvement in achievement, or the amount of effort a student puts forth. All of these procedures have problems that distort the meaning of grades.

Grading on the basis of *learning ability* has sometimes been used at the elementary level to motivate students with less ability. At first glance, it seems sensible to give a grade of A to students who are achieving all that they are capable of achieving. There are two major problems with this procedure, however. First, it is difficult, if not impossible, to get a dependable measure of learning ability apart from achievement. Both tests have similar type items and measure similar concepts. Second, the meaning of the grades become distorted. A low-ability student with average performance might receive an A, whereas a high-ability student with average performance receives a grade of C. Obviously, the grades are no longer very meaningful as indicators of achievement.

Using the amount of *improvement* as a basis for grading also has its problems. For one, the difference scores between measures of achievement over short spans of time are very unreliable. For another, students who score high on the entry test cannot possibly get a high grade because little improvement can be shown. Students who know about this grading procedure ahead of time can, of course, do poorly on the first test and be assured of a fairly good grade. This is not an uncommon practice where grades are based on improvement. Finally, the grades lack meaning as indicators of achievement when increase in achievement becomes more important than level of achievement. For example, a low-achieving student with considerable improvement might receive an A, while a high-achieving student with little improvement receives a B or C.

Grading on the basis of *effort,* or adjusting grades for effort, also distorts the meaning of the results. Low-achieving students who put forth great effort receive higher grades than their achievement warrants and high-achieving students who put forth little effort are likely to receive lower grades than deserved. Although such grading seems to serve a motivational function for low-achieving students, the grades become meaningless as measures of the extent to which students are achieving the intended learning outcomes.

In summary, assigning grades that take into account learning ability, amount of improvement, or effort simply contaminates the grades and distorts their meaning as indicators of student achievement. A letter grade is most useful when it represents achievement and only achievement. Other factors may be rated separately on a report card, but they should not be allowed to distort the meaning of the letter grade.

A Combination of Absolute and Relative Grading

Grades should represent the degree of which instructional objectives (i.e., intended learning outcomes) are achieved by students. Some of the objectives of instruction are concerned with minimum essentials that must be mastered if a student is to proceed to the next level of instruction. Other objectives are concerned with learning outcomes that are never fully achieved but toward which students can show varying degrees of progress. The first are called minimal objectives and the second developmental objectives.

Minimal objectives are concerned with the knowledge, skill, and other lower-level learning outcomes that represent the minimum essentials of the course. In order to receive a passing grade, a student must demonstrate that this basic knowledge and skill, which are prerequisite to further learning in the area, have been learned to a satisfactory degree. *Developmental objectives* are concerned with higher-level learning outcomes such as understanding, application, and thinking skills. Although we can identify degrees of progress toward these objectives, we cannot expect to ever fully achieve them. In science, for example, we might expect all students to master basic terms, concepts, and skills, but encourage each student to proceed as far as he or she can in understanding and applying the scientific process and in developing the intellectual skills used by scientists. Similarly, all students in math might be expected to master the fundamental operations, but show wide diversity in problem-solving ability and mathematical reasoning. In all instructional areas there are lower-level objectives that should be mastered by all students and higher-level objectives that provide goals that never can be fully achieved. Thus, with minimal objectives we attempt to obtain a uniformly high level of performance for all students, and with developmental objectives we encourage each student to strive for maximum development.

As indicated earlier, the pass-fail decision should be based on whether the minimal objectives have been mastered. Students demonstrating that they have achieved the minimal objectives, and thus have the necessary prerequisites for success at the next level of instruction, should be passed. Those who do not should fail. This requires an *absolute* judgment, not a relative one. Students should not be failed simply because their achievement places them near the bottom of some group. It is the nature of the achievement that is significant.

Above the pass-fail cutoff point, grades should be assigned on a relative basis. This is because students' scores will tend to be spread out in terms of their degree of development beyond the minimal level. Students cannot be expected to master the more complex learning outcomes described by developmental objectives, but they can show varying degrees of progress toward their attainment. Although it would be ideal to have a scale of achievement ranging from simple to complex so that absolute grading could be used, this is not possible at this time. The best we can do is obtain a spread of student achievement scores in terms of the complexity of the learning outcomes attained and use relative grading. If properly done, a grade of A would represent greater achievement of the higher-level learning outcomes and not simply a high relative position in the group. This would assume, of course, that tests and other assessment techniques would measure a range of achievement from simple to complex, and not just knowledge of factual information and simple skills.

In most cases the school will dictate the grading policy, including the basis on which the grades are to be assigned. Regardless of the system used, it is important to relate the grades back to student achievement so that different grades represent different levels of performance. Letter grades without an achievement referent tend to have little meaning.

Combining Data for Grading

Assigning grades typically involves combining results from various types of assessment, including such things as tests, projects, papers, and laboratory work. If each element is to be included in the grade in terms of its relative importance, the data must be combined in a way that proper weights are used. For example, if we want test scores to count 50 percent, papers 25 percent, and laboratory work 25 percent of the grade, we need a method that will result in grades that reflect this emphasis. The process is simplified if all assessment results are converted to numerical scores first. It is then simply a matter of following a systematic procedure of combining scores.

The method of combining scores so that proper weights are obtained for each element is not as simple as it seems. A common procedure is simply to add scores together if they are to have equal weight and to multiply by 2 if an element is to count twice as much as the other. This typically will not result in each element receiving its proper weight, even if the highest possible scores is the same for all sets of scores. How much influence each element has in a composite score is determined by the spread, or variability, of scores and not the number of total points.

The problem of weighting scores when combining them can be best illustrated with a simple example. Let's assume we only have two measures of achievement and we want to give them equal weight in a grade. Our two sets of achievement scores have score ranges as follows:

Test scores   20 to 100
Laboratory work   30 to 50

If we simply added together a student's test score and score on laboratory work, the grade the student received would be determined largely by the test score because of its wide spread of scores. This can be shown by comparing a student who had the highest test score and lowest laboratory score (Student 1) with a student who had the lowest test score and highest laboratory score (Student 2).

	Student 1	Student 2
Test score	100	20
Laboratory score	30	50
Composite score	130	70

It is quite obvious from the difference in composite scores that the weighting is not equal.

With sets of scores like those for our test and laboratory work, it is not uncommon for teachers to attempt to give them equal weight by making the top possible score equal. This can be done, of course, by multiplying the score on laboratory work by 2, making the highest possible score 100 for both measures. Here is how the two composite scores for our hypothetical students would compare under this system:

	Student 1	Student 2
Test score	100	20
Laboratory score (× 2)	60	100
Composite score	160	120

Our composite scores make clear that equalizing the maximum possible score does not provide equal weights either. As noted earlier, the influence a measure has on the composite score depends on the spread, or variability, of scores. Thus, the greater the spread of scores, the larger the contribution to the composite score.

We can give equal weight to our two sets of scores by using the **range** of scores in each set. Because our test scores have a range of 80 (100–20) and our laboratory scores have a range of 20 (50–30), we must multiply each laboratory score by 4 to equalize the spread of scores and, thus, given them equal weight in the composite score. Here are the composite scores for our two hypothetical students:

	Student 1	Student 2
Test score	100	20
Laboratory score (× 4)	120	200
Composite score	220	220

At last we have a system that gives the two measures equal weight in the composite score. Note that if we wanted to count our test score *twice* as much as the laboratory score, we would multiply it by 2 and the laboratory score by 4. However, if we wanted to have our laboratory score count twice as much as the test score, we would have to multiply each laboratory score by 8. Thus, when we originally multiplied our laboratory scores by 4, we simply adjusted the spread of those scores to match the spread of the test scores. When the two sets of scores have the same range of scores, we can then assign additional weights in terms of their relative importance (see Box 10.2).

The range of scores provides only a rough approximation of score variability but it is satisfactory for most classroom grading purposes. A more dependable basis for weighting grade components can be obtained with the standard deviation.

BOX 10.2 • *Computing Composite Scores for Grading*

1. Select assessments to be included in the composite score and assign percentages.
2. Record desired weight for each assessment.
3. Equate range of scores by using multiplier.
4. Determine weight to apply to each score by multiplying "desired weight" by "multiplier to equate ranges."

Components	Desired Weight	Range of Scores	Multiplier to Equate Ranges	Weight to Apply to Each Score
1. Test scores	50%	2	20 to 100	1	$2 \times 1 = 2$
2. Laboratory work	25%	1	30 to 50	4	$1 \times 4 = 4$
3. Homework	25%	1	0 to 10	8	$1 \times 8 = 8$

COMPUTING THE COMPOSITE SCORES

	Raw Scores			Weighted Scores			Composite
Students	1	2	3	1(×2)	2(×4)	3(×8)	1(w)+2(w)+3(w)
Nguyen	93	42	8	186	168	64	418
Derek	84	45	10	168	180	80	428
Maria	85	47	7	170	188	56	414
Jonus	95	35	10	190	140	80	410

Note that Derek had the highest composite score but would have had the lowest if the raw scores were simply added together, or even if the test score was multiplied by 2 (the desired weight). That is because the measure with the biggest range of scores has the greatest influence on the combined scores unless adjustments are made to equate the spread of scores. Compare Jonus's raw scores and composite scores to Derek's.

Some teachers obtain a composite grade by converting all test scores and other assessments to letter grades, converting the letter grades to numbers (e.g., A = 4, B = 3, C = 2, D = 1, F = 0) and then averaging them for a final grade. When this procedure is followed, information is lost because the data are reduced to only five categories. For example, a student with a high A and high B would receive the same average grade as a student with a low A and a low B. To overcome this problem, pluses and minuses are sometimes added (e.g., A+ = 12, A = 11, A– = 10, B+ = 9, B = 8, B– = 7, etc.). This provides more categories but some information is still lost. A better solution is to use numerical scores on all assessments and then combine these numerical scores into a composite score before assigning grades.

Guidelines for Effective and Fair Grading

Assigning grades that provide a valid measure of student achievement, that have a meaning beyond the classroom in which they are given, and that are considered to be fair by students is a difficult but important part of teaching. The following guidelines provide a framework that should help clarify and standardize the task.

1. *Inform students at the beginning of instruction what grading procedures will be used.* This should include what will be included in the final grade (e.g., tests, projects, laboratory work) and how much weight will be given to each element. It should also include a description, in achievement terms, of what each letter grade represents. A descriptive handout may be helpful.

2. *Base grades on student achievement, and achievement only.* Grades should represent the extent to which the intended learning outcomes were achieved by students. They should *not* be contaminated by student effort, tardiness, misbehavior, or other extraneous factors. These can be reported on separately, but they should not influence the achievement grade. If they are permitted to become a part of the grade, the meaning of the grade as an indicator of achievement is lost.

3. *Base grades on a wide variety of valid assessment data.* All too frequently, grades are based primarily, if not entirely, on test scores. If grades are to be sound indicators of achievement, all important learning outcomes must be assessed and the results included in the final grade. Evaluations of papers, projects, and laboratory work are not as reliable as objective test scores but to eliminate them lowers the validity of the grades.

4. *When combining scores for grading, use a proper weighting technique.* As noted earlier, the influence of a component on the overall grade is determined by the spread, or variability, of the scores. Thus, in combining scores

to obtain a composite for assigning grades, be sure the spread of scores is equalized before weighting and combining them.

5. *Select an appropriate frame of reference for grading.* If the entire instruction is based on mastery learning, it is necessary to use an *absolute* standard for grading and to define the grades in mastery terms. For conventional classroom instruction, the pass-fail distinction should be described in absolute terms and the grades above that determined by relative position in the group. However, these relative letter grades should have achievement referents representing learning outcomes ranging from simple to complex.

6. *Review borderline cases by reexamining all achievement evidence.* When setting cutoff points for each grade, there is typically a student or two just below the cutoff line. Measurement errors alone might be responsible for a student being just below (or above) the line. Also, the composite score may contain a clerical error, or one low test score contributing to the composite score may be due to illness or some other extraneous factor. In any event, it is wise to review the data for borderline cases and make any needed adjustments. When in doubt, fair grading would favor giving the student the higher grade.

Although in this chapter we focused on assigning grades, it does not imply that all student assignments and activities should be graded. Using brief tests, written assignments, and projects as learning tools is frequently more effective if the focus is on detecting and overcoming learning errors rather than on assigning grades. Formative assessment emphasizes this function of assessment results. Whether graded or not, however, all assessments of student achievement should include plans for the effective feedback of results along with suggestions for improving learning. Grading is an important and necessary task in teaching but it is secondary to our main purpose—improving student learning.

Reporting to Students and Parents

The letter grade is typically required for school records, but a more elaborate report is needed for describing achievement to students and parents. One method is to use a reporting system that provides a rating of performance on each of the major learning outcomes of a course of instruction. The example of a Science Performance Report shown in Box 10.3 illustrates a form for this purpose. The report could be made more informative by listing the specific learning outcomes for each major outcome. If the instructional objectives and specific learning outcomes are specified at the beginning of instruction, as they should be, the report form can be easily arranged and shared with students when instruction begins. Just don't make the list so long and

BOX 10.3 • *Science Performance Report*

The circled number indicates the student's level of performance on each of the major learning outcomes being evaluated. The numerical ratings are defined as follows:

4 — Outstanding performance.
3 — Good performance, some improvement needed.
2 — Inadequate performance, needs additional work.
1 — Did not achieve the intended outcome.

4 3 2 1   (a) Knows scientific terms and facts.
4 3 2 1   (b) Understands science concepts and processes.
4 3 2 1   (c) Applies science learning to new situation.
4 3 2 1   (d) Demonstrates reasoning ability.
4 3 2 1   (e) Demonstrates research skills.
4 3 2 1   (f) Demonstrates laboratory proficiency.
4 3 2 1   (g) Solves math problems needed in science.

---

cumbersome that it overwhelms students and confuses parents. It may be helpful to have a committee of teachers, students and parents work out a satisfactory report form for your grade level, department, or the entire school.

A comprehensive report form should contain a place for an achievement grade (uncontaminated by effort, tardiness, misbehavior, or similar factors), a separate grade for effort (if desired), and a list of the intended learning outcomes, work habits, and personal characteristics to be rated. The letter grade is useful as an overall measure of achievement and is easily recorded for administrative uses. But the ratings of intended learning outcomes and related characteristics provide the most valuable information for improving learning and instruction, and reporting progress to students and parents.

Using a Portfolio

As noted in Chapter 9, there is no better way of reporting student achievement than the use of a portfolio. The collected samples of work make clear to students and parents alike what students are learning and how well they are learning it. In conference with students and parents, you can present a summary of the students' achievements and then support it by showing actual samples of the students' work. This provides as comprehensive and complete a report of student achievement as is possible. The conference also provides for two-way communication that permits the student or parent to ask for clarification and to discuss ways to improve performance.

If portfolios are not used in the school, it is still wise to use samples of student work when discussing learning progress and level of achievement with students and parents. Combined with a report form, like the one described earlier, work samples can be very useful in clarifying student achievement.

Summary of Points

1. Grades should represent achievement of the intended learning outcomes and be uncontaminated by other factors.
2. Grades should be assigned in accordance with the grading policies and procedures of the school.
3. Absolute grading requires predetermined standards based on clearly specified learning tasks and measures designed for criterion-referenced interpretation.
4. If instruction is based on a mastery learning program, absolute grading should be used with defined cutoff points and a stated rationale for the selection of the cutoff points.
5. Relative grading is based on the ranking of individuals in a group but relative grades also should have content meaning. Higher grades should represent higher levels of understanding, application, thinking skills, and performance skills.
6. Where relative grading is used, the pass-fail decision still should be determined on an absolute basis. The important question is: Does this student have the minimum knowledge and skill needed to succeed at the next level of instruction?
7. A grading system based on minimal objectives (to determine the pass-fail decision) and developmental objectives that spread students out in terms of the difficulty and complexity of the material learned, provides a good compromise between absolute and relative grading for use in conventional classroom instruction.
8. Basing grades on achievement in relation to learning ability, amount of improvement, or effort will only distort the meaning of grades as measures of achievement.
9. Grades should be based on valid measures of achievement. Validity is built in during the construction of tests and other assessment procedures by designing instruments that measure the intended outcomes of instruction.
10. Grades should be based on a variety of achievement assessments. Test scores should be supplemented by various types of performance assessment that measure the intended outcomes of instruction more directly (e.g., writing samples, laboratory work).

11. Components entering into an overall grade should be adjusted for the spread of scores before weighting them in terms of their importance.

12. Borderline cases should be given the benefit of the doubt and assigned the higher grade, unless a review of the achievement data indicates otherwise.

13. Attitude, effort, misbehavior, and other nonachievement factors might be rated separately but should not be allowed to influence the achievement grade.

14. Some tests and assessment procedures can be used for learning purposes and need not be assigned a grade (e.g., formative use of learning assessments).

15. Reporting to students and parents involves informing them of the extent to which the intended learning outcomes are being achieved. Both detailed performance reports and portfolios are useful for this purpose.

16. Whatever grading and reporting system is used, the procedures should be made clear to students at the beginning of instruction. A descriptive handout may be useful for this.

References and Additional Reading

Airasian, P. W., *Classroom Assessment*, 3rd ed. (New York: McGraw-Hill, 1997).

Linn, R. L., and Gronlund, N. E., *Measurement and Assessment in Teaching*, 8th ed. (Upper Saddle River, NJ: Merrill/Prentice-Hall, 2000).

McMillan, J. H., *Classroom Assessment: Principles and Practices for Effective Instruction*. 2nd ed. (Upper Saddle River, NJ: Merrill/Prentice-Hall, 2001).

Oosterhoff, A. C., *Classroom Applications of Educational Measurement*, 3rd ed. (Upper Saddle River, NJ: Merrill/Prentice-Hall, 2001).

11

Interpreting Standardized Achievement Test Scores

Studying this chapter should enable you to

1. Distinguish between norm-referenced and criterion-referenced interpretation of standardized test results.
2. Describe the basic features of a standardized achievement test.
3. Explain the meaning of each of the scores used in norm-referenced interpretation and list the cautions when interpreting each one.
4. Describe how standard scores are derived from the mean and standard deviation.
5. Convert standard scores to each other and to percentile ranks, using the normal curve.
6. Explain the stanine system and describe the advantages of using stanine scores.
7. Describe the procedures for making criterion-referenced interpretations with standardized tests.
8. List the cautions to observe when making criterion-referenced interpretations with standardized tests.

Standardized achievement tests have been widely used in the schools as a means of determining how well schools are doing. These tests have been primarily norm-referenced tests that compared local student performance to the performance of a representative sample of students in a norm group (e.g., a group of students at the national, regional, or state level). In the past, the test items were selection-type items, primarily multiple choice. In recent years, the tests have been modified to provide for criterion-referenced interpretations as well (e.g., by including more items per task, using open-ended tasks, and providing for interpretation by clusters of tasks). Both types of interpretation will be discussed in turn.

Being able to interpret the various types of norm-referenced test scores and understand how criterion-referenced interpretations are used in standardized tests is important, if the tests are to play a role in the instructional program. It is also important, of course, to understand them well enough to be able to explain them to students and parents. To start with, it is important to keep in mind that norm-referenced interpretation indicates a student's relative level of performance in comparison to others and criterion-referenced interpretation describes the tasks a student can perform.

Features of Standardized Achievement Tests

Standardized achievement tests are designed to determine how well students are achieving a common set of broadly based goals. Well-constructed standardized achievement tests typically have the following features.

1. The content of the test is based on widely used textbooks and curriculum guides.
2. The test items are written by test experts in consultation with subject-matter experts, and are based on a clear set of specifications.
3. The test items are tried out, reviewed, analyzed for difficulty and discriminating power, and either revised or eliminated.
4. The final set of items is selected on the basis of the test specifications.
5. Directions for administering and scoring the test are rigidly prescribed.
6. The test is administered to select groups of students to establish national, regional, or statewide norms for interpretation of the test scores.
7. The final version of the test is published along with a test manual that describes the test's technical qualities and the procedures for administering, scoring, interpreting, and using the results.

Thus, a standardized test measures a standard set of broadly based educational outcomes, uses standard directions and standard scoring procedures, and provides for a comparison of a student's score to that of similar students who have taken the same test under the same conditions. If a **battery of tests** is used, and all tests have been standardized on the same norm group, a student's performance on the different tests can also be compared. On a basic skill battery, for example, we can determine a student's relative level of performance in reading, language, and mathematics. With comparable forms of the test, we can also examine learning progress over a series of grade levels. All of these norm-referenced interpretations and comparisons of standardized test scores requires an understanding of the various types of test scores that are used in describing students' test performance.

Interpreting Norm-Referenced Scores

The score a student receives when a test has been scored according to the directions is called the **raw score.** On a classroom test, this is typically the number of items a student answers correctly. Although raw scores are used in classroom testing, the interpretations and comparisons made with standardized tests require that the raw scores be converted to some type of **derived score.** Comparison of performance on two different tests (e.g., reading and math), for example, require that both tests be on the same scale. Raw scores won't work because the two tests may differ in the number of items in the test and the difficulty of the items. By converting both sets of raw scores to the same derived score scale, we provide a common basis for comparing relative performance. Although there are many different types of derived scores, the most common types used in school achievement testing are:

1. Percentile ranks
2. Grade equivalent scores
3. Standard scores

The raw scores on a standardized test are converted to derived scores during the norming of the test. Attempts are made to obtain norm groups that contain a sample of students like those for whom the test is intended. National **norms,** for example, typically include students from the various geographic regions of the United States, urban and rural schools, and schools of different size. A balance of boys and girls, socioeconomic levels, and ethnic groups is also sought. Thus, national norms should approximate as closely as possible the student population throughout the United States. The same care is typically also followed in obtaining regional, state, and special group norms (e.g., private schools). Despite the care in obtaining norm groups, however, the obtained sample of students only approximates the ideal sample, due to such constraints as the needed cooperation of selected schools to administer the tests and the time limits for obtaining the norm sample.

After the norm groups have been selected and the tests administered and scored, the raw scores are converted to derived scores and presented in the test manual in tables of norms. These tables present the raw scores and derived scores in columns so that a raw score can be converted into a derived score by going across the parallel columns from the raw score to the derived score. Of course, the printout from machine scoring will give both the raw score and the derived score.

Before using the derived scores from a standardized test, it is wise to consider the nature of the norm group. Does the norm group provide a relevant basis for interpreting student performance? How was the norm group obtained? When were the norms obtained? We can obtain the most meaningful norm-referenced interpretation of test scores when the norms are relevant, representative, and up to date.

A final caution. The scores in the norm group should not be viewed as goals or standards. They are simply the scores that a representative group of students have earned on the test. They aid in interpreting and comparing test performance but they do not represent levels of performance to strive for. They are average or typical scores obtained in average or typical schools.

Percentile Ranks

The percentile rank is one of the easiest scores to understand and to interpret to parents. A percentile rank indicates a student's relative position in a group in terms of the percentage of group members scoring at or below the student's raw score. For example, if a raw score of 33 equals a percentile rank of 80, it means 80 percent of the group members had raw scores equal to or lower than 33. By converting raw scores to percentile ranks, the raw scores are put on a scale that has the same meaning with different size groups and for different length tests.

To further clarify the meaning of percentile ranks, Table 11.1 illustrates how raw scores are converted to percentile ranks. The following steps illustrate the procedure.

1. The raw scores are ranked from high to low (column 1).
2. The number of students obtaining each score is listed in the frequency column (column 2).
3. The score frequencies are added from the bottom up (i.e., adding each score frequency to the total frequency of all lower scores) to obtain the cumulative frequency (column 3).
4. Applying the following formula at each score level to get the percentile rank for that raw score (column 4).

$$PR = \frac{CF\ below\ score + 1/2\ of\ frequency\ at\ score}{number\ in\ group\ (N)} \times 100$$

where   PR = percentile rank
   CF = cumulative frequency

To illustrate the computation, let's compute the percentile ranks for two scores.

Score 33 $PR = \dfrac{23 + 1}{30} \times 100 = 80$

Score 30 $PR = \dfrac{17 + .5}{30} \times 100 = 58.3$

TABLE 11.1 *Frequency Distribution and Percentile Ranks for an Objective Test of 40 Items*

1 Test Score	2 Frequency	3 Cumulative Frequency	4 Percentile Rank*
38	1	30	98
37	1	29	95
36	0	28	93
35	2	28	90
34	1	26	85
33	2	25	80
32	3	23	72
31	2	20	63
30	1	18	58
29	4	17	50
28	2	13	40
27	2	11	33
26	2	9	27
25	3	7	18
24	1	4	12
23	0	3	10
22	1	3	8
21	1	2	5
20	0	1	3
19	1	1	2
	N = 30		

*Rounded to nearest whole number.

Percentile ranks are rounded to the nearest whole number, so the percentile rank for the raw score of 30 is listed in Table 11.1 as 58. To be sure you understand this procedure, you can compute the percentile ranks of other raw scores in the table and check your answers.

When interpreting percentile ranks there are a number of cautions to be kept in mind. (1) Percentile ranks describe test performance in terms of the *percentage of persons* earning a lower score and *not* the percentage of items answered correctly. The **percentage correct score** is a criterion-referenced interpretation; **percentile rank** indicates relative standing and, therefore, is a norm-referenced score. (2) Percentile ranks are always specific to a particular group. For example, a percentile rank of 90 in a gifted group represents higher test performance than a percentile rank of 90 in an average group. Thus, whenever we are describing a student's relative performance, knowing the nature of the group is just as important as knowing the student's relative standing. (3) Percentile ranks are not equally spaced on the scale. A difference of 5 percentile ranks near the middle of the distribution of scores represents a smaller difference in test performance than a 5 percentile rank difference at the ends of the distribution. This is because percentile ranks are based on the percentage of persons being surpassed and there is a larger percentage of persons in the middle of a score distribution to surpass than at the ends of the distribution. For example, at the high end of the distribution, a raw score difference of several points will make little difference in percentile rank because there are so few high scores. Although this limits some uses of percentile ranks (e.g., they can't be directly averaged), they remain one of the most useful and easiest to interpret types of derived scores.

Percentile Bands

Some test manuals use **percentile bands** in presenting test norms. Instead of a specific percentile rank for each raw score, a range of percentile ranks is presented. For example, a table of norms may show that a raw score of 52 has a percentile band of 60–64. This allows for the possible error in the test score. The band tells us that we can be fairly certain that a student who earns a raw score of 52 on the test has a relative standing that falls somewhere between the 60th and 64th percentile rank. We cannot be more precise than this because our estimates of test performance (i.e., raw scores) always contain some error, due to such factors as fluctuations in attention, memory, effort, and luck in guessing during testing.

The width of the percentile band is determined by the reliability of the test. With a highly reliable test the band is narrow. With a test of low reliability the band is wide. The width of the band is computed by using the **standard error of measurement.** This is a statistic computed from the reliability coefficient and used to estimate the amount of error in an individual test score (see Chapter 12). These *error* bands can, of course, be computed for raw scores or for any type of derived score. They are sometimes called *confidence* bands because they indicate how much confidence we can have in the score representing a person's test performance. With a narrow band, we are more confident that the score represents the person's "true" or "real" level of achievement.

In addition to using percentile bands to interpret an individual's test performance, percentile bands can also be used to interpret differences in test performance on a battery of tests. In comparing percentile bands for the different tests, we can conclude that where the bands do *not* overlap there is probably a "real" difference in test performance and where they do overlap, the differences are likely to be due to error. For example, the following percentile bands from a test battery for Maria indicate that there is no "real" difference in her performance in reading and language, but she is lower in math.

	Reading	*Language*	*Math*
Maria's percentile bands	70–75	74–79	63–68

The use of percentile bands prevents us from over interpreting small differences in test scores. Test publishers that use percentile bands typically plot them as bars on students' test profiles, making it easy to determine when the ends of the bands overlap and when they don't.

Grade Equivalent Scores

Grade equivalent scores provide another widely used method of describing test performance. They are used primarily at the elementary school level. With these scores, a student's raw score on the test is converted to the grade level at which the score matches the average raw score of students in the norm group. As with other derived scores, tables in the test manual present parallel columns of raw scores and grade equivalents. Thus, all we need to do is consult the table and obtain the grade equivalent for any given raw score. Although it is easy to obtain and is apparently easy to interpret, it is probably one of the most misinterpreted types of score. Let's take a look at what the grade equivalent score means and what it doesn't mean.

To clarify the meaning of grade equivalents, let's assume that we obtained the following grade equivalent scores from a test battery for Dave, who is in the middle of the fourth grade.

Reading   4.5
Language   6.5
Math   7.8

First note that the grade equivalent score is expressed in terms of the grade level and the month in that school year. Thus, Dave's score in reading is equal to the average score earned by students (in the norm group) in the middle of the fourth grade. Because Dave is in the middle of the fourth grade, we interpret his performance in reading as average. In language, Dave is two years advanced, and in math, he is more than three years advanced. Does that mean that Dave can do the work at these levels? No, it most likely means that he does fourth-grade work in these areas faster and more efficiently than other fourth-graders. The tests probably did not include sixth- and seventh-grade material. The same misinterpretations can occur with low grade equivalents. If Dave had a math score of 2.0, for example, it wouldn't mean he could only do second-grade math problems. It would more likely mean that he did fourth-grade problems slower and with more errors than other fourth-graders. High and low grade equivalent scores are typically obtained by extrapolation and do not represent average scores earned by those groups. This is often necessary because students at lower grade levels may not have the knowledge and skill needed to take the test and students at higher grade levels may have moved beyond the types of skills measured by the test.

Grade equivalent scores provide a simple method of interpreting test performance, but when using them and interpreting them to parents, the following common misinterpretations should be avoided.

1. They are *not* standards to be achieved but simply the average scores of students in the norm group.
2. They do *not* indicate the grade level at which a student can do the work.
3. Extremely high and low grade equivalent scores are *not* as dependable indicators of test performance as those near the student's grade level.

In addition to these cautions to be observed when interpreting an individual's grade equivalent scores, a comparison of scores on tests in a test battery requires an additional caution. Growth in basic skills, for example, is uneven. In reading, growth is more rapid than in math, which depends more directly on the skills taught in school. Thus, a difference of a year in grade equivalent scores represents a larger difference in achievement on a reading test than on a math test. In addition, growth in achievement tends to slow down at different times for different skills, and when growth slows down, the differences in achievement between grade equivalent scores become smaller. Both the variations in growth of skills from one area to another and the variations in patterns of growth over time contribute to the unevenness of the units on our grade equivalent score scale. In comparing a student's grade equivalent scores on different tests from a test battery, it may be wise to look at the norm table to see how the raw scores spread out on each test. A high or low grade equivalent score might be discounted if the difference from other grade equivalent scores is based on relatively few raw score points.

Standard Scores

A **standard score** describes test performance in terms of how far a raw score is above or below average. It is expressed in units that are computed from the mean and the standard deviation of a set of scores. We are all familiar with the use of the **mean** as an average. It is obtained by summing the test scores and dividing by the number of scores. The standard deviation indicates the spread of scores in a set. The computation for obtaining the standard deviation is shown in Box 11.1, but that does not help us understand its meaning or its use in interpreting standard scores. This can best be done by describing its properties and showing how it is used as the basic unit for the various types of standard scores.

BOX 11.1 • *Computation of the Standard Deviation Using a Hand Calculator*

Steps to Follow
1. Square each score in the set.
2. Add these squared values to obtain a total.
3. Divide the total by the number of scores in the set.
4. Square the mean of the set of scores.
5. Subtract the squared mean in step 4 from the result obtained in step 3.
6. Take the square root of the difference obtained in step 5. This is the standard deviation (*SD* or *s*).

Formula for the Computational Steps

$$SD = \sqrt{\frac{\Sigma X^2}{N} - M^2}$$

where Σ = "sum of"
            X = a test score
            N = number of scores
            M = mean
            $\sqrt{}$ = "square root of"

The standard deviation (*SD* or *s*) is an important and widely applicable statistic in testing. In addition to its use as a basic unit in standard scores, it also serves as a basis for computing reliability coefficients and the standard error of measurement, as we shall see in the next chapter.

The Mean, Standard Deviation, and Normal Curve

The mean and the standard deviation can probably be best understood in terms of the **normal curve,** although a normal distribution is not required for computing them. The normal curve is a symmetrical bell-shaped curve based on a precise mathematical equation. Scores distributed according to the normal curve are concentrated near the mean and decrease in frequency the further one departs from the mean. A sample normal curve is presented in Figure 11.1.

It will be noted in Figure 11.1 that the mean falls at the exact center of a normal distribution. Note also that when the normal curve is divided into standard deviation (*SD*) units, which are equal distances along the baseline of the curve, each portion under the curve contains a fixed percentage of cases. Thus, 34 percent of the cases fall between the mean and +1 *SD*, 14 percent

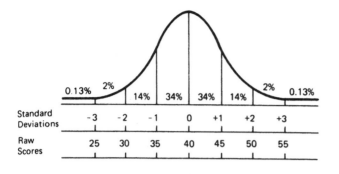

FIGURE 11.1   Normal curve with the approximate percentage of cases within each interval (percentages have been rounded).

between +1 *SD* and +2 *SD,* and 2 percent between +2 *SD* and +3 *SD.* Since the curve is symmetrical, the same percentages, of course, apply to the intervals below the mean. These percentages have been rounded to the nearest whole number, but only a small fraction of a percent (0.13 percent) of the cases fall above and below three standard deviations from the mean. Thus, from a practical standpoint, a normal distribution of scores falls between –3 and +3 standard deviations from the mean.

To aid in understanding the meaning of standard deviation, a set of raw scores with a mean of 40 and a standard deviation of 5 has been placed below the baseline of the curve in Figure 11.1. Note that the mean raw score of 40 has been placed at the zero point and that the distance of one standard deviation is 5 raw score points everywhere along the baseline of the curve. Thus, the point one standard deviation above the mean equals 45 (40 + 5) and the point one standard deviation below the mean equals 35 (40 – 5). In this particular set of scores, then, approximately 68 percent of the scores (about two-thirds) fall between 35 and 45, approximately 96 percent fall between 30 and 50, and approximately 99.7 percent fall between 25 and 55 (the figure shows 100 percent because numbers are rounded).

When the standard deviation is being computed for a set of normally distributed scores, we are essentially determining how far we need to go above (or below) the mean in raw score points to include 34 percent of the cases. The scores obtained with standardized tests typically approximate a normal distribution or are normalized by statistical means and thus permit the types of interpretations we are making here.

z-Scores

A number of standard scores are based on the standard deviation unit. The simplest of these and the one that is basic to the others is the z-score. This score simply indicates, in standard deviation units, how far a given raw score is above or below the mean. The raw score of 45 in Figure 11.1, for example, would be assigned a z-score of 1.0 because it is one standard deviation above the mean. The raw score of 30 in Figure 11.1 would be given a z-score of –2.0 because it is two standard deviations below the mean. The formula for z-scores is:

$$z\text{-score} = \frac{\text{Raw score} - \text{Mean}}{\text{Standard deviation}}$$

For example, z-scores for raw scores of 47 and 36 in Figure 11.1 would be computed as follows:

$$z\text{-score} = \frac{47 - 40}{5} = 1.4 \qquad z\text{-score} = \frac{36 - 40}{5} = -.8$$

Thus, a raw score of 47 is 1.4 standard deviations above the mean and a raw score of 36 is .8 of a standard deviation below the mean.

While used in research, z-scores are seldom used directly in test interpretation because of the use of decimal points and minus signs. Instead, z-scores are converted to other types of standard scores that use only whole numbers and positive values. Such scores are more convenient to use and avoid the possibility of misinterpretation due to a forgotten minus sign.

There are a number of different types of standard scores used in test interpretation. All one needs to do is select an arbitrary mean and standard deviation and convert the z-scores into the standard score units. To illustrate, we will describe the procedure for some common standard scores.

T-Scores

T-scores have a mean of 50 and a standard deviation of 10. They are obtained from z-scores by multiplying the z-score by 10 and adding the result to 50, as shown in the following formula.

$$T\text{-score} = 50 + 10 \, (z\text{-score})$$

Applying the formula to the various z-scores discussed earlier (1.0, –2.0, 1.4, –.8) we would obtain T-scores as follows:

$$T = 50 + 10 \, (1.0) = 60 \qquad T = 50 + 10 \, (-2.0) = 30$$
$$T = 50 + 10 \, (1.4) = 64 \qquad T = 50 + 10 \, (-.8) = 42$$

T-scores can be easily interpreted because they always have the same mean and standard deviation. A T-score of 60 always means one standard deviation above the mean and a *T*-score of 30 always means two standard deviations below the mean. Thus, with the use of *T*-scores, an individual's performance on different tests can be directly compared, and the scores can be combined or averaged without the distortion of different size standard deviations, which occur with the raw scores.

Where a normal distribution can be assumed, *T*-scores can also be interpreted in terms of percentile ranks because, in this case, there is a direct relationship between the two as shown in Figure 11.2. Note that a *T*-score of 30 is equivalent to a percentile rank of 2, a *T*-score of 40 is equivalent to a percentile rank of 16, and so on. This relationship makes it possible to use standard scores for those purposes where equal units are

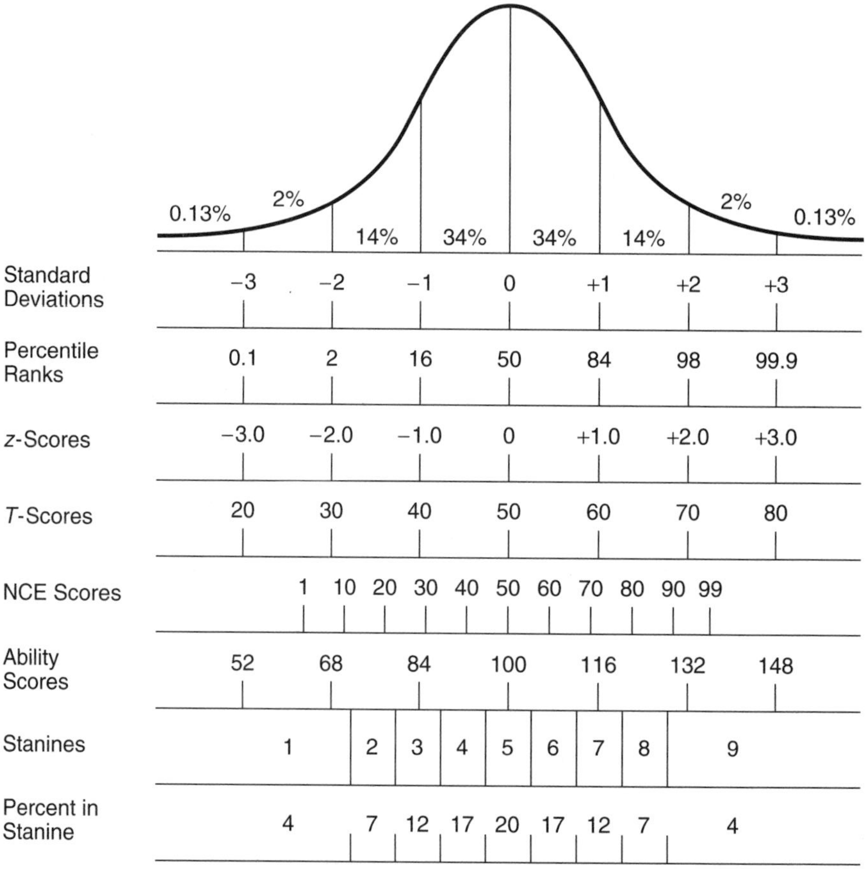

FIGURE 11.2 Corresponding percentile ranks, z-scores, *T*-scores, NCE scores, ability scores, and stanines in a normal distribution.

needed and to use percentile ranks when interpreting test performance to students and parents.

Because *T*-scores and percentile ranks both have a mean of 50 and use similar two-digit numbers, the two types of scores are often confused by those inexperienced in test interpretation. Thus, it is important to keep in mind that percentile rank indicates the percentage of individuals who fall at or below a given score, while a *T*-score indicates how many standard deviation units a given score falls above or below the mean. Note in Figure 11.2 that although percentile ranks and *T*-scores have the same mean value of 50, below the mean percentile ranks are smaller than *T*-scores and above the mean they are larger than *T*-scores. This is accounted for, of course, by the fact that percentile ranks are crowded together in the center of the distribution and spread out at the ends, while *T*-scores provide equal units throughout the distribution of scores.

Normal-Curve Equivalent Scores (NCE)

Another standard score that might be confused with both *T*-scores and percentile ranks is the **normal-curve equivalent score** (NCE). This set of scores also has a mean of 50, but a standard deviation of 21.06. This provides a set of scores with equal units, like the *T*-score, but the scores range from 1 to 99. Percentile ranks also range from 1 to 99, but they do not provide equal units. As can be seen in Figure 11.2, percentile ranks are smaller at the middle of the distribution (e.g., one *SD* = 34%) than at the ends (e.g., one *SD* = 2%). Thus, when interpreting NCE scores, don't confuse them with *T*-scores, which have a more restricted range of scores (typically 20 to 80), or with percentile ranks that have the same range of scores (1 to 99) but are based on unequal units.

Ability Scores

Publishers of achievement test batteries typically administer a test of learning ability (also called cognitive ability, school ability, or intelligence) to the same norm groups as the achievement battery to make comparisons of learning ability and achievement possible. The scores on these tests are now reported as standard scores with a mean of 100 and standard deviation of 16 (15 on some tests). These scores are to be interpreted like any other standard score (see Figure 11.2). A score of 116 means one standard deviation above the mean (percentile rank = 84). These scores were originally called deviation IQs, because they replaced the old ratio IQ (i.e., $\frac{MA}{CA} \times 100$). More recently, however, to avoid the confusion surrounding IQ scores, they have been given more appropriate names, such as school ability scores and standard age scores.

Stanine Scores

Test scores can also be expressed by single-digit standard scores called sta-nines (pronounced *stay-nines*). The stanine scale divides the distribution of raw scores into nine parts (the term **stanine** was derived from *standard nines*). The highest stanine score is 9, the lowest is 1, and stanine 5 is located in the center of the distribution. Each stanine, except 9 and 1, includes a band of raw scores *one-half of a standard deviation wide*. Thus, stanines are standard scores with a mean of 5 and a standard deviation of 2. The distribution of sta-nines and the percentage of cases in each stanine are shown in Figure 11.2.

The nine-point scale is simple to interpret to students and parents because of the single-digit score. It is easy to visualize where a person falls on a nine-point scale, where 5 is average. Because each stanine includes a band of raw scores, there is also less chance that test performance will be overinterpreted. When comparing scores on two different tests in a test bat-tery, a difference of two stanines is typically significant. Thus, in interpreting the following scores for a student, we would conclude that the student is higher in math but there is no difference between reading and language.

> Reading stanine = 5
> Language stanine = 4
> Math stanine   = 7

In addition to the ease of interpretation, stanines provide a simple method for combining and averaging test scores. The conversion of raw scores to stanines puts the scores from different tests on the same standard score scale, with equal units. Thus, they have uniform meaning from one part of the scale to another and from one test to another. A difference between stanine 5 and stanine 7 is the same as a difference between a stanine of 4 and a stanine of 6. A difference of two stanines is also the same, if we are referring to a reading test, a language test, a math test, or any other test. Like other standard scores, they provide equal units that can be readily com-bined. Unlike other standard scores, they are easy to interpret and to explain to others. See Box 11.2 for suggestions on how to interpret test results.

Criterion-Referenced Interpretation

To make standardized achievement test batteries more useful for instruc-tional purposes, some test publishers have modified the multiple-choice items to include more real-life situations, added open-ended performance tasks, and made provisions for criterion-referenced interpretation of test performance.

BOX 11.2 • *Interpreting Standardized Test Results to Students and Parents*

1. Describe in general terms what the test measures and how it relates to the local curriculum (e.g., The test measures computational skills only. It does not include measures of math reasoning, which is the main focus of our curriculum.).
2. When interpreting percentile ranks, keep the description simple (e.g., The percentile rank of 87 means 87 percent of students in the norm group had lower scores. It is not a percentage-correct score.).
3. When interpreting grade equivalents, make statements that are unlikely to be misinterpreted (e.g., The grade equivalent of 6.5 for a fifth-grader means he can do fifth-grade work as rapidly and efficiently as students in the middle of the sixth grade.).
4. When interpreting stanines, use brief, simple statements (e.g., The stanine of 6 on the reading test is one stanine above average on a scale from 1 to 9, and the stanine of 4 on the math test is one stanine below average.).
5. When interpreting differences between test scores use percentile bands or other ways to take error into account (e.g., The percentile bands for reading and math do not overlap, so there is probably a "real" difference in performance. Or, the stanines indicate a "real" difference because they differ by two stanines.).

One of the best known methods of reporting criterion-referenced test results is the *percentage-correct score.* This simply reports the percentage of test items in a test, or subtest, answered correctly. The report can be for individual students, the class, the school, or the entire school district. Percentage-correct scores for the various school groups are compared to the percentage-correct scores in the national norm sample as one basis for evaluating the schools.

Scores for individuals can also be presented by clusters of items representing a content area, skill, or objective, with an indication of the level of performance (e.g., above average, average, below average). Care must be taken in interpreting these results where a small number of items is included in the item clusters.

Some test batteries provide reports that include standards of performance. The standards are typically set by panels of educators and the report indicates a student level of performance by categories ranging from lack of mastery to superior performance.

When making criterion-referenced interpretations of test performance there are a number of questions to keep in mind.

1. Do the objectives the tests were designed to measure match the school's objectives for these subjects (e.g., routine skills versus reasoning)?
2. Are the skills and content measured by the tests appropriate for the grade levels tested?
3. Did elimination of the easy items from the test, to obtain greater discrimination among students for norm-referenced interpretation, result in inadequate description of what low-achieving students can do?
4. Was there a sufficient number of test items in each item cluster to permit criterion-referenced interpretation?
5. Was the procedure in setting performance standards adequate for this type of interpretation?

Criterion-referenced interpretation of standardized tests can be useful in classroom instruction but they must be cautiously made.

Summary of Points

1. Standardized achievement tests have been widely used in the schools to determine how student performance compared to that of a sample of students (i.e., a norm group) at the national, regional, or state level.
2. Standardized tests were carefully constructed to fit a set of test specifications, tried out and improved, and administered to a norm group for norm-referenced test interpretation.
3. The most common types of norm-referenced scores used with standardized tests are percentile ranks, grade equivalent scores, and various types of standard scores.
4. A percentile rank indicates relative position in a group in terms of the percentage of group members scoring at or below a given score. It should not be confused with the percentage of items answered correctly (a criterion-referenced interpretation).
5. Percentile bands are used in reporting test performance to allow for possible error in test scores. The width of the band indicates the amount of error to allow for during interpretation, and it prevents the overinterpretation of small differences in test scores.
6. A grade equivalent score indicates relative test performance in terms of the grade level at which the student's raw score matches the average score earned by the norm group. Thus, a grade equivalent score of 4.5 indicates performance equal to the average student in the middle of the fourth grade. Grade equivalent scores are easy to interpret but they are subject to numerous misinterpretations.

7. Standard scores are based on the mean (*M*) and standard deviation (*SD*) of a set of scores. To fully understand them it is necessary to understand the meaning of these statistics.
8. Standard scores indicate the number of standard deviations a raw score falls above and below the mean. They are more difficult to understand and interpret to others but they have the advantage of providing equal units.
9. The standard scores discussed in this chapter have the following means (*M*) and standard deviations (*SD*). The third column shows the score for one standard above the mean.

	M	*SD*	*+1SD*
z-scores	0	1	1
T-scores	50	10	60
NCE scores	50	21.06	71
Ability scores	100	16	116
Stanines	5	2	7

10. In a normal distribution, any standard score can be converted to percentile rank for easy interpretation. For example, one standard deviation above the mean (see column 3) has a percentile rank of 84, no matter what type of standard score is used to express test performance.
11. Because *T*-scores, NCE scores, and percentile ranks all have a mean of 50 and use similar two-digit numbers, care must be taken not to confuse them when interpreting test performance.
12. Stanines are single-digit standard scores that range from 1 to 9. They are easily explained to students and parents and a difference of two stanines typically indicates a significant (i.e., "real") difference in test performance.
13. Stanines and percentile ranks using percentile bands are the two types of scores that are favored when interpreting test results to others and judging differences between test scores.
14. Criterion-referenced interpretations of test performance have been added to many standardized tests. These include percentage correct scores, the use of performance standards and interpretation by item clusters representing a content area, skill, or objective.
15. Criterion-referenced interpretations of standardized tests require a check on how well the objectives, content, and skills of the test match the local instructional program; whether the construction of the test favors criterion-referenced interpretation; whether there is a sufficient number of test items for each type of interpretation; and how the performance standards are determined.

References and Additional Reading

American Educational Research Association, *Standards for Educational and Psychological Testing* (Washington, DC: AERA, 1999).

Chase, C. I., *Contemporary Assessment for Educators* (New York: Longman, 1999).

Linn, R. L., and Gronlund, N. E., *Measurement and Assessment in Teaching*, 8th ed. (Upper Saddle River, NJ: Merrill/Prentice-Hall, 2000).

Lyman, H. B., *Test Scores and What They Mean*, 6th ed. (Boston: Allyn and Bacon, 1998).

Oosterhoff, A. C. *Classroom Applications of Educational Measurement*, 3rd ed. (Upper Saddle River, NJ: Merrill/Prentice-Hall, 2001).

12

Validity and Reliability

Studying this chapter should enable you to

1. Distinguish between validity and reliability.
2. Describe the essential features of the concept of validity.
3. Describe how content-related evidence of validity is obtained.
4. List factors that can lower the validity of achievement assessments.
5. Describe procedures for obtaining criterion-related evidence of validity.
6. Describe procedures for obtaining construct-related evidence of validity.
7. Describe the role of consequences of using an assessment procedure on its validity.
8. Describe the methods for estimating test reliability and the type of information provided by each.
9. Describe how the standard error of measurement is computed and interpreted.
10. Explain how to determine the reliability of a performance-based assessment.

The two most important questions to ask about a test or other assessment procedure are: (1) to what extent will the interpretation of the results be appropriate, meaningful, and useful?, and (2) to what extent will the results be free from errors? The first question is concerned with *validity*, the second with *reliability*. An understanding of both concepts is essential to the effective construction, selection, interpretation, and use of tests and other assessment instruments. Validity is the most important quality to consider in the preparation and use of assessment procedures. First and foremost, we want the results to provide a representative and relevant measure of the achievement domain under consideration. Our second consideration is reliability, which refers to the consistency of our assessment results. For example, if we tested individuals at a different time, or with a different sample of equivalent items, we would like to obtain approximately the same results. This consistency of results is important for two reasons. (1) Unless the results are fairly stable we cannot expect them to be valid. For example, if an individual scored high on a test one time and low another time, it would be impossible to validly describe the achievement. (2) Consistency of results indicates smaller errors of measurement and, thereby, more dependable results. Thus, reliability provides the consistency needed to obtain validity and enables us to interpret assessment results with greater confidence.

Although it is frequently unnecessary to make elaborate validation and reliability studies of informal assessment procedures, an understanding of these concepts provides a conceptual framework that can serve as a guide for more effective construction of assessment instruments, more effective selection of standardized tests, and more appropriate interpretation and use of assessment results.

Validity

Validity is concerned with the interpretation and use of assessment results. For example, if we infer from an assessment that students have achieved the intended learning outcomes, we would like some assurance that our tasks provided a relevant and representative measure of the outcomes. If we infer that the assessment is useful for predicting or estimating some other performance, we would like some credible evidence to support that interpretation. If we infer that our assessment indicates that students have good "reasoning ability," we would like some evidence to support the fact that the results actually reflect that construct. If we infer that our use of an assessment had positive effects (e.g., increased motivation) and no adverse effects (e.g., poor study habits) on students, we would like some evidence concerning the consequences of its use. These are the kinds of considerations we are concerned with when considering the validity of assessment results (see the summary in Figure 12.1).

The meaning of *validity* in interpreting and using assessment results can be grasped most easily by reviewing the following characteristics.

1. Validity is *inferred* from available evidence (not measured).
2. Validity depends on *many different types* of evidence.
3. Validity is expressed by *degree* (high, moderate, low).
4. Validity is specific to a particular *use*.
5. Validity refers to the *inferences drawn,* not the instrument.
6. Validity is a *unitary concept.*
7. Validity is concerned with the *consequences of using the assessments.*

Describing validity as a unitary concept is a basic change in how validity is viewed. The traditional view that there were several different "types of

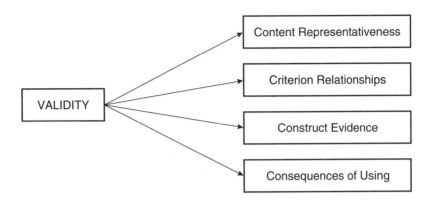

FIGURE 12.1   Types of considerations in determining the validity of assessment results.

validity" has been replaced by the view that validity is a single, unitary concept that is based on various forms of evidence. The former "types of validity" (content, criterion-related, and construct) are now simply considered to be convenient categories for accumulating evidence to support the validity of an interpretation. Thus, we no longer speak of "content validity," but of "content-related evidence" of validity. Similarly, we speak of "criterion-related evidence" and "construct-related evidence."

For some interpretations of assessment results only one or two types of evidence may be critical, but an *ideal* validation would include evidence from all four categories. We are most likely to draw valid inferences from assessment results when we have a full understanding of: (1) the nature of the assessment procedure and the specifications that were used in developing it, (2) the relation of the assessment results to significant criterion measures, (3) the nature of the psychological characteristic(s) or construct(s) being assessed, and (4) the consequences of using the assessment. Although in many practical situations the evidence falls short of this ideal, we should gather as much relevant evidence as is feasible within the constraints of the situation. We should also look for the various types of evidence when evaluating standardized tests (see Table 12.1).

Content-Related Evidence

Content-related evidence of validity is critical when we want to use performance on a set of tasks as evidence of performance on a larger domain of tasks. Let's assume, for example, that we have a list of 500 words that we expect our students to be able to spell correctly at the end of the school year. To test their spelling ability, we might give them a 50-word spelling test. Their performance on these words is important only insofar as it provides

TABLE 12.1   *Basic Approaches to Validation*

Type of Evidence	Question to Be Answered
Content-Related	How adequately does the sample of assessment tasks represent the domain of tasks to be measured?
Criterion-Related	How accurately does performance on the assessment (e.g., test) predict future performance (predictive study) or estimate present performance (concurrent study) on some other valued measure called a criterion?
Construct-Related	How well can performance on the assessment be explained in terms of psychological characteristics?
Consequences	How well did use of the assessment serve the intended purpose (e.g., improve performance) and avoid adverse effects (e.g., poor study habits)?

evidence of their ability to spell the 500 words. Thus, our spelling test would provide a valid measure to the degree to which it provided an adequate sample of the 500 words it represented. If we selected only easy words, only difficult words, or only words that represented certain types of common spelling errors, our test would tend to be unrepresentative and thus the scores would have low validity. If we selected a balanced sample of words that took these and similar factors into account, our test scores would provide a representative measure of the 500 spelling words and thereby provide for high validity.

It should be clear from this discussion that the key element in content-related evidence of validity is the adequacy of the *sampling.* An assessment is always a sample of the many tasks that could be included. Content validation is a matter of determining whether the sample of tasks is representative of the larger domain of tasks it is supposed to represent.

Content-related evidence of validity is especially important in achievement assessment. Here we are interested in how well the assessment measures the intended learning outcomes of the instruction. We can provide greater assurance that an assessment provides valid results by (1) identifying the learning outcomes to be assessed, (2) preparing a plan that specifies the sample of tasks to be used, and (3) preparing an assessment procedure that closely fits the set of specifications. These are the best procedures we have for ensuring the assessment of a representative sample of the domain of tasks encompassed by the intended learning outcomes.

Although the focus of content-related evidence of validity is on the adequacy of the sampling, a valid interpretation of the assessment results assumes that the assessment was properly prepared, administered, and scored. Validity can be lowered by inadequate procedures in any of these areas (see Box 12.1). Thus, validity is "built in" during the planning and preparation stages and maintained by proper administration and scoring. Throughout this book we have described how to prepare assessments that provide valid results, even though we have not used the word validity as each procedure was discussed.

The makers of standardized test follow these same systematic procedures in building achievement tests, but the content and learning outcomes included in the test specifications are more broadly based than those used in classroom assessment. Typically, they are based on the leading textbooks and the recommendations of various experts in the area being covered by the test. Therefore, a standardized achievement test may be representative of a broad range of content but be unrepresentative of the domain of content taught in a particular school situation. To determine relevance to the local situation, it is necessary to evaluate the sample of test items in light of the content and skills emphasized in the instruction.

In summary, content-related evidence of validity is of major concern in achievement assessment, whether you are developing or selecting the assessment procedure. When constructing a test, for example, content relevance and representativeness are built in by following a systematic procedure for specifying and selecting the sample of test items, constructing high quality items, and arranging the test for efficient administration and scoring. In test selection, it is a matter of comparing the test sample to the domain of tasks to be measured and determining the degree of correspondence between them. Similar care is needed when preparing and using performance assessments. Thus, content-related evidence of validity is obtained primarily by careful, logical analysis.

BOX 12.1 • *Factors That Lower the Validity of Assessment Results*

1. Tasks that provide an inadequate sample of the achievement to be assessed.
2. Tasks that do not function as intended, due to use of improper types of tasks, lack of relevance, ambiguity, clues, bias, inappropriate difficulty, or similar factors.
3. Improper arrangement of tasks and unclear directions.
4. Too few tasks for the types of interpretation to be made (e.g., interpretation by objective based on a few test items).
5. Improper administration—such as inadequate time allowed and poorly controlled conditions.
6. Judgmental scoring that uses inadequate scoring guides, or objective scoring that contains computational errors.

Criterion-Related Evidence

There are two types of studies used in obtaining criterion-related evidence of validity. These can be explained most clearly using test scores, although they could be used with any type of assessment result. The first type of study is concerned with the use of test performance to predict future performance on some other valued measure called a *criterion*. For example, we might use scholastic aptitude test scores to predict course grades (the criterion). For obvious reasons, this is called a *predictive* study. The second type of study is concerned with the use of test performance to estimate current performance on some criterion. For instance, we might want to use a test of study skills to estimate what the outcome would be of a careful observation of students in an actual study situation (the criterion). Since with this procedure both measures (test and criterion) are obtained at approximately the same time, this type of study is called a *concurrent* study.

Although the value of using a predictive study is rather obvious, a question might be raised concerning the purpose of a concurrent study. Why would anyone want to use test scores to estimate performance on some other measure that is to be obtained at the same time? There are at least three good reasons for doing this. First, we may want to check the results of a newly constructed test against some existing test that has a considerable amount of validity evidence supporting it. Second, we may want to substitute a brief, simple testing procedure for a more complex and time-consuming measure. For example, our test of study skills might be substituted for an elaborate rating system if it provided a satisfactory estimate of study performance. Third, we may want to determine whether a testing procedure has *potential* as a predictive instrument. If a test provides an unsatisfactory estimate of current performance, it certainly cannot be expected to predict future performance on the same measure. On the other hand, a satisfactory estimate of present performance would indicate that the test may be useful in predicting future performance as well. This would inform us that a predictive study would be worth doing.

The key element in both types of criterion-related study is the *degree of relationship* between the two sets of measures: (1) the test scores and (2) the criterion to be predicted or estimated. This relationship is typically expressed by means of a correlation coefficient or an expectancy table.

Correlation Coefficients.   Although the computation of correlation coefficients is beyond the scope of this book, the concept of correlation can easily be grasped. A **correlation coefficient** (r) simply indicates the degree of relationship between two sets of measures. A *positive* relationship is indicated when high scores on one measure are accompanied by high scores on the other; low scores on the two measures are similarly associated. A *negative* relationship is indicated when high scores on one measure are accompanied by low scores on the other. The extreme degrees of relationship it is possible to obtain between two sets of scores are indicated by the following values:

1.00 = perfect positive relationship
.00 = no relationship
−1.00 = perfect negative relationship

When a correlation coefficient is used to express the degree of relationship between a set of test scores and some criterion measure, it is called a *validity coefficient.* For example, a validity coefficient of 1.00 applied to the relationship between a set of aptitude test scores (the predictor) and a set of achievement test scores (the criterion) would indicate that each individual in the group had exactly the same relative standing on both measures, and would thereby provide a perfect prediction from the aptitude scores to the achievement scores. Most validity coefficients are smaller than this, but the extreme positive relationship provides a useful bench mark for evaluating validity coefficients. The closer the validity coefficient approaches 1.00, the higher the degree of relationship and, thus, the more accurate our predictions of each individual's success on the criterion will be.

A more realistic procedure for evaluating a validity coefficient is to compare it to the validity coefficients that are *typically* obtained when the two measures are correlated. For example, a validity coefficient of .40 between a set of aptitude test scores and achievement test scores would be considered small because we typically obtain coefficients in the .50 to .70 range for these two measures. Therefore, validity coefficients must be judged on a relative basis, the larger coefficients being favored. To use validity coefficients effectively, one must become familiar with the size of the validity coefficients that are typically obtained between various pairs of measures under different conditions (e.g., the longer the time span between measures, the smaller the validity coefficient).

Expectancy Table. The expectancy table is a simple and practical means of expressing criterion-related evidence of validity and is especially useful for making predictions from test scores. The **expectancy table** is simply a twofold chart with the test scores (the predictor) arranged in categories down the left side of the table and the measure to be predicted (the criterion) arranged in categories across the top of the table. For each category of scores on the *predictor,* the table indicates the percentage of individuals who fall within each category of the *criterion.* An example of an expectancy table is presented in Table 12.2.

Note in Table 12.2 that of those students who were in the above-average group (stanines 7, 8, and 9) on the test scores, 43 percent received a grade of A, 43 percent a B, and 14 percent a C. Although these percentages are based on this particular group, it is possible to use them to predict the future performance of other students in this science course. Hence, if a student falls in

TABLE 12.2 *Expectancy Table Showing the Relation between Scholastic Aptitude Scores and Course Grades for 30 Students in a Science Course*

Grouped Scholastic Aptitude Scores (Stanines)	Percentage in Each Score Category Receiving Each Grade				
	E	D	C	B	A
Above Average (7, 8, 9)			14	43	43
Average (4, 5, 6)		19	37	25	19
Below Average (1, 2, 3)	57	29	14		

the above-average group on this scholastic aptitude test, we might predict that he or she has 43 chances out of 100 of earning an A, 43 chances out of 100 of earning a B, and 14 chances out of a 100 of earning a C in this particular science course. Such predictions are highly tentative, of course, due to the small number of students on which this expectancy table was built. Teachers can construct more dependable tables by accumulating data from several classes over a period of time.

Expectancy tables can be used to show the relationship between any two measures. Constructing the table is simply a matter of (1) grouping the scores on each measure into a series of categories (any number of them), (2) placing the two sets of categories on a twofold chart, (3) tabulating the number of students who fall into each position in the table (based on the student's standing on both measures), and (4) converting these numbers to percentages (of the total number in that row). Thus, the expectancy table is a clear way of showing the relationship between sets of scores. Although the expectancy table is more cumbersome to deal with than a correlation coefficient, it has the special advantage of being easily understood by persons without knowledge of statistics. Thus, it can be used in practical situations to clarify the predictive efficiency of a test.

Construct-Related Evidence

The construct-related category of evidence focuses on assessment results as a basis for inferring the possession of certain psychological characteristics. For example, we might want to describe a person's reading comprehension, reasoning ability, or mechanical aptitude. These are all hypothetical qualities, or *constructs*, that we assume exist in order to explain behavior. Such theoretical constructs are useful in describing individuals and in predicting how they will act in many different specific situations. To describe a person as being highly intelligent, for example, is useful because that term carries with it a series of associated meanings that indicate what the individual's behavior is likely to be under various conditions. Before we can interpret assessment results in terms of these broad behavior descriptions, however, we must first establish that the constructs that are presumed to be reflected in the scores actually do account for differences in performance.

Construct-related evidence of validity for a test includes (1) a description of the theoretical framework that specifies the nature of the construct to be measured, (2) a description of the development of the test and any aspects of measurement that may affect the meaning of the test scores (e.g., test format), (3) the pattern of relationship between the test scores and other significant variables (e.g., high correlations with similar tests and low correlations with tests measuring different constructs), and (4) any other type of evidence that contributes to the meaning of the test scores (e.g., analyzing the mental process used in responding, determining the predictive effectiveness of the test). The specific types of evidence that are most critical for a particular test depend on the nature of the construct, the clarity of the theoretical framework, and the uses to be made of the test scores. Although the gathering of construct-related evidence of validity can be endless, in practical situations it is typically necessary to limit the evidence to that which is most relevant to the interpretations to be made.

The construct-related category of evidence is the broadest of the three categories. Evidence obtained in both the content-related category (e.g., representativeness of the sample of tasks) and the criterion-related category (e.g., how well the scores predict performance on specific criteria) are also relevant to the construct-related category because they help to clarify the meaning of the assessment results. Thus, the construct-related category encompasses a variety of types of evidence, including that from content-related and criterion-related validation studies (see Figure 12.2).

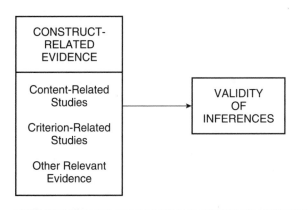

FIGURE 12.2   Construct validation includes all categories of evidence.

The broad array of evidence that might be considered can be illustrated by a test designed to measure mathematical reasoning ability. Some of the evidence we might consider is:

1. Compare the sample of test tasks to the domain of tasks specified by the conceptual framework of the construct. Is the sample relevant and representative (content-related evidence)?
2. Examine the test features and their possible influence on the meaning of the scores (e.g., test format, directions, scoring, reading level of items). Is it possible that some features might distort the scores?
3. Analyze the mental process used in answering the questions by having students "think aloud" as they respond to each item. Do the items require the intended reasoning process?
4. Determine the internal consistency of the test by intercorrelating the test items. Do the items seem to be measuring a single characteristic (in this case mathematical reasoning)?
5. Correlate the test scores with the scores of other mathematical reasoning tests. Do they show a high degree of relationship?
6. Compare the scores of known groups (e.g., mathematical majors and nonmajors). Do the scores differentiate between the groups as predicted?
7. Compare the scores of students before and after specific training in mathematical reasoning. Do the scores change as predicted from the theory underlying the construct?
8. Correlate the scores with grades in mathematics. Do they correlate to a satisfactory degree (criterion-related evidence)?

Other types of evidence could be added to this list, but it is sufficiently comprehensive to make clear that no single type of evidence is adequate. Interpreting test scores as a measure of a particular construct involves a comprehensive study of the development of the test, how it functions in a variety of situations, and how the scores relate to other significant measures.

Assessment results are, of course, influenced by many factors other than the construct they are designed to measure. Thus, construct validation is an attempt to account for all possible influences on the scores. We might, for example, ask to what extent the scores on our mathematical reasoning test are influenced by reading comprehension, computation skill, and speed. Each of these factors would require further study. Were attempts made to eliminate such factors during test development by using simple vocabulary, simple computations, and liberal time limits? To what extent do the test scores correlate with measures of reading comprehension and computational skill? How do students' scores differ under different time limits? Answers to these and similar questions will help us to determine how well the test scores reflect the construct we are attempting to measure and the extent to which other factors might be influencing the scores.

Construct validation, then, is an attempt to clarify and verify the inferences to be made from assessment results. This involves a wide variety of procedures and many different types of evidence (including both content-related and criterion-related). As evidence accumulates from many different sources, our interpretations of the results are enriched and we are able to make them with great confidence.

Consequence of Using Assessment Results

Validity focuses on the inferences drawn from assessment results with regard to specific uses. Therefore, it is legitimate to ask, What are the consequences of using the assessment? Did the assessment improve learning, as intended, or did it contribute to adverse effects (e.g., lack of motivation, memorization, poor study habits)? For example, assessment procedures that focus on simple learning outcomes only (e.g., knowledge of facts) cannot provide valid evidence of reasoning and application skills, are likely to narrow the focus of student learning, and tend to reinforce poor learning strategies (e.g., rote learning). Thus, in evaluating the validity of the assessment used, one needs to look at what types of influence the assessments have on students. The following questions provide a general framework for considering some of the possible consequences of assessments on students.

1. Did use of the assessment improve motivation?
2. Did use of the assessment improve performance?
3. Did the use of the assessment improve self-assessment skills?
4. Did the use of the assessment contribute to transfer of learning to related areas?
5. Did the use of the assessment encourage independent learning?
6. Did the use of the assessment encourage good study habits?
7. Did the use of the assessment contribute to a positive attitude toward schoolwork?
8. Did use of the assessment have an adverse effect in any of the above areas?

Judging the consequences of using the various assessment procedures is an important role of the teacher, if the results are to serve their intended purpose of improving learning. Both testing and performance assessments are most likely to have positive consequences when they are designed to assess a broad range of learning outcomes, they give special emphasis to complex learning outcomes, they are administered and scored (or judged) properly, they are used to identify students' strengths and weaknesses in learning, and the students view the assessments as fair, relevant, and useful for improving learning.

Reliability

Reliability refers to the consistency of assessment results. Would we obtain about the same results if we used a different sample of the same type task? Would we obtain about the same results if we used the assessment at a different time? If a performance assessment is being rated, would different raters rate the performance the same way? These are the kinds of questions we are concerned about when we are considering the reliability of assessment results. Unless the results are generalizable over similar samples of tasks, time periods, and raters, we are not likely to have great confidence in them.

Because the methods for estimating reliability differ for tests and performance assessments these will be treated separately.

Estimating the Reliability of Test Scores

The score an individual receives on a test is called the *obtained score, raw score,* or *observed score.* This score typically contains a certain amount of error. Some of this error may be *systematic error,* in that it consistently inflates or lowers the obtained score. For example, readily apparent clues in several test items might cause all students' scores to be higher than their achievement would warrant, or short time limits during testing might cause all students' scores to be lower than their "real achievement." The factors causing systematic errors are mainly due to inadequate testing practices. Thus, most of these errors can be eliminated by using care in constructing and administering tests. Removing systematic errors from test scores is especially important because they have a direct effect on the validity of the inferences made from the scores.

Some of the error in obtained scores is *random error,* in that it raises and lowers scores in an unpredictable manner. Random errors are caused by such things as temporary fluctuations in memory, variations in motivation and concentration from time to time, carelessness in marking answers, and luck in guessing. Such factors cause test scores to be inconsistent from one measurement to another. Sometimes an individual's obtained score will be higher than it should be and sometimes it will be lower. Although these errors are difficult to control and cannot be predicted with accuracy, an estimate of their influence can be obtained by various statistical procedures. Thus, when we talk about estimating the *reliability* of test scores or the amount of *measurement error* in test scores, we are referring to the influence of random errors.

Reliability refers to the *consistency* of test scores from one measurement to another. Because of the ever present measurement error, we can expect a certain amount of variation in test performance from one time to another, from one sample of items to another, and from one part of the test to another. Reliability measures provide an estimate of how much variation we might expect under different conditions. The reliability of test scores is typically reported by means of a *reliability coefficient* or the *standard error of measurement* that is derived from it. Since both methods of estimating reliability require score variability, the procedures to be discussed are useful primarily with tests designed for norm-referenced interpretation.

As we noted earlier, a correlation coefficient expressing the relationship between a set of test scores and a criterion measure is called a *validity coefficient*. A *reliability coefficient* is also a correlation coefficient, but it indicates the correlation between two sets of measurements taken from the same procedure. We may, for example, administer the same test twice to a group, with a time interval in between (*test-retest* method); administer two equivalent forms of the test in close succession (*equivalent-forms* method); administer two equivalent forms of the test with a time interval in between (*test-retest with equivalent forms* method); or administer the test once and compute the consistency of the response within the test (*internal-consistency* method). Each of these methods of obtaining reliability provides a different type of information. Thus, reliability coefficients obtained with the different procedures are not interchangeable. Before deciding on the procedure to be used, we must determine what type of reliability evidence we are seeking. The four basic methods of estimating reliability and the type of information each provides are shown in Table 12.3.

TABLE 12.3   *Methods of Estimating Reliability of Test Scores*

Method	Type of Information Provided
Test-retest method	The stability of test scores over a given period of time.
Equivalent-forms method	The consistency of the test scores over different forms of the test (that is, different samples of items).
Test-retest with equivalent forms	The consistency of test scores over *both* a time interval and different forms of the test.
Internal-consistency methods	The consistency of test scores over different parts of the test.

Note: Scorer reliability should also be considered when evaluating the responses to *supply-type* items (for example, essay tests). This is typically done by having the test papers scored independently by two scorers and then correlating the two sets of scores. Agreement among scorers, however, is not a substitute for the methods of estimating reliability shown in the table.

Test-Retest Method   The test-retest method requires administering the same form of the test to the same group after some time interval. The time between the two administrations may be just a few days or several years. The length of the time interval should fit the type of interpretation to be made from the results. Thus, if we are interested in using test scores only to group students for more effective learning, short-term stability may be sufficient. On the other hand, if we are attempting to predict vocational success or make some other long-range predictions, we would desire evidence of stability over a period of years.

Test-retest reliability coefficients are influenced both by errors within the measurement procedure and by the day-to-day stability of the students' responses. Thus, longer time periods between testing will result in lower reliability coefficients, due to the greater changes in the students. In reporting test-retest reliability coefficients, then, it is important to include the time interval. For example, a report might state: "The stability of test scores obtained on the same form over a three-month period was .90." This makes it possible to determine the extent to which the reliability data are significant for a particular interpretation.

Equivalent-Forms Method   With this method, two equivalent forms of a test (also called **alternate forms** or **parallel forms**) are administered to the same group during the same testing session. The test forms are equivalent in the sense that they are built to measure the same abilities (that is, they are built to the same set of specifications), but for determining reliability it is also important that they be constructed independently. When this is the case, the reliability coefficient indicates the adequacy of the test sample. That is, a high reliability coefficient would indicate that the two independent samples are apparently measuring the same thing. A low reliability coefficient, of course, would indicate that the two forms are measuring different behavior and that therefore both samples of items are questionable.

Reliability coefficients determined by this method take into account errors within the measurement procedures and consistency over different samples of items, but they do not include the day-to-day stability of the students' responses.

Test-Retest Method with Equivalent Forms   This is a combination of both methods. Here, two different forms of the same test are administered with time intervening. This is the most demanding estimate of reliability, since it takes into account all possible sources of variation. The reliability coefficient reflects errors within the testing procedure, consistency over different samples of items, and the day-to-day stability of the students' responses. For most purposes, this is probably the most useful type of reliability, since it enables us to estimate how generalizable the test results are over the various conditions. A high reliability coefficient obtained by this method would indicate that a test score represents not only present test performance but also what test performance is likely to be at another time or on a different sample of equivalent items.

Internal-Consistency Methods   These methods require only a single administration of a test. One procedure, the *split-half* method, involves scoring the odd items and the even items separately and correlating the two sets of scores. This correlation coefficient indicates the degree to which the two arbitrarily selected halves of the test provide the same results. Thus, it reports on the internal consistency of the test. Like the equivalent-forms method, this procedure takes into account errors within the testing procedure and consistency over different samples of items, but it omits the day-to-day stability of the students' responses.

Since the correlation coefficient based on the odd and even items indicates the relationship between two halves of the test, the reliability coefficient for the total test is determined by applying the Spearman-Brown prophecy formula. A simplified version of this formula is as follows:

$$\text{Reliability of total test } = \frac{2 \times \text{reliability for } \frac{1}{2} \text{ test}}{1 + \text{reliability for } \frac{1}{2} \text{ test}}$$

Thus, if we obtained a correlation coefficient of .60 for two halves of a test, the reliability for the total test would be computed as follows:

$$\text{Reliability of total test } = \frac{2 \times .60}{1 + .60} = \frac{1.20}{1.60} = .75$$

This application of the Spearman-Brown formula makes clear a useful principle of test reliability; the reliability of a test can be increased by lengthening it. This formula shows how much reliability will increase when the length of the test is doubled. Application of the formula, however, assumes that the test is lengthened by adding items like those already in the test.

Another internal-consistency method of estimating reliability is by use of the **Kuder-Richardson Formula 20** (KR-20). Kuder and Richardson developed other formulas but this one is probably the most widely used with standardized tests. It requires a single test administration, a determination of the proportion of individuals passing each item, and the standard deviation of the total set of scores. The formula is not especially helpful in understanding how to interpret the scores, but knowing what the coefficient means is important. Basically, the KR-20 is equivalent to an average of all split-half coefficients when the test is split in all possible ways. Where all items in a test are measuring the same thing (e.g., math reasoning), the result should approximate the split-half reliability estimate. Where the test items are measuring a variety of skills or content areas (i.e., less homogeneous), the KR-20 estimate will be lower than the split-half reliability estimate. Thus, the KR-20 method is useful with homogeneous tests but can be misleading if used with a test designed to measure heterogeneous content.

Internal-consistency methods are used because they require that the test be administered only once. They should not be used with speeded tests, however, because a spuriously high reliability estimate will result. If speed is an important factor in the testing (that is, if the students do not have time to attempt all the items), other methods should be used to estimate reliability.

Standard Error of Measurement   The standard error of measurement is an especially useful way of expressing test reliability because it indicates the amount of error to allow for when interpreting individual test scores. The standard error is derived from a reliability coefficient by means of the following formula:

Standard error of measurement $= s\sqrt{1 - r_n}$

where s = the standard deviation and r_n = the reliability coefficient. In applying this formula to a reliability estimate of .60 obtained for a test where s = 4.5, the following results would be obtained.

$$
\begin{aligned}
\text{Standard error of measurement} &= 4.5\sqrt{1 - .60} \\
&= 4.5\sqrt{.40} \\
&= 4.5 \times .63 \\
&= 2.8
\end{aligned}
$$

The standard-error of measurement shows how many points we must add to, and subtract from, an individual's test score in order to obtain "reasonable limits" for estimating that individual's true score (that is, a score free of error). In our example, the standard error would be rounded to 3 score points. Thus, if a given student scored 35 on this test, that student's *score band*, for establishing reasonable limits, would range from 32 (35 – 3) to 38 (35 + 3). In other words, we could be reasonably sure that the score band of 32 to 38 included the student's true score (statistically, there are two chances out of three that it does). The standard errors of test scores provide a means of allowing for error during test interpretation. If we view test performance in terms of score bands (also called *confidence bands*), we are not likely to overinterpret small differences between test scores.

For the test user, the standard error of measurement is probably more useful than the reliability coefficient. Although reliability coefficients can be used in evaluating the quality of a test and in comparing the relative merits of different tests, the standard error of measurement is directly applicable to the interpretation of individual test scores.

Reliability of Criterion-Referenced Mastery Tests   As noted earlier, the traditional methods for computing reliability require score variability (that is, a spread of scores) and are therefore useful mainly with norm-referenced tests. When used with criterion-referenced tests, they are likely to provide misleading results. Since criterion-referenced tests are not designed to emphasize differences among individuals, they typically have limited score variability. This restricted spread of scores will result in low correlation estimates of reliability, even if the consistency of our test results is adequate for the use to be made of them.

When a criterion-referenced test is used to determine mastery, our primary concern is with how consistently our test classifies masters and nonmasters. If we administered two equivalent forms of a test to the same group of students, for example, we would like the results of both forms to identify the same students as having mastered the material. Such perfect agreement is unrealistic, of course, since some students near the cutoff score are likely to shift from one category to the other on the basis of errors of measurement (due to such factors as lucky guesses or lapses of memory). However, if too many students demonstrated mastery on one form but nonmastery on the other, our decisions concerning who mastered the material would be hopelessly confused. Thus, the reliability of mastery tests can be determined by computing the percentage of consistent mastery-nonmastery decisions over the two forms of the test.

The procedure for comparing test performance on two equivalent forms of a test is relatively simple. After both forms have been administered to a group of students, the resulting data can be placed in a two-by-two table like that shown in Figure 12.3. These data are based on two forms of a 25-item test administered to 40 students. Mastery was set at 80 percent correct (20 items), so all students who scored 20 or higher on both forms of the test were placed in the upper right-hand cell (30 students), and all those who scored below 20 on both forms were placed in the lower left-hand cell (6 students). The remaining students demonstrated mastery on one form and nonmastery on the other (4 students). Since 36 of the 40 students were con-

| | | FORM B | |
		NONMASTERS	MASTERS
FORM A	MASTERS	2	30
	NONMASTERS	6	2

FIGURE 12.3   Classification of 40 students as masters or nonmasters on two forms of a criterion-referenced test.

sistently classified by the two forms of the test, we apparently have reasonably good consistency.

We can compute the percentage of consistency for this procedure with the following formula:

$$\% \text{ Consistency } = \frac{\text{Masters (both forms)} + \text{Nonmasters (both forms)}}{\text{Total number in group}} \times 100$$

$$\% \text{ Consistency } = \frac{30 + 6}{40} \times 100 = 90\%$$

This procedure is simple to use but it has a few limitations. First, two forms of the test are required. This may not be as serious as it seems, however, since in most mastery programs more than one form of the test is needed for retesting those students who fail to demonstrate mastery on the first try. Second, it is difficult to determine what percentage of decision consistency is necessary for a given situation. As with other measures of reliability, the greater the consistency, the more satisfied we will be, but what constitutes a minimum acceptable level? There is no simple answer to such a question because it depends on the number of items in the test and the consequences of the decision. If a nonmastery decision for a student simply means further study and later retesting, low consistency might be acceptable. However, if the mastery-nonmastery decision concerns whether to give a student a high school certificate, as in some competency testing programs, then a high level of consistency will be demanded. Since there are no clear guidelines for setting minimum levels, we will need to depend on experience in various situations to determine what are reasonable expectations.

More sophisticated techniques have been developed for estimating the reliability of criterion-referenced tests, but the numerous issues and problems involved in their use go beyond the scope of this book. See Box 12.2 for factors that lower reliability of test scores.

BOX 12.2 • *Factors That Lower the Reliability of Test Scores*

1. Test scores are based on too few items. (*Remedy:* Use longer tests or accumulate scores from several short tests.)
2. Range of scores is too limited. (*Remedy:* Adjust item difficulty to obtain larger spread of scores.)
3. Testing conditions are inadequate. (*Remedy:* Arrange opportune time for administration and eliminate interruptions, noise, and other disrupting factors.)
4. Scoring is subjective. (*Remedy:* Prepare scoring keys and follow carefully when scoring essay answers.)

Estimating the Reliability of Performance Assessments

Performance assessments are commonly evaluated by using scoring rubrics that describe a number of levels of performance, ranging from high to low (e.g., outstanding to inadequate). The performance for each student is then judged and placed in the category that best fits the quality of the performance. The reliability of these performance judgments can be determined by obtaining and comparing the scores of two judges who scored the performances independently. The scores of the two judges can be correlated to determine the consistency of the scoring, or the proportion of agreement in scoring can be computed.

Let's assume that a performance task, such as writing sample, was obtained from 32 students and two teachers independently rated the students' performance on a four-point scale where 4 is high and 1 is low. The results of the ratings by the two judges are shown in Table 12.4. The ratings for Judge 1 are presented in the columns and those for Judge 2 are presented in the rows. Thus, Judge 1 assigned a score of 4 to seven students and Judge 2 assigned a score of 4 to eight students. Their ratings agreed on six of the students and disagreed by one score on three of the students. The number of rating agreements can be seen in the boxes on the diagonal from the upper righthand corner to the lower lefthand corner. The percentage of agreement can be computed by adding the numbers in these diagonal boxes (6 + 7 + 6 + 5 = 24), dividing by the total number of students in the group (32), and multiplying by 100.

$$\text{Rater agreement} = \frac{24}{32} \times 100 = 75\%$$

TABLE 12.4 *Classification of Students Based on Performance Ratings by Two Independent Judges*

		Ratings by Judge 1				
	Scores	*1*	*2*	*3*	*4*	*Row Totals*
	4			2	6	8
Ratings by Judge 2	**3**		3	7	1	11
	2	2	6			8
	1	5				5
Column Totals		7	9	9	7	32

By inspection, we can see that all ratings were within one score of each other. The results also indicate that Judge 2 was a more lenient rater than Judge 1 (i.e., gave more high ratings and fewer low ratings). Thus, a table of this nature can be used to determine the consistency of ratings and the extent to which leniency can account for the disagreements.

Although the need for two raters will limit the use of this method, it seems reasonable to expect two teachers in the same area to make periodic checks on the scoring of performance assessments. This will not only provide information on the consistency of the scoring, but will provide the teachers with insight into some of their rating idiosyncrasies. See Box 12.3 for factors that lower the reliability of performance assessment.

The percentage of agreement between the scores assigned by independent judges is a common method of estimating the reliability of performance assessments. It should be noted, however, that this reports on only one type of consistency—*the consistency of the scoring.* It does not indicate the consistency of performance over similar tasks or over different time periods. We can obtain a crude measure of this by examining the performance of students over tasks and time, but a more adequate analysis requires an understanding of **generalizability** theory, which is too technical for treatment here.

BOX 12.3 • *Factors That Lower the Reliability of Performance Assessments*

1. Insufficient number of tasks. (*Remedy:* Accumulate results from several assessments. For example, several writing samples.)
2. Poorly structured assessment procedures. (*Remedy:* Define carefully the nature of the tasks, the conditions for obtaining the assessment, and the criteria for scoring or judging the results.)
3. Dimensions of performance are specific to the tasks. (*Remedy:* Increase generalizability of performance by selecting tasks that have dimensions like those in similar tasks.)
4. Inadequate scoring guides for judgmental scoring. (*Remedy:* Use scoring rubrics or rating scales that specifically describe the criteria and levels of quality.)
5. Scoring judgments that are influenced by personal bias. (*Remedy:* Check scores or ratings with those of an independent judge. Receive training in judging and rating, if possible.)

Summary of Points

1. Validity is the most important quality to consider in assessment and is concerned with the appropriateness, meaningfulness, and usefulness of the specific inferences made from assessment results.
2. Validity is a *unitary concept* based on various forms of evidence (content-related, criterion-related, construct-related, and consequences).
3. Content-related evidence of validity refers to how well the sample of tasks represents the domain of tasks to be assessed.
4. Content-related evidence of validity is of major concern in achievement assessment and is built in by following systematic procedures. Validity is lowered by inadequate assessment practices.
5. Criterion-related evidence of validity refers to the degree to which assessment results are related to some other valued measure called a *criterion*.
6. Criterion-related evidence may be based on a predictive study or a concurrent study and is typically expressed by a correlation coefficient or expectancy table.
7. Construct-related evidence of validity refers to how well performance on assessment tasks can be explained in terms of psychological characteristics, or constructs (e.g., mathematical reasoning).
8. The construct-related category of evidence is the most comprehensive. It includes evidence from both content-related and criterion-related studies plus other types of evidence that help clarify the meaning of the assessment results.
9. Consequences of using the assessment is also an important consideration in validity—both positive and negative consequences.
10. Reliability refers to the consistency of scores (i.e., to the degree to which the scores are free from measurement error).
11. Reliability of test scores is typically reported by means of a reliability coefficient or a standard error of measurement.
12. Reliability coefficients can be obtained by a number of different methods (e.g., test-retest, equivalent-forms, internal-consistency) and each one measures a different type of consistency (e.g., over time, over different samples of items, over different parts of the test).
13. Reliability of test scores tends to be lower when the test is short, range of scores is limited, testing conditions are inadequate, and scoring is subjective.
14. The standard error of measurement indicates the amount of error to allow for when interpreting individual test scores.
15. Score bands (or *confidence bands*) take into account the error of measurement and help prevent the over interpretation of small differences between test scores.

16. The reliability of criterion-referenced mastery tests can be obtained by computing the percentage of agreement between two forms of the test in classifying individuals as masters and nonmasters.
17. The reliability of performance-based assessments are commonly determined by the degree of agreement between two or more judges who rate the performance independently.

References and Additional Reading

American Educational Research Association, *Standards for Educational and Psychological Testing* (Washington, DC: AERA, 1999).

Linn, R. L., and Gronlund, N. E., *Measurement and Assessment in Teaching*, 8th ed. (Upper Saddle River, NJ: Merrill/Prentice-Hall, 2000).

Oosterhoff, A. C., *Classroom Applications of Educational Measurement*, 3rd ed. (Upper Saddle River, NJ: Merrill/Prentice-Hall, 2001).

Thorndike, R., *Measurement and Evaluation in Psychology and Education*, 6th ed. (Upper Saddle River, NJ: Prentice-Hall, 1997).

Glossary

This glossary of assessment terms focuses primarily on the terms used in this book.

Achievement Assessment A procedure that is used to determine the degree to which individuals have achieved the intended learning outcomes of instruction. It includes both paper-and-pencil tests and performance assessments, plus judgments concerning learning progress.

Achievement Test An instrument that typically uses sets of items designed to measure a domain of learning tasks and is administered under specified conditions (e.g., time limits, open or closed book).

Alternate Forms Two or more forms of a test or assessment that are designed to measure the same abilities (also called *equivalent* or *parallel forms*).

Alternative Assessment An assessment procedure that provides an alternative to paper-and-pencil testing.

Analytic Scoring The assignment of scores to individual components of a performance or product (e.g., Evaluate a writing sample by using separate scores for organization, style, mechanics, etc.).

Anecdotal Record A brief description of some significant student behavior, the setting in which it occurred, and an interpretation of its meaning.

Authentic Assessment An assessment procedure that emphasizes the use of tasks and contextual settings like those in the real world.

Battery of Tests Two or more tests standardized on the same sample of students, so that performance on the different tests can be compared using a common norm group.

Checklist A list of dimensions of a performance or product that is simply checked present or absent.

Content Standard A broad educational goal that indicates what a student should know and be able to do in a subject area.

Correlation Coefficient A statistic indicating the degree of relationship between two sets of test scores or other measures.

Criteria A set of qualities used in judging a performance, a product, or an assessment instrument.

Criterion-Referenced Interpretation A description of an individual's performance in terms of the tasks he or she can and cannot perform.

Derived Score A score that results from converting a raw score to a different score scale (e.g., percentile rank, standard score).

Difficulty Index Percentage of individuals who obtain the correct answer on a test item or task.

Discrimination Index The degree to which a test item or task discriminates between high and low scorers on the total test.

Expectancy Table A twofold chart that shows the relationship between two sets of scores. It can be used to predict the chances of success on one measure (the criterion) for any given score on the other measure (the predictor), and it can be used for obtaining criterion-related evidence of validity.

Generalizability The extent to which an assessment procedure provides comparable results over different samples of similar tasks, different settings, and different administrations.

Grade Equivalent Score A derived score that indicates the grade level at which an individual's score matches the average score (e.g., a grade equivalent score of 4.5 indicates the raw score matches the average score of students in the middle of the fourth grade).

Holistic Scoring The assignment of a score based on an overall impression of a performance or product rather than a consideration of individual elements. The overall judgment is typically guided by descriptions of the various levels of performance or scoring rubrics.

Item Analysis Traditionally, a method for determining the difficulty and discriminating power of test items. It can also be used to determine the responsiveness of test items to instructional effects.

Kuder-Richardson Formula 20 (KR-20) A method for estimating reliability based on the internal consistency of a test (i.e., on the extent to which the test items correlate with each other).

Mastery Test An assessment method used to determine whether an individual has met some predetermined level of performance.

Mean The arithmetic average that is determined by adding together a set of scores and dividing by the number of scores.

Norm-Referenced Interpretation A description of an individual's performance in terms of how it compares to the performance of others (typically those in a norm group).

Normal Curve A symmetrical bell-shaped curve based on a precise mathematical equation. It is widely used in interpreting standardized test scores because of its fixed mathematical properties (e.g., when standard deviations are plotted along the baseline of the curve, each portion of the curve contains a fixed percentage of scores).

Normal-Curve Equivalent Score A normalized standard score that ranges from 1 to 99 with a mean of 50. It is used for reporting performance on standardized achievement tests.

Norms Data that describe the performance of individuals in some reference group (e.g., national norms, local norms). Norms represent average or typical performance and are not to be interpreted as standards.

Objective Test A test that can be consistently scored by equally competent scorers (i.e., they obtain the same scores). This contrasts with subjective tests where the scores are influenced by scorer judgment (e.g., essay tests).

Percentage Correct Score The percentage of items that an individual answers correctly on a test, or the percentage of tasks an individual performs correctly on a performance assessment.

Percentile Band A range of percentile ranks that sets reasonable limits within which an individual's true score is likely to fall. It takes into account the inconsistency of obtained scores due to errors of measurement (also called an *error band* or *confidence band*).

Percentile Rank The percentage of individuals in a group scoring at or below a given score. Not to be confused with the percentage-correct score.

Performance Assessment A procedure that requires individuals to perform tasks and the process or product of the performance is judged using prespecified criteria.

Portfolio Assessment A preplanned collection of samples of student work, assessment results, and other data that represent the student's accomplishments. It is viewed by some as a basic type of performance assessment and by others as merely a convenient method for accumulating evidence of student performance.

Range The difference between the highest score and the lowest score in a distribution of scores.

Rating Scale A systematic procedure for guiding and recording judgments concerning the degree to which the characteristics of a performance or behavior are present.

Raw Score The score that is obtained when first scoring a test or performance task (also called an obtained score). The raw score is frequently converted to some type of derived score for interpretation (e.g., percentile rank or standard scores).

Reliability The degree to which assessment results are consistent from one measurement (or assessment) to another. Reliability estimates typically indicate the consistency of scores or judgments over different forms, different time periods, different parts of the instrument, or different raters. High reliability indicates greater freedom from error.

Scoring Rubric A set of scoring guidelines that describe the characteristics of the different levels of performance used in scoring or judging a performance.

Standard A prespecified level of performance that is considered satisfactory for the use to be made of the assessment results (e.g., minimum standards, mastery standards).

Standard Error of Measurement A method of expressing reliability that estimates the amount of error in test scores. It is the standard deviation of the errors of measurement and is used to compute the error bands (e.g., percentile bands) used in interpreting test scores.

Standard Score A term used to describe a variety of derived scores that convert raw scores to a standard scale for a more useful interpretation of test results.

Standardized Achievement Test A test constructed to fit detailed specifications, administered under prescribed conditions to selected groups, and scored using definite rules of scoring. Published standardized tests typically include a test manual that contains rules for administration and scoring, norms for interpretation, and validity and reliability data.

Stanine A standard score that ranges from 1 to 9 with a mean of 5. Each stanine is one-half of a standard deviation wide, except 1 and 9 at the ends of the distribution.

T-Score A standard score with a mean of 50 and standard deviation of 10.

Table of Specifications A two-way chart that specifies the number or proportion of test items (or assessment tasks) to be designed for each area of content and each type of intended learning outcome when planning a test (or other assessment procedure).

Task An assessment exercise that requires students to demonstrate a knowledge, skill, or combination of attributes, by means of a performance or product (see *performance assessment*).

Validity The extent to which inferences made from assessment results are appropriate, meaningful, and useful in terms of the purpose for the assessment. Validity is a unitary concept that depends on a variety of types of evidence, is expressed by degree (high, low), and refers to the inferences drawn (not the instrument itself).

Index